Karate Goju Ryu Meibukan

Karate Goju Ryu Meibukan

Lex Opdam

P.O. Box 491788, Los Angeles, CA 90049

Disclaimer

Please note that the author and publisher of this book are NOT RESPONSIBLE in any manner whatsoever for any injury that may result from practicing the techniques and/or following the instructions given within. Since the physical activities described herein may be too strenuous in nature for some readers to engage in safely, it is essential that a physician be consulted prior to training.

First published in 2007 by Empire Books
Copyright © 2007 by Empire Books

All rights reserved. No part of this publication may be reproduced or utilized in any form or by any means, electronic or mechanical, including photocopying, recording, or by any information storage and retrieval system, without prior written permission from Empire Books.

First edition
06 05 04 03 02 01 00 99 98 97 1 3 5 7 9 10 8 6 4 2

Printed in the United States of America.

Empire Books
P.O. Box 491788
Los Angeles, CA 90049

ISBN-13: 978-1-933901-29-9
ISBN-10: 1-933901-29-2

    Library of Congress Cataloging-in-Publication Data

Opdam, Lex.
  Karate Goju ryu Meibukan / by Lex Opdam. -- 1st ed.
    p. cm.
  Includes index.
  ISBN 978-1-933901-29-9 (pbk. : alk. paper)
  1. Karate. I. Title.
  GV1114.3.O63 2007
  796.815'3--dc22

2007011678

Acknowledgements

I thank my students for the energy and inspiration they gave me to produce this book, and in particular Mark Hemels and Iwan Meij, who made the necessary text corrections in the Dutch version. Iwan, together with Peter Versteeg, also assisted in translating the original book into English. Without their help, it would have taken me considerably more time to finish the translation. I thank my students, Pascal de Haan, René van de Deyl, Iwan Meij, Maarten Arends, Léontine Veenhuis, and Tim Baartmans, who served as models for the photos within.

My good friend Teun Meeuwesse, a professional photographer, gave his patience and insight, and shared his expert knowledge with me. His background as a Goju-ryu karateka and experience as a photographer provided a unique understanding of my vision for this project, which he expertly depicted through his photographic work in this book.

I also thank Peter and Heather Andritsakis for their time and energy for their help in copyediting and their assistance in the process to finalize the work before sending the final manuscript to the publisher. Mathieu Ravignat was very helpful with his comments on the manuscript before I finished the final edit.

Keiko Sato and Hing-Poon Chan helped with translations; Sifu Eric Tuttle shared his interview with Sensei Mirakian; and author Mark Schoene and Terry O'Neill, publisher of Fighting Arts International, gave permission to republish one of the best in-depth series of Goju-ryu interviews of Sensei Mirakian. These contributions to this book are most appreciated.

Finally, I thank my teacher, Sensei Anthony Mirakian, for his approval to publish this book and permission to reprint many photos from his private collection. I am grateful for the time, energy, and attention he has given to me, and still is giving, as my teacher in Okinawan Meibukan Goju-ryu Karate-do. In my eyes, he is the living embodiment of traditional Meibukan Goju-ryu Karate-do, and I am proud to serve as his representative in the Meibukan in preserving this Goju-ryu tradition.

Foreword by Anthony Mirakian

It is an honor to have the opportunity to write a foreword for this informative book on Okinawan Meibukan Goju-ryu Karate-do. Sensei Lex Opdam, now my representative in the Netherlands, decided after much diligent research to travel from the Netherlands and train in my dojo, the United States headquarters for Okinawan Meibukan Goju-ryu Karate-do. Since his initial visit, Sensei Lex Opdam has returned to my dojo many times to continue to train and broaden his knowledge and understanding of the martial arts in general, and Meibukan Goju-ryu Karate-do in particular.

Over the years Sensei Opdam has shown loyalty, dedication and enthusiasm in his karate training. He upholds a high standard of karate dojo etiquette and maintains a very high level of quality technical training at his Netherlands dojo. For his accomplishments, Sensei Lex Opdam has rightfully earned the rank of Sixth Degree Black Belt, Rokudan, Renshi, which was issued by me.

This book contains information on the historical, philosophical, and technical aspects of Okinawan Goju-ryu Karate-do. The reader will find many historical photographs of great Okinawan Goju-ryu karate masters who were the pioneers of this unique martial art, as well as present-day photographs of those dedicated masters who still are promoting and expanding the art of Goju-ryu Karate-do. This book gives an overall informative view of Meibukan Okinawan Goju-ryu Karate-do. I know that the reader will find the information in this book very valuable in many ways.

I highly commend Sensei Lex Opdam for his tireless efforts in organizing and compiling all the information included herein, and published, for the first time, in a format that is easily understood by both novice and advanced students of the martial arts.

Anthony Mirakian
Karate Master 9th Degree
Hanshi, Kudan
U.S.A. Headquarters
Meibukan Goju-ryu Karate-do
Watertown, Massachusetts, U.S.A.

Preface by Lex Opdam

In recent years, I have come to the conclusion that there was a need for a broad survey and concrete technical information for both novice and more experienced students in the martial arts. With my own students, I sensed a longing for historical, philosophical, and technical explanations of the martial arts that could be internalized in written form as well as on the dojo floor. To support this positive need for knowledge and insight, I decided to write a book in the form of a technical manual, or syllabus, on Meibukan Goju-ryu Karate-do.

After its first publication in a limited edition in Dutch, Sensei Mirakian suggested that I consider making it available in English. Broadening the work's scope to an international audience was a great honor and privilege, and I readily agreed to do so. Consequently, some of the content contained in the original has been edited, expanded, and rewritten to serve the needs of this broader readership.

The syllabus before you serves as a technical manual in which history, origins, practice, and techniques are arranged in an orderly way, allowing the identity of the style to emerge. This syllabus offers deep background that not only will serve beginning karatedokas by giving them a rational framework to grasp this martial art, but also more experienced karatedokas who may reinforce or augment their existing understanding of the style's unique subtleties.

Without pretending to be a complete technical work about Goju-ryu Karate-do, or a learning tool for karate techniques, this book is meant for all who are interested in Goju-ryu Karate-do, especially those who follow the education of the Meibukan School of the late Dai Sensei Meitoku Yagi.

Lex Opdam
Karate Sensei, 6th Degree
Renshi, Rokudan
Meibukan Goju-ryu Karate-do Netherlands
Nijmegen/Lent, Gelderland
Netherlands

Contents

Foreword by Anthony Mirakian	vi
Preface by Lex Opdam	vii
Introduction	1

History of Goju-ryu Karate-do — 3

Kanryo Higaonna	4
Chojun Miyagi	5
Meitoku Yagi	6
The Birth and Succession of Goju-ryu	7
Meitoku Yagi's students	10
The International Meibukan Goju-ryu Karate-do Association	11
Anthony Mirakian	11
Hanshi Anthony Mirakian's history	12
The branches of Hanshi Anthony Mirakian	15
Meibukan Goju-ryu Karate-do Netherlands	17
Notes	18
Supplements	26
Interview—Memories of my father, Chojun Miyagi	26
The Meibukan Crest	30

The Meibukan Syllabus — 32

Overview of Meibukan Goju-Ryu Karate-Do System	32

KATA — 35

Heishu kata — 36

Sanchin kata	36
Origins and history	37
Adjustments to Sanchin kata	39
Physiological applications	40
Muscular system	40
Muscle protection	41
Muscle tension	41
Respiration/Breathing	44
The bio-energetic aspect	46
Ki/Qi	46
Hard Qi exercise	47

Heightened tension through muscle focus	47
Qi flow	48
Internal and external Qi practice	49
The mental aspect	50
Visualization of breathing	51
Visualization of stance, movement and fighting applications	53
Sanchin testing	54
Execution of the Kanryo Higaonna Sanchin kata	56
Embusen of the Kanryo Higaonna Sanchin kata	63
Attentions concerning general posture	64
Execution of breathing	70
Important key points in the training method of Sanchin kata	71
Afterword Sanchin kata	72
Tensho kata	72
Breathing	72
Motion	73
Naihanchi kata	73
Notes	75

Kaishu kata — 79

Fukyu kata	79
Origin and development	79
Basic Meibukan Goju-ryu Fukyu kata survey	81
Execution of the Fukyu kata Jodan	83
Embusen of the Fukyu kata Jodan	87
The origins of the Goju-ryu kata	89
Gekisai kata	89
Meibukan Gekisai dai ichi and Gekisai dai ni kata	91
Execution of the Gekisai dai ichi kata	92
Embusen of the Gekisai dai ichi kata	97
Saifa kata	98
Shisochin kata	98
Sanseru kata	99
Sesan kata	100
Seiunchin kata	100
Sepai kata	101
Kururunfa kata	101
Suparinpei kata	102
The Meibuken kata	102
Notes	104

KUMITE 109
Kumite kata 110
   About kumite 110
      Attack and defense 111
      Alertness 113
      Close-in fighting 113
      Misunderstanding of body contact 114
   Yakusoku kumite 115
      Yakusoku Ippon kumite 115
      Yakusoku Nippon kumite 116
      The deeper grounds of the ritualized fighting stances and etiquette 116
      The fighting postures of the Yakusoku kumite's 117
         Neko Ashi No Kamae 117
         Morote Gedan Heiko No Kamae 118
         Saifa No Kamae 119
      Measuring and movement regarding Yakusoku kumite 119
         Short distance 119
         Long Distance 120
      Remarks upon the execution of Yakusoku kumite 120
      Execution of the Yakusoku Ippon kumite 124
      Execution of the Yakusoku Nippon kumite 130
   Renzoku kumite 134
      General 134
      Yakusoku Renzoku Fukyu kumite 135
         Execution of the Yakusoku Renzoku Fukyu kumite 135
      Yakusoku Renzoku Fukyu Kakomi kumite 139
   Bunkai kumite 140
   Kake Uke kumite 142
      Sensitivity 143
      Stability 143
      Basic exercise 143
      Advanced exercise 144
      Power exercise 144
   Ude Tanren kumite 146
      The basic exercise 149
      Execution of the basic Ude Tanren kumite exercise 150

UNDO 153
Hojo undo 154
   General 154
   Clarification of terms and concepts 155

Isolating	155
Muscle chain/collaborating	155
Concentric	155
Eccentric	156
Static	156
Dynamic	156
Percentage Maximum Force	156
Training	157
What is training?	157
Repetition method	157
Duration method	157
Interval method	157
Power/weight training	158
General power training	158
Specific power training	158
Appearance of force	158
Dynamic force	158
Static force	158
Hojo undo training apparatus	159
Chi'shi	159
Nigiri game	160
Ishi sashi	160
Tetsuarei	161
Kogoken	161
Tan	162
Makiwara	162
Tetsu geta	163
Tou	163
Makiage kigu	163
Sashi Ishi	163
Sari bako	164
The three most abounded and trained components	165
Employment of the Makiwara	165
Employment Chi'shi	169
Employment Nigiri game	170
General indications for training	171
Target schedule weight training	173

Yobi, Seiri and Junan undo — 174
Yobi undo and Seiri undo — 174
    Breathing and concentration — 176

Junan undo	177
Slight stretch	177
Increasing stretch	178
Breathing	178
Stretch reflex	178
Practical stretching exercises	179

APPENDICES — 191

Dojo-etiquette	192
The law and self-defense	196
Vital points	199
Examples of natural weapons (of the body)	204
Basic stances	213
Lineage of Okinawan Goju-Ryu Karate Meibukan Association	215
Terminology	216
General	216
Titles and names	219
Ceremony	220
Technical	221
General	221
Stances	224
Fighting postures	224
Movements	224
Body parts	225
Specific techniques	226
Punch, pinch and strike techniques	226
Kicking techniques	227
Throwing techniques	227
Defense techniques	227
Fighting drills	228
Supporting training	229
Counting	229
Graduations	229
Kyu-grades	229
Dan-grades	230
Physical appearance of the obi's	230

Suggested readings on Meibukan Goju-ryu Karate-do	231
Contact addresses for branches of Hanshi Anthony Mirakian	233
Interviews with Master Anthony Mirakian	234
The Golden Age of Okinawan Karate (1990)	234
Eric Tuttle interviews Anthony Mirakian (1997)	284
Karate-do, its purpose and responsibility (2005)	295
Photo credits	311

Introduction

This work, KARATE GOJU RYU MEIBUKAN, reflects the system of education from the School of Dai Sensei Meitoku Yagi, named the Meibukan. The Meibukan, in an educational sense, originated from the teachings of "the Empty Hand" that Chojun Miyagi adopted in his Goju-ryu Karate system and passed on to his student Meitoku Yagi. In turn, Meitoku Yagi developed the Goju-ryu system further and gave these teachings a personal interpretation. The core of Miyagi's Goju-ryu remained, and Meitoku Yagi's additions, personal methods, and didactic structures made the system alive. Its evolution did not stop with Dai Sensei Meitoku Yagi but continues on through his student Hanshi Anthony Mirakian, and me.

My interpretation of the core of the Goju-ryu system originates out of my personal training and experience, plus verbal and visual transfer and research that is reflected accordingly in this syllabus and the structure of my own classes in the Netherlands. Although the core clearly is Meibukan Goju-ryu, as taught by Dai Sensei Meitoku Yagi, you also will find content reflecting my own influences and that of my teacher, Sensei Mirakian.

This book is written as a supplementary educational resource in a way that I deem appropriate to support a student of the art. The first part of the book briefly explains the history of Meibukan Goju-ryu Karate-do, because I believe it important that all students know the roots of their martial arts. I want to prompt readers to begin their own investigations and, by means of this text, reach out for knowledge and consider their training as a beginning of this great journey.

The next part represents the syllabus, and we begin to cover the technical components of the Goju-ryu system, with special attention to those components as reflected in the Meibukan School. These components consist of kata, kumite, and undo (additional and supplementary exercises). The Appendices contain examples of techniques and stances presented with pictures and Japanese names to serve as a useful reference tool. There also is extra information at hand, including a glossary, vital points, dojo etiquette (kun), three interviews with Sensei Mirakian, and a short discourse on law and self-defense. Note: all readers are well advised to research the laws governing self-defense in their own countries and communities.

There is a lot to say about my reasons why certain subcomponents are or are not present in this book (for example, presenting certain kata as a photo-series). My main goal has been to write a book for the beginner and intermediate karate-doka, who will benefit the most from such a text. I do not support the notion that one can learn karate from a book, but am trying to meet the need that many beginners have—to overcome their uncertainty in this unknown activity in movement, breathing, posture, and mental state of mind. For them, this book contains photos of the first forms that they learn, forms better understood as kata, like Sanchin kata, Gekisai Dai Ichi kata, and Fukyu kata. Also, the specific forms of kumite, or fighting drills with partner, like Ippon kumite and Nippon kumite, are given so that they can function as a reminder. Furthermore, there are examples of additional and supplementary exercises, supported by pictures, to build up an arsenal of knowledge from which the karatedoka can start training more independently. Exercise components are detailed and explained in more depth to provide greater value in establishing a broad training regimen.

I hope that the publication of this book contributes to the awareness and self-activation of the karatedoka.

History of Goju-ryu Karate-do

People, because of such parlor antics as breaking wood and stone, often misinterpret the purpose of karate. This is but a small part of the overall art and essence of karate. In peacetime, karate should be used as a tool to train the mind. In cases of emergency and in times where lawlessness is at hand, the practitioner could use one's body as a defense against a potential opponent.

It is not easy to define the real nature of karate-do. Like other forms of Budo, its deep meaning cannot be explained with words. Its essence lies beyond rationality.

The origin of karate can be found in Chinese kempo. However, documentation concerning the evolution of Chinese kempo is very poor. There is no hard evidence to prove the origin and development of karate before Chinese kempo existed. One theory suggests that kempo originated in Central Asia and spread to India and China. Another theory explains the existence of kempo as coming from China more than 5,000 years ago, during the time of the Yellow Emperor. Whatever theory, we are certain only that ancient people of combative nature and a sense of rivalry cultivated fighting skills.

—Chojun Miyagi, 1934

HISTORY OF GOJU-RYU KARATE-DO

The history of Goju-ryu Karate-do goes further than this book represents. The goal of this book is to explain the core history, with some added information. The most important period concerning the formation of Goju-ryu Karate-do is when the ryu (style) begins with the legendary Kanryo Higaonna.

Grandmaster Kanryo Higaonna.

Kanryo Higaonna

In 1853, the Okinawan Kanryo Higaonna (Chinese name Shin Zen Yen) was born in the district Nishimura of Naha, Okinawa. Kanryo Higaonna was the fourth son of Kanyo Higaonna (1823–1867) who belonged to the Okinawan Shin clan. Kanryo's father, Kanyo, earned his living transporting goods, especially firewood, between Okinawa and neighboring islands. Kanyo possessed a yabarusen (little boat) that he used for his business. He also was a crewmember of a larger ship that ferried goods and passengers between the Ryukyu Islands and China. On these trips, Kanyo Higaonna heard many stories about China, its culture and its fighting arts from businessmen, traders and public officers who regularly traveled between the mainland and the Ryukyu Islands. Those stories were passed down from father to son.

As a youth, Kanryo Higaonna became interested in the martial arts and he began studying tegumi (wrestling) and to-de (the name for the martial arts that was practiced those days). When he was approximately twenty years old, Higaonna began training under the tutelage of Arakaki, Seisho (1). Later, he traveled to Fuzhou, a providence of China, where he started training under Kung Fu Master Ryoto (2). Master Ryoto, impressed by Higaonna's rapid progress, introduced him to Chinese Master Liu Liu Ko (3) (Ryu Ryu Ko). After studying many years in China and learning the martial and healing arts, Kanryo Higaonna returned home to Okinawa. Research indicates that he may have trained with other teachers; however, his focus and influence remained Master Liu Liu Ko. Several years after his return from China, Kanryo Higaonna began to accept several students whom he would teach the martial arts from his home. He went on to teach martial arts at the local high school, and the royal family of King Sho-Tei–O also observed his teaching and instruction.

History of Goju-ryu Karate-do

Chojun Miyagi

At this time, fourteen-year-old Chojun Miyagi (born 1888 at Higashi-machi, Okinawa) was introduced to Kanryo Higaonna by his martial arts teacher of three years, Ryuko Arakaki. Master Ryuko Arakaki trained in the martial arts, described as Tomari-te, that stressed body conditioning, makiwara, and Hojo undo, as preparation and support for the actual practice of karate. The name Tomari-te comes from the geographical location of its origin, which is similar to Naha-te and Shuri-te. Chojun Miyagi, son of Chosho Miyagi, was of nobility and, because of the family's financial means, had a lot of time to devote to the study of martial arts. During school time, he participated in Okinawan wrestling and succeeded in almost every physical activity because of his athletic ability.

Grandmaster Chojun Miyagi, Founder of Goju-ryu Karate. Born on April 15, 1888, Died October 8, 1953.

Chojun Miyagi remained loyal to his teacher until Kanryo Higaonna's death on October 15, 1915; Higaonna died in his sleep at the age of 62.

Chojun Miyagi continued his study in the martial arts. In 1915, he journeyed to Fuzhou, China, where his teacher, Kanryo Higaonna, had received his core teachings in the martial arts. This journey was shared with Eisho Nakamoto, an English teacher at the Fuzhou City Commercial School. In 1917, upon his return from China, Chojun Miyagi became instructor at the educational center of the Okinawan police, taught at several high schools, and was connected to the Prefecture Health Center. In the years between then and World War II, he undertook journeys to research and share his martial arts. An important travel companion on several of these journeys was Master Go Ken Kin, who was a Chinese Master in White Crane Boxing, a tea merchant, and a good friend of Chojun Miyagi since 1915, when the two met in China. Go Ken Kin's influence on Chojun Miyagi's martial art was significant.

Go Ken Kin performing Nepai Kata with on the left Kenwa Mabuni.

Chojun Miyagi taught karate-do until 1943. He taught mostly in Okinawa; however, he occasionally taught in Japan. In 1934, he spent one year in Hawaii. By invitation of Chinyei Kinjo, president of the Hawaiian newspaper Yoen Jihosha, and with the cooperation of the Okinawan society on Hawaii, Chojun Miyagi instructed his Goju-ryu Karate-do. After World War II, he resumed his teaching activities. Health problems (4) brought about a decline in his teaching activities, and on February 8, 1953, Chojun Miyagi passed away from a heart attack.

Meitoku Yagi

Grandmaster Meitoku Yagi.

On March 6, 1912, Meitoku Yagi was born in Naha, Okinawa. At the age of fourteen, he was introduced by his grandfather to Chojun Miyagi. Meitoku Yagi's grandfather told Chojun Miyagi during the introduction that his grandson descended from the "Thirty-six families" who emigrated from China to Okinawa in 1392 (5). Due to this fact, and the honorable way of his introduction, Chojun Miyagi accepted the young Meitoku Yagi as his student. In 1926, when Meitoku Yagi joined the circle of personal students, five or six students were already training at the dojo. A few amongst them were Seiko Higa (1898–1966), Genkai Nakaima (1911–1984), Azami, and Tatsutoku Sakiyama.

The training that Meitoku Yagi received was hard, intensive, and often selectively pointed toward simple and essential basics. In the beginning, Meitoku Yagi was taught only Sanchin kata (6) and supplementary exercises. Slowly, and after many hours of training, other kata from the curricula were introduced to Meitoku Yagi and other students. The majority of the training was geared toward building up a strong physical body suitable for Goju-ryu.

At the age of sixteen, Meitoku Yagi started to assist under Master Chojun Miyagi. He was a natural in physical movements. Several years later, Chojun Miyagi began instructing the remaining kata of his system to Meitoku Yagi. Meitoku Yagi was one of the first who was privileged to learn the whole system by the age of eighteen.

Chojun Miyagi carried out testing during the performance of Sanchin kata by Meitoku Yagi and other students. This testing, called shimé, literally was testing the body through contact by means of pressure, pushes, and punches. These tests usually left visible marks and bruising on the bodies of the students. Chojun Miyagi stressed training on the wooden punching board called makiwara. Meitoku Yagi developed such a strong punching technique from the makiwara that often he was called the makiwara breaker.

History of Goju-ryu Karate-do

Famous Master Seiko Higa.

Meitoku Yagi received many awards during his life for his activities in the martial arts. On April 29, 1986, Dai (7) Sensei Meitoku Yagi was declared as a patron of the Japanese Cultural Heritage. He also was awarded by Japan's late Emperor Hirohito with "The Fourth Order of Merit" and given the title "Nigen Kohuho," (Living National Treasure) for his exceptional contribution towards karate and Okinawa.

On August 26, 1997 Meitoku Yagi (Goju-ryu), Shoshin Nagamine (8) (Matsubayashi-ryu) and Seiko Itokazu (9) (Uechi-ryu), were declared as Intangible Assets by the Okinawan government.

Meitoku Yagi not only taught his direct and personal students, but also instructed and informed other teachers and masters of different styles and schools, like Gogen Yamaguchi (10), who, at the end of the 1930s, spread a slightly different Goju-ryu curriculum in mainland Japan. His organization, the Goju-kai, is one of the biggest Goju-ryu organizations in the world.

The Birth and Succession of Goju-ryu

Just before World War II, although not made public, Chojun Miyagi was considering his top student, Jin'nan Shinzato as a possible inheritor of his Goju-ryu Karate-do system. Jin'nan Shinzato started training with Chojun Miyagi in 1920. In both words and actions, Chojun Miyagi groomed Jin'nan Shinzato toward stewardship of his Goju-ryu. According to students of Chojun Miyagi, Jin'an Shinzato was a genius in the martial arts. His knowledge and skill exceeded his fellow students. His role as an assistant teacher, his participation at various meetings and gatherings, in addition to performing at many martial arts demonstrations representing Chojun Miyagi, all pointed towards Jin'an Shinzato as likely successor of Chojun Miyagi.

Chojun Miyagi is testing the Sanchin kata performance.

While demonstrating in Tokyo on May 5, 1930 at the "All Japan Martial Arts Demonstration" in honor of the Crown Prince Hirohito's succession to the throne of Japan, Jin'an Shinzato was asked what he

Jin'an Shinzato.

called his style. He was unable to answer. This prompted him, upon his return from the demonstration, to discuss this query with Chojun Miyagi. Miyagi eventually named his martial art 'te' 'Goju-ryu' and registered this name at the All Japan Martial Arts Association or the Dai Nippon Butokai, the oversight body of the developing martial arts. Chojun Miyagi gave the name "Goju" to his martial arts because of the meaning Go (hard/external) and 'ju' (soft/internal), as mentioned in one of the most important manuscripts he possessed on the Chinese Martial Arts titled the "Bubishi," and probably because many Fujian-based Kung Fu systems identify themselves as "soft-hard" styles in relation to the Ki theory (see Chapter Kihon). In the Bubishi, or manual for the art of military science, the words go and ju express the very essence of Chojun Miyagi's karate-do in its phrase, "Ho go ju donto" (the way of breathing in and out is a way of softness and hardness).

The new name for Chojun Miyagi's martial art was registered with the Okinawa Kenritsu Taiiku Kyokai (Okinawa Prefecture Athletic Association) on November 21, 1930. This date is significant because Goju-ryu became the first officially recorded karate style with the Okinawa Prefecture Athletic Association. Jin'an Shinzato's significant role in this historical event provides further evidence of his potential appointment as successor to Chojun Miyagi.

World War II interrupted the development and growth of standardizing the karate syllabus and the development of karate in general. Miyagi taught karate for the last time before the war in 1943 at the famous Ritsumeikan University, making this a special occasion.

Tragically, however, just before his formal appointment as successor to Chojun Miyagi, Jin'an Shinzato died in 1945 due to heavy bombing of Okinawa and his village Kin-son during

Kanryo Higaonna (front, second from the right) and Chojun Miyagi (back, middle).

World War II. His premature death left a void as to who would be appointed the honorable task of inheriting the Goju-ryu system. As time went on and the war ended, many of Chojun Miyagi's students were busy rebuilding the infrastructure of Okinawa. During and after this postwar reconstruction, karate training slowly revived. Meitoku Yagi, who, after the war, worked for the civil services, first as a policeman and eventually as the commissioner of customs, began teaching karate with the permission of Chojun Miyagi in 1952. Meitoku Yagi had assisted in teaching at Chojun Miyagi's garden training sessions. He also had participated at many demonstrations with Jin'nan Shinzato, representing what became to be known as Goju-ryu. The dojo that Meitoku Yagi opened was in a fenced garden located in the district of Daido, Naha-city, Okinawa. His first student at this outdoor dojo was Yushun Tamaki, a former student of Seiko Higa.

Chojun Miyagi at the Naha Commercial High School in 1942.

Chojun Miyagi passed away in 1953, leaving no apparent successor. Chojun Miyagi's top students organized a meeting in the home of a fellow student, Genkai Nakaima, to decide who would be named the successor of Chojun Miyagi. There was a lot of disagreement and the meeting ended without a result. Miyagi's wife, Makato, and daughter Yasuko decided to name Eiichi Miyazato to take over the training and become head of the dojo. They also named Koshin Iha assistant and administrator. These appointments were transitional in nature until a permanent successor could be named.

Meitoku Yagi decided to break away and called his dojo and educational methods "Meibukan." Other important students followed suit and founded their own styles to differentiate their

Goju-ryu Masters Toguchi, Miyazato, and Yagi in front of bust of Miyagi.

Group photo taken in Okinawa in 1963 with some of the members of Grandmaster Chojun Miyagi's family. Seated in the center is his widow, Mrs. Miyagi. Second from the left kneeling is one of his sons, Mr. Ken Miyagi. Standing in the rear, fifth from the left is the daughter of Grandmaster Chojun Miyagi, Mrs. Yasuko Kogi.

own teaching and methods/philosophy from each other. For example, Seikichi Toguchi went with Shoreikan; Eiko Miyazato followed with his Gokenkan; and, in 1957, Eiichi Miyazato, whom Chojun Miyagi's wife and daughter had appointed as interim leader, built a large dojo attached to his house, and, to differentiate this dojo and educational methods, called it the Jundokan.

In 1963, ten years after the death of Chojun Miyagi, the Miyagi family publicly appointed Meitoku Yagi "Menkyo Kaiden" or heir of the style. During this official ceremony, the Miyagi family bestowed Grandmaster Miyagi's karate-uniform and belt to Meitoku Yagi to signify his inheritance of Chojun Miyagi's Goju-ryu. With this tremendous responsibility, Dai Sensei Meitoku Yagi embarked on a mission to pass on the traditions of Goju-ryu Karate-do in the spirit of his teacher Chojun Miyagi.

In 1978, during an interview at the "25th commemoration of Chojun Miyagi" in Tokyo, the daughter of Chojun Miyagi, Yasoku (1912–1987) expressed clearly why the Miyagi family named Meitoku Yagi as successor to Chojun Miyagi and the Goju-ryu system: "Mr. Yagi started learning karate when he was fourteen years old. Mr. Yagi studied karate for a long time and was dedicated to my father. My mother and I decided to give my father's training uniform and belt to Mr. Yagi. The most important person who has developed the way of Goju-ryu is Mr. Yagi. I think the person who does one's best for Goju-ryu should be the leader. My father would also be pleased with this decision."

Meitoku Yagi's students

Although Meitoku Yagi had many students, his most senior students (11) started in the 1950s and 60s. These students included Yushun Tamaki (12), Shosei Shiroma, Anthony Mirakian, Tsuioshi Nakasone, Meitatsu Yagi, Shigetoshi Senaha, Meitetsu Yagi, and Kyoshi Nakamoto. Later came Seisho Kuniyoshi, Kyoshi Horikawa, Masaaki Ikemiyagi, Masami Odo, and Tananori Shiki. Other students were Tamaki Tami, Arakaki Moshin, Higa Masagi, Ota Fumiyaki, Taira Sadyuki, Miyazato Masanaou, and Yasonori Yonamine.

History of Goju-ryu Karate-do

International Meibukan Goju-ryu Karate-do Association

With the growth of Meibukan Goju-ryu Karate-do outside Okinawa, principally through the efforts of Anthony Mirakian, Dai Sensei Meitoku Yagi founded the "International Meibukan Goju-ryu Karate-do Association."

After World War II, especially in the 50s and 60s, many Okinawan karate organizations and schools made contact with American soldiers stationed on Okinawa, one of the biggest operational military bases in the Far East. Intrigued by the martial arts, these servicemen were exposed to Okinawan karate as both individuals and groups. As Westerners and foreigners to Okinawa, not having the same value system, standards, and cultural identity, it was difficult to be accepted by an Okinawan teacher, especially in the beginning.

Leading Meibukan Goju-ryu karate masters seated from left to right: Grandmaster Meitoku Yagi, 10th Degree Judan (Hanshisai), the world's foremost authority of Okinawan Goju-ryu Karate-do; Master Anthony Mirakian, 9th Degree Hanshi; Master Shigetoshi Senaha, 9th Degree Hanshi; Master Meitatsu Yagi, 9th Degree Hanshi, the older son of Grandmaster Meitoku Yagi and President of the Meibukan Goju-ryu Karate-do Association, August 28, 1990.

Gradually the karate schools opened their doors and accepted Westerners (if they complied with the proper etiquette and other conditions set by the teacher). This development caused many schools to create international organizations and to adopt guidelines for the education and structure of their martial art because they knew that, eventually, their art would go overseas and foreign influence could have a negative impact on their cultural treasure.

Hanshi Anthony Mirakian.

The foremost senior active student of Dai Sensei Meitoku Yagi is Anthony Mirakian. As one of these servicemen, he grasped the opportunity during his military service on Okinawa to come in contact with this unique martial art and make it his own.

Anthony Mirakian

In the early 50s, Anthony Mirakian started training Goju-ryu Karate-do at the Shoreikan of Seikichi Toguchi. Mirakian trained under Toguchi and other prominent masters. Introduced by his second teacher on Okinawa, Ryuritsu Arakaki, Anthony Mirakian came to the Meibukan of Dai Sensei Meitoku Yagi. As the only Westerner in this dojo, mentioned by Ryuritsu Arakaki as the dojo lead by the leading authority in Goju-ryu, it would become the dojo where Anthony Mirakian found his definite school and master. After meticulous and thorough examination of his personality by Master Meitoku Yagi, Anthony Mirakian was accepted as a student. When Anthony Mirakian began training at the Meibukan, only a few students were training, among whom were Yushun Tamaki, Shosei Shiroma, Meitatsu Yagi, Shigetoshi Senaha, and Tsuioshi Nakasone.

Sensei Anthony Mirakian, Okinawan Meibukan Goju-ryu Karate Master demonstrates.

Anthony Mirakian returned to the United States in November 1959, and on March 15, 1961, he officially was granted permission by his teacher, Meitoku Yagi, to open his dojo, called the "Okinawan Karate-do Academy, Meibukan Goju-ryu" as the U.S. headquarters of the "Okinawan Meibukan Goju-ryu Karate-do Association." This dojo was the first foreign dojo in the history of the Meibukan, and one of the first dojos outside Japan in the history of Okinawan Goju-ryu.

On March 6, 1972, Hanshi Anthony Mirakian was appointed by Dai Sensei Meitoku Yagi as "Overseas General Manager" of the Okinawan Meibukan Karate-do Association—an honor that seldom is given from an Okinawan master, especially to a Westerner.

Years later, more students of Meitoku Yagi opened dojos, including Shiki Tadanori, Shigetoshi Senaha, Ikemiyagi Masaaki, and Meitoku Yagi's sons Meitatsu and Meitetsu. Later, in the 80s and 90s, international branches were formed under the supervision of Meitatsu Yagi and Meitetsu Yagi, who took over their father's role concerning the Meibukan. Today, Meitatsu Yagi is president of the International Meibukan Goju-ryu Karate-do Association, and Meitetsu Yagi is its vice president.

Hanshi Anthony Mirakian's history

On November 12, 1933, Anthony Mirakian was born in Cuba, of Armenian background. In his early years, Mirakian immigrated to the United States and joined the Air Force. Some time later he became stationed at the air base (13) on Okinawa.

There, Mirakian's interest in karate grew and happenstance brought him and

History of Goju-ryu Karate-do

an Air Force friend to the dojo of Master Seikichi Toguchi. It was here that young Mirakian had his first contact with the intensive trainings of Goju-ryu.

The training that Anthony Mirakian received was conducted six days a week, an average of four to five hours a day. This form of training challenged the physical ability of the students. The training included additional and supplementary exercises in the form of weight training, interval training, warm-ups, and aerobic training, all combined with relaxation exercises and stretching.

Grandmaster Meitoku Yagi (center) with his two sons, Meitetsu (left) and Meitatsu (right) at the honbu dojo in Kume, Naha-city, Okinawa, in 1985.

In the dojo of Toguchi at the district of Nakanomachi, there was no free fighting and, to use the words of Anthony Mirakian: "When you practiced with the advanced Okinawans, you had to remain alert, because they were fast, strong, and skilled; they also had control. The attitude was very serious. The students practiced kumite as if their lives depended on it, as if a mistake could be fatal." The level of karate more than forty years ago was exceptionally high, and this standard of karate practice in general cannot be compared to nowadays.

After an intensive period of training at the Toguchi dojo, Anthony Mirakian met his second karate Master, Ryuritsu Arakaki, who was a student of Chojun Miyagi and Seiko Higa and treated Anthony Mirakian as a protégé. Through this man, young Mirakian was introduced to the inner circle of Okinawan karate. Because of his openness, the intensity by which he approached the Okinawan culture, and his study and practice of the martial arts, Anthony Mirakian became accepted in the Okinawan karate culture—an exceptional position in those days for a Westerner. Seeing his serious approach, character, and determination in his study and practice of Goju-ryu, Ryuritsu Arakaki introduced Mirakian to Meitoku Yagi, one of the most important authorities on Goju-ryu and a top student of Chojun Miyagi. On the recommendation of Ryuritsu Arakaki, Anthony

Anthony Mirakian performs Sepai kata.

Anthony Mirakian attending one of the meetings of the Goju-ryu Karate-do Association held in the dojo of the late Grandmaster Seiko Higa in the city of Itoman, southern Okinawa in the 1950's. Standing left to right: Master Seikichi Toguchi, Anthony Mirakian, Grandmaster Seiko Higa, Grandmaster Meitoku Yagi, Master Tamaki, Master Yushun Tamaki, and Master Ishimine. Kneeling in front: Master Fukuji and Mr. Mitsugi Kobayashi.

Mirakian was accepted by Meitoku Yagi as a student. After his acceptance, Mirakian's training started at the Meibukan School.

Training at the Meibukan dojo of Sensei Meitoku Yagi always took place in a mystical atmosphere. No talking was allowed and no macho behavior was tolerated. Grandmaster Meitoku Yagi led the training in a strict and disciplined way, but with a warm and friendly attitude. The way Mirakian received his training at the Meibukan was characteristic of the level of individual instructions. Directions to students were given in a manner that would fit that particular student; in this way, instructed techniques, once understood, could become natural.

Although the official training at the Meibukan dojo averaged four hours a day, five days a week, Mirakian would add two additional hours per day if his work schedule allowed him to do so. Being responsible for the technical maintenance of heavy weapons at the air base, Mirakian had to carry and lift very heavy items many times during the day. Coupled with his karate training, he developed a strong physique that helped him excel in his martial arts training.

In the time that Anthony Mirakian lived on Okinawa, he was permitted to take part in meetings and gatherings of diverse Okinawan martial arts organizations, and he even was permitted to make unique films of famous masters of Okinawan karate. On many occasions, Mirakian also would demonstrate Goju-ryu during public martial arts events on Okinawa.

Mirakian was promoted to Sandan, Third-degree Black Belt, in 1959 by Meitoku Yagi. Before returning to the United States, Mirakian traveled intensively throughout the Orient, including visits to Taiwan and Hong Kong. Here, he met prominent masters in external and internal Eastern martial arts like Dr. Kwan Tak Hing (14). During his years on Okinawa, Mirakian also conducted many private and semi-private trips to Japan, where he met people like Juhatsu Kiyoda (15). Mirakian's love, dedication, and research, together with his willingness and openness

History of Goju-ryu Karate-do

regarding the Eastern cultures and way of thinking, have been the hallmarks that make him one of the most important historical figures of martial arts in the West.

Sensei Mirakian, now Hanshi Kudan, Ninth-degree Black Belt, upon his return from Okinawa, has introduced Okinawan Goju-ryu karate to the Western world. As an historian of Okinawan karate, in particular Goju-ryu, he is a remarkable man with a great knowledge and expertise in the martial arts.

From 1960 until now, Hanshi Anthony Mirakian has instructed authentic Goju-ryu Karate-do in his Okinawan Karate-do Academy Meibukan Goju-ryu (16). During these years, Sensei Mirakian always has taught in an honest way and offered people the opportunity to receive instruction in this art form. Regrettably, through the growth of competition- and sport karate, commerce, and misinterpretation of the philosophical concepts of karate-do, the correct way of presenting and teaching this art form is beginning to disappear. Hanshi Anthony Mirakian has never made compromises, gained no financial profit from karate, and kept his art as pure as possible. In his modest dojo of today, several dozen of his students, some of whom have received instruction for more than 30 years, work out the way Mirakian himself worked out back on Okinawa.

Karate Master Shigetoshi Senaha, Ninth Degree (Hanshi), President of the Meibukan Goju-ryu dojo at Tomigusuku, Okinawa, and one of the top students of Grandmaster Meitoku Yagi.

Personal representatives of Master Anthony Mirakian for Okinawan Meibukan Goju-ryu Karate-do. (Left) Renshi Hing-Poon Chan and (right) Renshi Lex Opdam at the Headquarters of the Meibukan Overseas General Manager.

The Branches of Hanshi Anthony Mirakian

In 1996, for the first time in 36 years, Sensei Mirakian gave someone permission to be his personal representative in Meibukan Goju-ryu Karate-do outside the United States. Joining the Meibukan in 1993, and becoming the official Branch-representative (17) in the same year and head instructor of Meibukan Goju-ryu Karate-do in the Netherlands, I have, as the writer of this book, received the honor to become that personal representative. In that same year, Hanshi Anthony Mirakian appointed a second personal representative for his branch in Canada, Sensei Hing Poon-Chan.

Both representatives of Hanshi Anthony Mirakian were members of other Goju-ryu schools and organizations, tracing back to the Jundokan school of Eiichi Miyazato. Sensei Hing Poon-Chan started in Hong Kong under Sensei Kim-Hung Wong, student of Hanshi Masafumi Suzuki (Seibukan), student of Hanshi Eiichi Miyazato (Jundokan). I started with Goju-ryu karate under Sensei Harry de Spa (IOGKF), student of Hanshi Morio Higaonna (IOGKF), student of Hanshi Eiichi Miyazato (Jundokan).

Master Meitatsu Yagi and Lex Opdam in front of the Meibukan Headquarters on Okinawa, December 1993.

Sensei Lex Opdam and some of his students visiting the Okinawan Karate-do Academy Meibukan Goju-ryu of Hanshi Anthony Mirakian in 1999. From left to right: Jacqueline Abbenhuis, Léontine Veenhuis, Gerald Pikkemaat, Master Anthony Mirakian, Lex Opdam, Vilmar Honing, Pascal de Haan, Stephan Finschi and Rene van der Deijl.

History of Goju-ryu Karate-do

Meibukan Goju-ryu Karate-do Netherlands

The Honbu (headquarters) dojo Meibukan Netherlands was founded in August of 1993 after my first training period under Sensei Meitatsu Yagi, and with that the Meibukan in June 1993 in Israel. Officially, the existence of this Dutch Honbu dojo was confirmed and acknowledged during my visit on Okinawa in December 1993.

The Honbu dojo Meibukan Netherlands is seated in Lent, a little village next to the town of Nijmegen, in the province of Gelderland.

In 1995, during intensive training periods under Hanshi Anthony Mirakian and after carefully observation, I was accepted as a student. One year later, after my second training period in this USA Honbu dojo, I was officially named "Personal Representative" of Hanshi Anthony Mirakian for Meibukan Goju-ryu Karate-do in the Netherlands. In 2005, I was, like Sensei Hing Poon-Chan, promoted by Hanshi Anthony Mirakian to Rokudan, Sixth-Degree Black Belt.

Master Anthony Mirakian displays this gold handmade certificate certifying that Alexander Coenraad Opdam, is authorized to be his Representative in the Netherlands, for Okinawan Meibukan Goju-ryu Karate-do, dated and issued July 12, 1996.

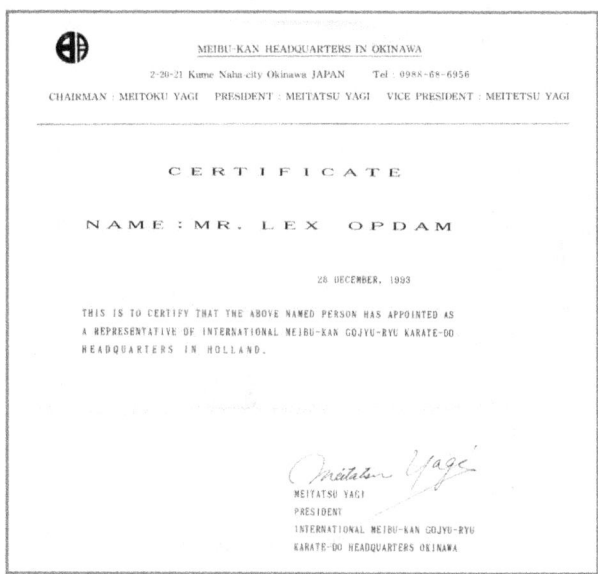

Certificate signed by Meitatsu Yagi in 1993 saying that Lex Opdam is appointed representative of International Meibu-kan Gojyu-ryu Karate-do in Holland.

In this Dutch Meibukan dojo, there has taken place a symbiosis between the Eastern and Western training cultures and their didactical and methodical coherence. In this environment, I try to integrate the art of karate-do into the Dutch society. With this, the concepts of the Budo- philosophy as a moral philosophy leading to martial virtue are brought to expression (18), especially in training and workouts of karate-do in the dojo. My personal experience and insight influence the way in which I pass down this martial art; Karate-do uses the body's training to develop the mind and guides one to spiritual development.

Notes

(1) In his book, "Tales of Okinawa's Great Masters," Shoshin Nagamine (reference note 8), founder of Matsubayashi-ryu Karate-do, writes: "In 1873, when he was about twenty years old, Higaonna began training rigorously under the astute martial arts Master Maya Arakaki (Arakaki Seisho, 1840–1920).

Grandmaster Shoshin Nagamine.

Renowned researcher P. McCarthy points out that not only Seisho Arakaki, but also Taite Kojo, was among the first martial arts teachers of Kanryo Higaonna, although he also states that Kanryo Higaonna was receiving instruction from Seisho Arakaki as early as 1867 until 1870.

P. McCarthy shares the opinion of researcher M. Bishop concerning one of the main teachers of Seisho Arakaki in China, called Wai Xinxian, Kung Fu teacher in Fuzhou. Some theories suggest that Kanryo Higaonna would have studied under Taite Kojo. Taite Kojo, like Meitoku Yagi, descends from the "Thirty-six Families" who came from China to Okinawa in 1392. Taite Kojo was a nephew of Isei Kojo, son of Sho Sai (second generation Kojo-ryu). Taite Kojo and Seisho Arakaki studied Chinese boxing. A teacher of Taite Kojo was Wai Xinxian (according to P. McCarthy, a possible teacher of Kanryo Higaonna, who stood in connection with Liu Liu Ko.

(2) Meitetsu Yagi writes in his book "Okinawan Karate-do Gojyu-ryu Meibu-kan": "What I have learned from Dai Sensei Yagi Meitoku about Gojyu-ryu history was that, at first, he (Kanryo Higaonna) learned Kempo from a man called Ryoto, who worked with plaster for a living. Ryoto was astonished by his rapid progress and introduced him to the famous Chinese Kempo Master Liu Ko."

Goju-ryu Master Meitoku Yagi and Uechi-ryu Master Kanei Uechi.

History of Goju-ryu Karate-do

(3) Little is know about Liu Liu Ko. Research throughout the years did not lead to concrete information; only oral transmissions and theories have given different speculations concerning Liu Liu Ko's martial art as well as his status and social position.

Anthony Mirakian, karate master, researcher, and historian in the field of Okinawan karate, states that Liu Liu Ko was of the Chinese nobility and had been tested to become the equivalent of a knight at an advanced age.

Chojun Miyagi sitting in the middle.

Researcher and karate master Morio Higaonna writes in his book "The history of Karate" that Liu Liu Ko could have been in service of the government as a "court official." Also, there are sources that claim Liu Liu Ko was a basket weaver.

It is not clear if Kanryo Higaonna had masters (see note 1) in China other than Liu Liu Ko (and Ryoto), and there also is a lot of uncertainty concerning the martial arts form(s) that he learned. Even the date of departure from Okinawa to China (between 1866 and 1877), his stay in China (between 6 and 30 years) and return from China to Okinawa (between 1881 and 1896) are disagreed upon. The date Sensei Mirakian gives for Kanryo Higaonna's departure to China is 1867–1868 (about the same date Morio Higaonna states). He also would remain there for more than twenty years.

The reason for Kanryo Higaonna's departure to learn martial arts in China, or in the underlying examples how his contact with Liu Liu Ko was established, has a range of different stories.

Mario Higaonna.

Morio Higaonna (student of Ei'ichi Miyazato and An'ichi Miyagi [no relation to Chojun Miyagi], both students of Chojun Miyagi) gives as the reason for the departure of Kanryo Higaonna to China a story written in his book, "The history of Karate": "In 1867, when Kanryo Higaonna was fourteen, his father was killed in a fight. The reason for this fight is not known, but his sudden and violent death was a terrible blow to the entire family, not least to the young Kanryo. He was overcome by tremendous grief, which was transformed into rage and eventually into a desire for revenge. At first, he was uncertain as to how he would achieve this, but the stories he had heard of the southern Chinese fighting arts and their devastating combative techniques were in his mind. He decided to travel to China to learn these deadly arts, and then return to Okinawa to avenge his father's death."

Seikichi Toguchi, a senior student of Chojun Miyagi, writes in his book "Okinawan Goju-ryu—Fundamentals of Shorei-kan Karate": "Master Kanryo Higashionna (Higaonna) began his studies in the martial arts as a child. As a young man, however, he became a sailor on the Shinko-sen, a vessel engaged in regular trading and cultural expeditions to China. On one of these regular trading and cultural expeditions, he bravely rescued a drowning child. When he returned the child to its parents, he discovered that Master Ryu, a renowned Chinese martial artist, was the boy's father. When a grateful Master Ryu offered Master Higashionna a reward, Master Higashionna asked for instruction in the art of Chinese boxing. Master Higashionna trained under Master Ryu for thirty years."

It is important to mention here that most of the oral traditions deliver a message that (amongst acknowledgements from senior students of Chojun Miyagi and other prominent martial arts master on Okinawa) Liu Liu Ko was the most important teacher in China to Kanryo Higaonna.

Clues point out that the specific techniques the kata Kanryo Higaonna brought from China to Okinawa have the strongest similarities with White Crane Boxing, Tiger Boxing, and Monk Boxing.

Oral tradition says that Kanryo Higaonna learned the Chinese kata (quan), and therefore pre-Goju-ryu kata or parts of the kata and techniques, from Liu Liu Ko. But still it is unclear if all the (Goju-ryu) kata and techniques came from Liu Liu Ko, since there is no hard evidence. There are theories that Kanryo Higaonna learned from other masters, and theories that he changed the Chinese kata he had learned.

In addition to learning the martial arts in China, which included Hojo undo, training methods, and mastery of weapons, he also studied Chinese medicine, in particular herbal medicine.

(4) According to Yasu Miyagi, Chojun Miyagi had developed health issues with his heart that would lead to his unfortunate passing in 1953: see interview on page 27.

Yasu Miyagi: "The third year after the first heart attack seems most dangerous. He died in this dangerous period of a heart attack."

Seikichi Toguchi mentions in his book "Okinawan Goju-ryu 2—

Advanced Techniques of Shorei-Kan Karate": "Beginning in 1952, Miyagi's health severely declined. When he taught us, he always sat on a chair and orally instructed us one at a time. I believe that in the beginning of 1953, he felt death was near. His blood pressure was very high and I noticed that his strength and stamina were low."

(5) In 1392 a large group of Chinese emigrated from China to Okinawa to encourage the cultural exchange. This group consisted of people with different backgrounds, crafts, and trades. Individuals and families made up the group that became known as the "Thirty-six families."

(6) Kata is a form of movement, performed solo, which technically consists of a chorographical pattern of fighting techniques that have defensive and offensive techniques demonstrated upon an imaginary opponent.

(7) Dai has the meaning of grandmaster (inheritor) of a ryu (style). In Japan, sometimes the letter "O" (O Sensei) is put before a name to give a certain prestige to a person (or object) to indicate importance.

(8) Shoshin Nagamine founded Matsubayashi-ryu in 1947. This Shorin-ryu style (Shorin Matsubayashi-ryu) was founded as homage to Kosaku Matsumora and Sokon Matsumora, who had been of great influence upon Nagamine and his martial art. Shoshin Nagamine's teachers included Ankichi Arakaki, Taro Shimabaku, Kohatsu Iha, Chotoku Kyan, Chokki Motobu, and Chojin Kuba. Although he opened his first dojo in 1942, this dojo did not survive the war. His present school, de Kodokan (originally Kodokan Karate-do and Kobujutsu Dojo), was founded in 1953.

(9) Seiko Itokazu was a student of Kanei Uechi (son of Kanbun Uechi and founder of Uechi-ryu). The martial art that Kanbun Uechi (1877–1948) mainly studied under his master Chou-tzu-ho was called Pangai-noon (meaning hard-soft). After the death of Kanbun Uechi, his son, Kanei Uechi (1911–1991), took over the role as Menkyo Kaiden (successor, inheritor). In 1949, Kanei Uechi changed the name Pangai-noon in Uechi-ryu to honor his father. Top students of Kanbun Uechi included Kanei Uechi, Ryuyu Tomoyose, Saburo Uehara, Kai Akamine, Shuei Sakihama, Isamu Uehara, Seiyu Shinjo, Seiko Toyama, and Seiryo Shinjo.

Master Kanbun Uechi.

Sensei Shintetsu Kuniyoshi (senior student of Meitetsu Yagi) and Lex Opdam on Camp Kinser, Okinawa 1993.

Important students of Kanei Uechi included Kanmei Uechi, Kansei Uechi, Ryuko Tomoyose, Kosuke Yonamine, Shigeru Takamiyagi, Ken Nakamatsu, Soryu Furugen, Seiki Itokazu, Yoshitoku Iraha, Takenobu Uehara, and Seiko Itokazu. Seiko Itokazu dissociated from Kanei Uechi in 1980, together with other students, and changed and enlarged the curriculum of their Pangai-noon-ryu. His organization was founded as the Pangai-noon Ryu Kiyokai, and he shared the leadership of this organization with Takashi Kinjo.

Also, Takenobu Uehara started his own organization in 1983 with the name Uechi-ryu Oroku Shinkokai. Later, others also would split off and form their own organizations, like Ryuko Tomoyose, president of the Shohei-ryu organization.

(10) Gogen Yamaguchi (1909–1989) was introduced to Chojun Miyagi by Jitsuei Yogi (student of Chojun Miyagi) in 1929. Gogen Yamaguchi stayed for a short time (approximately two to three months) on Okinawa, where he was instructed by Chojun Miyagi. Gogen Yamaguchi, with the verbal approval of Chojun Miyagi, began spreading Goju-ryu in mainland Japan. In 1935, he founded the All Japan Goju-Kai Karate-do Association. This organization is one of the largest Goju-ryu organizations in the world. In 1936, he changed the Goju-ryu curriculum with a form of free-fighting from which the present sport karate sprang. Although Gogen Yamuchi claims in his book, "Goju ryu karatedo kykohan," that he received a Tenth- degree Black Belt from Chojun Miyagi, Chojun Miyagi never issued a Dan rank of any kind to anyone. In the period after World War II, Gogen Yamaguchi, together with his sons Gosei and Goshi, visited Okinawa and the dojo of Meitoku Yagi, the Meibukan, to be instructed and informed in the advanced techniques and forms of Goju-ryu. In return, Meitoku Yagi, with his sons Meitatsu and Meitetsu, visited mainland Japan, especially Tokyo, to strengthen the ties between the Yagi and the Yamaguchi family and to instruct Goju-ryu.

(11) At the end of the 1950s, the ranks were as follows: Yushun Tamaki 4th Dan, Anthony Mirakian, 2nd Dan, Shosei Shiroma 1st Dan, Tsuioshi Nakasone, brown belt, Meitatsu Yagi, green belt, and Shigetoshi Senaha, white belt. In

History of Goju-ryu Karate-do

Hanshi Meitatsu Yagi demonstrating Kururunfa kata in Israel in the summer of 1993.

1959, Sensei Anthony Mirakian received his 3rd Dan Black Belt from Meitoku Yagi. In 1960, Yushun Tamaki was promoted to 5th Dan Black Belt, Shigetoshi Senaha and Tsuishi Nakasone, both to 2nd Dan Black Belt, and Kyoshi Nakamoto and Meitatsu Yagi to 1st Dan Black Belt.

(12) After World War II, the American Navy established a huge military base on Okinawa (until the 1980s) with about 50,000 military personal. In the 1960s and early 1970s, this Okinawan base often was used for the Vietnam War. In 1972, after 27 years, Okinawa was officially returned to Japan. At the moment there is some resistance from the Okinawan community against the presence of this foreign military base, which has decreased in troop strength throughout the years.

(13) Kwan Tak Hing was a famous Chinese Hung Kung-Fu master and film actor in Hong Kong, China.

(14) Juhatsu Kiyoda (1887–1969) was a top student of Kanryo Higaonna. He was senior to Chojun Miyagi. Juhatsu Kiyoda founded his own ryu with the name Tou'on-ryu (Tou'on is the pronunciation of the last kanji in the name of Kanryo Higaonna). After World War II, he moved to Beppu, Japan. Juhatsu Kiyoda also studied under Yabu Kentsu and Itosu Anko. Juhatsu Kiyoda was one of the important promoters of Okinawan karate. He received his "trained warrior" certification (Kyoshi) from the Okinawan governor in 1934. Kiyoda was one of those who fought to bring the licensing system from the Butoku-kai to Okinawan karate. Kiyoda was chief director and head instructor of the Butoku-kai (Great Japan Martial Virtues Association) in Naha.

Grandmaster Juhatsu Kiyoda.

Among the organizations Kiyoda was involved in was the Okinawa-ken Karate-do Shinko-Kai (Okinawan Prefectural Karate-do Promotion Society), in which Chojun Miyagi also participated. Although the influence of his teacher, Kanryo Higaonna, upon Kiyoda's martial art was overwhelming, it is striking that his style named Tou'on-ryu differs from the Goju-ryu of Chojun Miyagi. His

Front of the Okinawan Karate-do Academy Meibukan Goju-ryu of Hanshi Anthony Mirakian.

The cellar of the Okinawan Karate-do Academy Meibukan Goju-ryu of Hanshi Anthony Mirakian.

Tou'on-ryu can be called light in comparison with the Goju-ryu of Higaonna. Also, Kiyoda's style is much more circular and fluid.

After the death of Yuhatsu Kiyoda, four of his students passed on his system: Juko Kiyoda (1926–1983), Choko Iraha (1901–1986), Katsumi Murakami (1927–) and Shigekazu Kanzaki (1927–). Today, the only active student is Kanzaki Shigekazu, who lives in Beppu, Japan.

(15) The Okinawan Karate-do Academy, Meibukan Goju-ryu, can be found in the city of Watertown near Boston, Massachusetts, USA. This dojo has a wooden floor on the first floor, where most of the training takes place. In the cellar, as big as the first floor, you can find training equipment such as makiwara, modern and traditional weigh training apparatus, and other supplementary Hojo undo materials. Also, an arsenal of traditional weapons is at hand.

(16) The branch representative is the person who is responsible for all facets of the organization/school, with connection to an appointed area. This status is the highest that someone can reach over an area (province, state, land, or continent).

(17) Budo philosophy: In a nutshell, the essence of budo deals with the inner conflict we create in ourselves, like a fight between life and death. The purpose of the martial arts is to develop self-knowledge, where self-defense can be used in a physical necessity. By means of cultivation, by controlling the physical body and directing the mind, we try to create a state of mind where we can let go of the ego—a condition where energy flows freely and is not blocked by thinking; a state of mind that is free of fear and where thoughts are absent (Mushin), thereby creating direct consciousness of reality; to be one with the world surrounding us, to unite with the universe, touching the nature of things.

Supplements

Additive enclosure note 4.

(Interview) Yasuko Kojiro (Thuruko Miyagi-old name) 30 March, 53rd year of Showa (1978)

Literally translated by Keiko Sato (1999) for the Headquarters Meibukan Goju-ryu Karate-do Netherlands from the Booklet "Commemoration of Chojun Miyagi" of the publishing house Denryokushinposha (1978). Edited by Hing-Poon Chan and Lex Opdam.

Grandmaster Chojun Miyagi, founder of Goju-ryu karate.

The Memory of my father, Chojun Miyagi

My father, Chojun, loved his children very much. Though my name is Yasu now, my old name was Thuru before I was married. As I used to be very active and gymnastic, my father's students, Mr. Matama and others, said to me, "Could you do Karate? Please do it." At that time, I wore Koshimaki (the cloth) instead of pants. I imitated my father's Karate with wearing only Koshimaki in front of these people. They really enjoyed and clapped enthusiastically. After having four daughters, my father got a son, his name is Kei. My sisters were quiet, but I was very active. I have always imitated my father's Karate. I have ten brothers and sisters. The oldest sister used to be a teacher in kindergarten. Her husband was also a teacher in a school and became a director before he retired. She died of fever after the delivery of the girl when she was only 28 years old. I am the second child and four years younger than my oldest sister. My father went to the War (First World War) when he was 21 years old. I was born after his return when my parents were both 25 years old. They were both born in the year of the mouse and so was I. After me, there were two daughters and then the first son, Kei, was born.

My father was very pleased and loved the son incredibly. It seemed that he could not feel any pain, even though he takes his son in his eyes (Japanese expres-

History of Goju-ryu Karate-do

*Original: Interview with Yasu Miyagi (1).
From the Goju-kai booklet
'Commemoration of Chojun Miyagi.'
Publishing house Denryokushinposha.*

sion). I used to be jealous as a child for the fact that a boy was very important in family. So I forced Kei to enter the Japanese cabinet to make him cry when my parents were not at home. I am seven years older than Kei and 19 years older than my youngest brother; his name is Ken-Bou (Bou is used for children only). When I walked with Ken-Bou, some people asked, "When did you get married and have a child?" My father loved his children very much. This morning (30th March, 1978) I tried to cut my nails. Usually my grandson cuts my nails, but he has gone skating today. It reminded me that my father used to wash our hair on every Saturday evening when we were small. At that time we did not have shampoo like today; instead we used the washing powder. After that we took a bath and he cut our nails. The way he cut the nails was so short that it hurt. Also, as my hand has been tensed by it, he has hit me gently with the scissors. When I cut my nails, I always remember that my father used to cut my nails every week. So the memory makes me embarrassed if I have long nails.

He was strict about cleaning and organizing. He would become angry when I did not put my books on the shelves properly. When I did not know how to read Kanji (Chinese character), I put Hiragana (Japanese alphabet) along the Kanji. He was angry that I could not even memorize the Kanji.

He was adopted by another family and then changed his name from Matsu to Chojun. He started learning Karate because when he was small he was not very healthy. The house where he was born was a pharmacy. They sold the medicines to the royal households. They imported the medicines from China and had two ships. When I was small, I found natural medicines, for example, the sweet plants (licorice) which cleanse the toxins after childbirth. There was a medicine, Saikaku (rhino horn), that was sold solely to the royal households in the region. My father was adopted to the main house of his family (his uncle, his father's oldest brother) when he was 3 or 4 years old. My father's name used to be Matsu (pine tree). But his rich neighbor gave him his new name, Chojun. His new family was very rich. My father has been in China many times to learn Karate. I have been having good memory since I was 3 years old. Although he had a master in Okinawa, Kanryo Higaonna Sensei, he wanted to go to China to learn Karate. This was because Karate came from China originally. But Chinese people hesitated to teach him Karate. So he paid money to learn. I was always looking forward to get the souvenirs from China.

My father died of a heart attack

My father died in October, the 28th year of Showa (1953), of a heart attack. He was 66 years old. I was in Tokyo when he passed away. At that time, I had a house in Kyoto and some medical students who came from Okinawa were living in my house. When they went to Okinawa, I asked them to bring some unusual souvenirs for my father. I have heard that he was not going to live more than three years. Just one year before he died, I received the telegraph from him, and I went back to Okinawa to see him. He was very pleased and called all his students, "Yasu has come back. Could you come to see her?" It was very surprising when I saw all these people. But it was very good that I went back to see him before he died. The third year of the first heart attack seems most dangerous. He died in the dangerous period. He was too young to die. I wanted him to live longer. He used to tell to my mother, "The people, who do Karate in Shuri can live longer, but not in Naha. So I really want to live long." (He lived in Naha. So he wanted to prove that someone who did Karate could live long in Naha.)

He collected many materials about Karate. He wished to write the book of Karate. When I asked if he wants to write the book, he said he has to do more research in China again. Unfortunately the Second World War had started and all materials were burnt and destroyed. He regretted this very much.

My father's training was dedicated to Meitoku Yagi

Here is Meitoku Yagi Sensei. He is same age as me. When we were small, I called him, "Yagi, Yagi." Then he said, "As I am a man, you should use the polite words." So I was against him and said, "It is not necessary. We are same age!" My mother and I decided to give my father's training wear to Mr. Yagi. When my mother was still alive, we tried to decide to whom we should give this training wear. Should we give it to Kei (the oldest son), or not? But finally we decided to give it to the person who has been doing Karate for a long time and dedicated to my father. That was Mr. Yagi. My brother, Kei, did not come back to Okinawa when my father died, even though he has an obligation, as the oldest son, to come back when one's parents die. I preferred to give this training wear to Mr. Yagi instead of Kei, because of this reason. Mr. Yagi started learning Karate when he was 14 years old. My father would be also pleased for this decision.

Karate uniform and belt of the late Grandmaster, Chojun Miyagi, the founder of Goju-ryu karate, which was given by his widow and family to his successor, Grandmaster Meitoku Yagi, on Okinawa in 1963.

Memorial of Chojun Miyagi in Naha-city, Okinawa.

In September this year, it will be the thirteenth anniversary of my mother's death. We gave my father's training wear to Mr. Yagi two to three years before my mother died. My father wrote his name, Master Miyagi, on his training wear. Kei wanted it and still thought that he can take the way of Goju-ryu, because he is the oldest son. But I do not think so. The most important person who has developed the way of Goju-ryu is Mr. Yagi. I think the person who does one's best for Goju-ryu should be the leader. The leader is not necessary to be the son of my father. But Kei cannot understand what I mean. At the beginning, the students could not understand as well. So I said to my brothers, "You have to think. Though you are the son, you have not done Karate. Have you learnt Karate from our father more than Mr. Yagi?" I am sure that my father would have agreed with me. This is the only way to follow the will of my father. Ken-Bou (the youngest brother) can understand. He said that they should not say anything about who should become the leader. The person who will take Goju-ryu will follow the way of Karate, not the position of my father.

Additive enclosure.

The Meibukan Family Crest

The text below is a translation (by Hing-Poon Chan) and interpretation of page 37 of Meitatsu Yagi's book (My Travels in Karate, published in 1985 in Japanese) of Meibukan Goju-ryu.

Crest Meibukan.

'Meibukan no hatajiruschi o (crest) to suru.'
We of the Meibukan have decided upon this symbol.

'Mei to wa akaraka de tsuji o tosu i'.
'Mei' of Meibukan means 'clear,' 'pure,' 'without doubt sticking to one's principles.'

'In Yo (hi to tsuki).'
'Mei' (crest) combines the sun (crest) and the moon (crest) and refers to the principles of positive and negative.

'A-um (crest) hi wa shimari tsuki wa hiraku.'
The principles of 'ah' and 'oom' refer to a quick response, without interference and interval from open to closed, like an open moon and closed sun.

'Goju (crest) hi was futoku tsuki was goju to arawasu.'
The sun is constant, fixed, and heavy. The moon is mobile, flexible, and light. Yin and Yang principles like night and day are expressed like the sun being thick and the moon being thin (referring to the Meibukan crest) and reveals itself in the essence of Goju, which means hard and soft.

'Ichigi hissatsu (crest) hi tsuki (hitotsuki suna wachi ichigi hissatsu o arawasu).'
The character Mei (crest) consists of the sun and the moon.
Together the sun and the moon mean 'one strike' or 'one punch.'

Sensei Meitatsu Yagi explained to me (the author of this book) in an interview on Okinawa in 1993 the complex meaning of Meibukan in understandable words. A part of that interview concerning this topic follows:

Character Meibukan.

Lex Opdam: Sensei, could you tell us something about the Meibukan, why it is founded and what the meaning of its name is?

Meitatsu Yagi: "The Meibukan is founded to spread the tradition of Goju-ryu Karate-do the best possible way. Meibukan literally means "House of the Pure Martial Art." Mei means 'clear' or 'pure', Bu means 'martial arts' and Kan means 'house.' Mei also means Meitoku, Meitatsu, and Meitetsu. It is a direct reference toward our family. The names of my father, brother, and me are connected.

Karate Master Meitatsu Yagi, Ninth Degree, (Hanshi) older son of Grandmaster Meitoku Yagi and President of the Meibukan Goju-ryu Karate-do Association.

Just like the meaning of Go, which means (in simple terms) hard, and Ju (in simple terms) means soft, the Meibukan crest also has two elements of hard and soft. The Meibukan crest exists out of the sun, which stands for 'inhaling' and 'outside' and the moon which stands for 'breathing out' and 'inside.'"

Lex Opdam: The sun shines by day, which represents Yang and the moon that shines by night represents Yin. These two positive and negative elements have a very deep meaning. It includes a harmonious being in the world where there is always a struggle between the two opposites. Sensei draws the crest together with the kanji and explains where the kanji of the sun or 'hi' and the moon or 'tsuki' becomes the strong-fused crest. The character of the sun is closed and the character of the moon is open, which means the breath control of inhale and exhale.

The Meibukan Syllabus
Overview of Meibukan Goju-ryu Karate-do System

KATA	**Heishu* Kata**	Sanchin (Kihon kata)
		Tensho (Kihon kata)
	Kaishu Kata**	Fukyu (Taikyoko)
		Gekisai ichi
		Gekisai ni
		Saifa
		Shisochin
		Sanseru
		Sesan
		Seiunchin
		Sepai
		Kururunfa
		Suparinpei
		Tenshi
		Seiryu
		Byakko
		Shujakku
		Genbu
KUMITE	**Yakusoku Kumite**	Ippon
		Nippon
	Renzoku Kumite	Fukyu
		Kakomi
	Bunkai Kumite	
	Kake Uke Kumite	
	Ude Tanren Kumite	
UNDO	**Hojo Undo**	
	Yobi Undo	Seiri Undo
		Junan Undo

Heishu Kata (Heishugata)

The heishu kata include Sanchin and Tensho. The kanji (Japanese character) for heishu means "closed" or, in this context, "closed hand." In the heishu kata, muscle tension is almost constant and held for long periods of time. Closed also refers to the fact that the Qi is circulated in a closed circuit, the intention being to train the body energetically and physically with a strictly limited (closed) set of repetitive movements.

**Kaishu Kata (Kaishugata)*

The kaishu kata include the katas from Gekisai to Suparinpei to Genbu. The kanji (Japanese character) for "kaishu" means "open" or, in this context, "open hand." Unlike the heishu kata, kaishu kata uses muscular tension in shorter time frames. The contraction and relaxation of the muscles is intermittent and is not constrained to a single given pattern or purpose. Also, in kaishu kata, the Qi is left to circulate normally, or "openly."

KATA

> # Heishu Kata
>
> *Sanchin, Tensho, and Naihanchi are all kihon kata that aim to cultivate a strong physical body and to be the vessel of the budo-spirit. Without expanding on each specific form, one learns to regulate breathing in conjunction with the strength one possesses within a correct posture.*
>
> —Chojun Miyagi, 1934

SANCHIN KATA

Sanchin kata is a fundamental part of Goju-ryu Karate-do, but also of Okinawa Karate-do. There is no other Japanese Martial Art that practices a form like the Sanchin kata.

The name Sanchin consists of the words 'San,' meaning three, and 'Chin,' meaning fight or conflict. The meaning of the word Sanchin, three fights or three conflicts, signifies the deeper physical and mental growth processes, which unify a man. The three conflicts signify the forces that have to cooperate within the Martial Arts. Body, mind, and spirit should embrace movement, breathing, the control of 'Ki,' the general physical and mental balance, and the tactics and strategy of the Martial Arts. In Sanchin kata, all these aspects are expressed.

'San' also refers to the three physical levels of the body: upper, center, and lower (explained in more detail later). Sanchin kata is of key importance in practicing the Goju-ryu Karate-do system. The different postures and associated muscle tensions, with a special focus on internal energy to create a "suit of armor," breathing and mental focus, give the practitioner a direct insight into the core elements of the Martial Art of karate-do, which facilitate growth and may lead to intuitive self-knowledge.

Through physical and mental training, it is possible to achieve such a high level of concentration/energy that a "natural" balance is formed, which harmonizes one with the world around.

Sanchin is preeminently a form, a kata, that leads one toward the achievement of spiritual growth through physical and mental power. In this form, the true goal of karate-do can be readily found: to reach such a high level of physical and mental energy through practice that the practitioner is brought into contact with the creational force. In other words, one returns to the center or the core of life.

Sanchin is an active way to strengthen the mind by the use of the body and to create an inner harmony.

Origins and history

The origins of Sanchin kata are difficult to trace; however, the small amounts of documented material and oral transmission do give us some understanding of its history. Sanchin is not exclusively a Goju-ryu Karate-do kata. Other Okinawan karate styles, such as Uechi-ryu and Shorin-ryu (originally), also include Sanchin in their curriculum, although there are some external differences. The history of the Goju-ryu Sanchin kata can be traced back to the Okinawan Kanryo Higaonna (1853-1915) who was taught Sanchin kata, among other things (the Fuzhou-dialect for Sanchin is San Chen and the Mandarin-dialect San Chan), during the first few years of his stay in China by his teacher Liu Liu Ko. Subsequently, Kanryo Higaonna passed on this knowledge to another Okinawan called Chojun Miyagi (1888–1953), the founder of Goju-ryu Karate-do.

If one reviews the principles behind the practice of Sanchin kata, they can be traced back to the Chinese Martial Arts (1) that already were in practice a substantial amount of time before Kanryo Higaonna's journey to China. (The name Sanchin even can be found back in several Chinese Kung-Fu styles that have a tradition that dates back from before Goju-ryu, Shorin-ryu, and Uechi-ryu). Chojun Miyagi viewed Sanchin kata as a fundamental part of his fighting art. In his work, "An outline of Karate-do" (1934), he mentions that in 1828 a "style" was introduced on Okinawa that originated from Fuzhou (the province of Fujian, China), which served as a basis for Goju-ryu karate kempo. Therefore, the question can be asked whether Kanryo Higaonna might have come into contact with Sanchin kata even before he went to China. Although many theories and speculations remain, for now the most tangible evidence concerning the introduction of the "pre-Goju-ryu" Sanchin kata remains the oral transmissions by Chojun Miyagi to his students. These state that Kanryo Higaonna, during his first few years of practice, was only taught Sanchin kata by his teacher Liu Liu Ko, together with additional exercises to strengthen the body and to prepare it for learning the rest of the self-defense system.

A probable predecessor of Sanchin kata called Happoren is mentioned in the Bubishi, a classical work on Chinese Kung Fu regarding its history and philosophy, (herbal) medicine and applications within the fighting arts. (The instructions concerning Happoren that are given in the Bubishi show strong resemblances to those used in Sanchin kata). The Bubishi ('Wu Bei Zhi') was considered by Chojun Miyagi to be the most valuable document from the past for Goju-ryu Karate-do. Estimates concerning the origin of the Bubishi range between 1644 and 1911 (Qing dynasty). There are several theories as to how the Bubishi was introduced on Okinawa. As far as the Goju-ryu history is concerned, it is believed that Kanryo Higaonna brought back (a copy of) the Bubishi to Okinawa (2) when he returned from his journey to China (between 1867 and 1896, see note 3, Chapter History of Goju-ryu Karate-do). He subsequently passed on his knowledge (not just of Sanchin kata, but also of [herbal] medicine) to his students. His top students were Juhatsu Kiyoda and Chojun Miyagi.

Chojun Miyagi again passed Sanchin kata on to his students, but he did create a variation of it later.

Some elements of Sanchin (Happoren) kata freely translated from the Bubishi:

Development of mind, body & spirit through the form.

Eliminate all internal and external distractions. Concentrate on the here and now. Regulate your breathing and discard any random thoughts. The mind should be focused and as calm as still water throughout the kata.

The practitioner must coordinate his breathing and synchronize it with muscle activity. During inhalation, the body grows light. During exhalation the body becomes rooted. There is a slight pause between inhalation and exhalation. Never exhale all your air reserves.

Listen to your breathing and become aware of every part of your body during all movements.

A constant, but pliable, muscle tension in the upper back and pectoral muscle groups exists throughout the kata. The spine is kept parallel to the stomach in order to accomplish correct abdominal breathing.

The starting point of all Sanchin kata techniques is where the elbow meets the hip. The arm "rubs" along the rib cage during movement and all movement is executed in a dynamic fashion

Principal elements of Sanchin movement.

The moving of the foot should be similar to walking. The advancing (or retreating) step is started in a natural way and finished in a dynamic and solid stance—firmly rooted to the ground, retaining a slight inner bend at the knees at the completion of the movement.

Each step is to be made smoothly and quickly and must be identical to the previous step. The large toe of the rear foot aligns to the heel of the forward foot and they should be shoulder width from each other.

Whether moving in a forward or backward direction, the forward foot creates a swiping crescent shape. Turn the forward foot / knee at the ball of the foot and lift the foot just a hair's height off the floor to allow movement or "gliding" along the floor. The forward or backward step is executed rapidly.

The leg muscles should be firm but also flexible. If the muscles are too tense, then the ability to transition from one movement to the next will be affected.

Adjustments to Sanchin kata

Sanchin kata was originally practiced with open hands (nukite), as it is still taught today in China (3). Kanryo Higaonna had been taught Sanchin kata with open hands by Liu Liu Ko, but Kanryo Higaonna also taught Sanchin kata as a closed fist form. The exact reason for this is not known, but there are several theories that try to explain it.

One of these theories is that the Okinawan people had been familiar for generations with the use of the "makiwara'" (see Hojo undo), onto which mainly fist-techniques were practiced as a form/part of self-defense training. To better integrate Sanchin kata into Okinawan culture, Kanryo Higaonna changed the open hand technique (nukite, spear hand) into a "seiken" (fist-technique), more common to the Okinawan fighting arts.

Another theory involves the release of external "ki" (Chinese "Qi"), which could influence bystanders, but also the practitioner when he or she had insufficient knowledge of these matters. The bystander may be affected from the outside by the flows of energy that are generated by the practitioner. When carried out incorrectly, the Sanchin practitioner's own energy balance may also be negatively influenced. Although a combination of these two theories cannot be ruled out, the second is very inconceivable. There is, however, a third theory, which appears to be the most plausible. The fact that Kanryo Higaonna started to teach publicly at a school (Naha Kuritsu Shogyo Koto Gakko) in 1905 has led to another, very straightforward, explanation. Until 1901, the practice of karate had been limited to a small circle of practitioners. Since then, adjustments were made to make karate more accessible to larger groups of people, so that it also could be fitted into the system of public schools. Considering the youthful age of the students, and the educational character of the school-system, it is probable that Kanryo Higaonna focused more on the general physical and mental development of his students and placed the deadly and dangerous fighting techniques more to the background.

In light of this last theory, it is important to mention that Kanryo Higaonna taught only the "closed hand" form of Sanchin kata to the larger groups of students, whereas he taught both the "closed" and the "open" hand form to his small circle of direct students.

Some Goju-ryu organizations discriminate between two sorts of Sanchin kata (4) and practice both within their curriculum. Within the Meibukan school of Sensei Meitoku Yagi, the closed hand form of the Kanryo Higaonna Sanchin kata is mainly practiced, and can be considered the core of Meibukan's curriculum.

The core of the practice of Sanchin kata can be found both on a mental and on a physical level. It is an exercise in which the highest goal is the focus of physical and mental energy that one tries to control by disciplined training.

Hing-Poon Chan is checked for proper execution (shimé) of Sanchin Kata by Renshi Paul Zarzour.

Physiological applications
The muscular system

On a physiological level, Sanchin kata is a form of conditioning the body. The muscles reach a form of isometric (static), concentric (tightening), and eccentric (opposing) tension. The concentric and eccentric contractions coexist during the movements and are virtually always carried out isokinetically (with a constant speed).

This is one way to maintain muscle power while increasing muscle endurance and still prepare the body in the form of a warm-up exercise. Through this way of tightening the muscles, one learns to invoke an internal resistance and to integrate this with one's breathing. The movements in these techniques are made in such a way that the practitioner experiences opposing forces that act upon the body from all possible angles. The opposing forces created should correspond to one's breathing. This means that the amount of work—moving with a certain intention, strength and speed, invoked by the resistance created—should equal the amount of energy that is available. One learns to match movement and breathing, and vice versa. The consciousness gained about these two forces during practice can lead to a perfect harmony. The right balance between the two could be termed a harmony of forces.

Through the correct tightening of muscles, one learns to set the joints in the correct position and also strengthens the so-called "end postures" of the joints by controlled focusing of the muscles. These end postures that recur during kimé-moments (maximal tension/focus of muscle chains) within techniques, but also on the way towards the final posture, are central key points (5) that are important in the growth process toward the right techniques and postures of Goju-ryu Karate-do.

Muscle protection

Sanchin kata also teaches us to tighten the muscles in order to serve as protective armor. Either as a part of tactics or allowing for an unexpected attack to the body, one needs to take into consideration that one may be hit. The Goju-ryu Karate-do system aims to fight close to the opponent and take impacts to the body into account. By tightening the muscles in various regions of the body, one can prevent an impact, which might otherwise cause more damage with various consequences, from penetrating too deep. In practicing the muscle tension during Sanchin kata, one trains for this result.

Muscle tension

During the practice of Sanchin kata, it is of great importance to use the correct muscle tension in the body. Incorrect muscle tension leads to passing over the actual goal of the practice of Sanchin—or worse, to negative consequences for the practitioner.

From a practical point of view, it is virtually impossible to describe in great detail the postures (with accompanying muscle tension) and the movements with their relationship to breathing. The practical side of karate-do can take place in only one way: in the dojo, supervised by a Sensei. He or she must accompany the student step by step in the way in which, in this case Sanchin kata, is exercised. In this way, the Sensei can give individual instructions to each student adjusted to his or her physical and mental characteristics. If an error is detected, the Sensei can intervene immediately and prevent any damage that might otherwise occur. Although this book also has much to offer to the semi-advanced karateka, it is written mainly for novices of Goju-ryu Karate-do, especially the Meibukan School of Dai Sensei Meitoku Yagi. In light of this, only a general overview is given of Sanchin kata and, among other things, muscle tension.

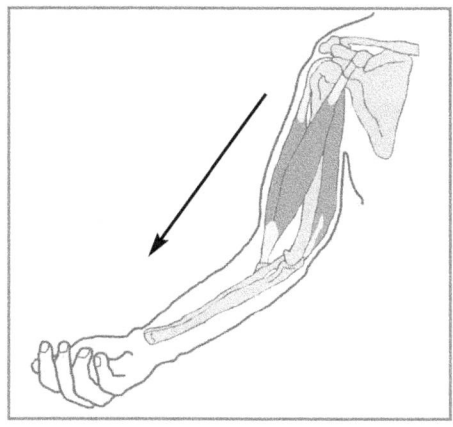
Eccentric movement of the biceps.

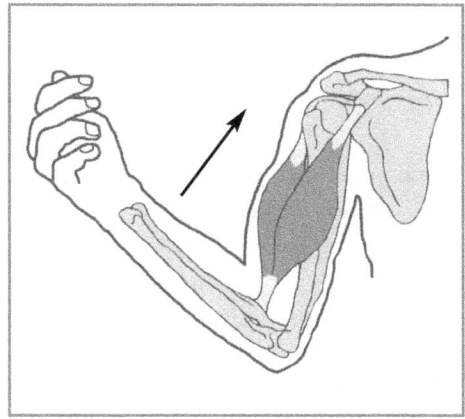
Concentric movement of the biceps.

During the practice of Sanchin kata, there is a continuous muscle tension in the body that varies in intensity from one muscle to the other. During walking, moving the body to a different position, there is a "natural" tension/relaxation in the lower part of the body, especially the legs, which allows them to move freely. The upper part of the body, roughly the rump, arms, and neck, have a tension that is somewhat higher than needed to maintain the postures of Sanchin kata (as described and shown in the photographs). As soon as the legs start to dig in (the leg has moved to its next position), they create a muscle tension that is greater than that needed to stand in this stance "naturally." When the rooting is completed (brought to its maximum strength), the leg muscles are strongly tightened and keep this tension until they need to relax to facilitate the next shift of a foot/leg. At the moment of focus or kimé, there is a maximal tightening of various muscle chains and muscles in the body. This is a very simple and rough description of the muscle tension present during the practice of Sanchin kata.

Static. The feet/leg muscles, as an example, stay tensed by muscle contraction. The muscle tension is high and spread in such a way that stability is guaranteed. No movement is made.

The cooperative interaction between muscle tension and breathing should be fine-tuned in such a way that the amount of energy used by the tightening of the muscles is supported by (among other things) the respiration (oxygen). The tightening of muscles, i.e., during the execution of a punching technique, starts at exactly the same time that exhalation starts. Retraction of the punch towards the "chamber" (side of the body; hikite) starts at exactly the same time that inhalation starts. Both the intention (amount of force, speed, time/pace) and the aim of techniques that are carried out must correlate with (abdominal) respiration (amount of force, speed, time/pace).

Some guidelines are as follows:
- During exhalation, some spare air/breath must be conserved in the body. Besides abdominal respiration, there also is chest respiration (used, for example, after a 100-meter sprint; additional respirational muscles are employed in order to pull up the chest so that more oxygen can be taken up and more carbon dioxide can be removed). In Sanchin, one does not address chest respiration. The tendency to use chest respiration is an indication that probably too much energy is being used in muscle power, which needs to be

Kata

Concentric. In the Sanchin movement seen on these two photos, the arm is pulled back by raising the concentric tension in the biceps among other muscles. The tension in the triceps, amongst other muscles, is lowered and therefore the movement in pulling the arm to the chamber is permitted. Strong tension remains present in the triceps amongst other muscles at all times.

Eccentric. In the Sanchin movement seen on these two photos, the arm is put forward by raising the concentric tension in the triceps among other muscles. The tension in the biceps, amongst other muscles, is lowered and therefore the movement in pushing the arm forward to the front of the body is permitted. Strong tension although remains present in the biceps amongst other muscles at all times.

compensated for by an increased inhalation of oxygen and/or an increased exhalation of carbon dioxide. Another indication pointing to this unbalance is craving for breath or yawning after Sanchin kata.
- Another way to focus the intensity is the "testing" (see page 53) that is applied to the practitioner. This needs to be adjusted to each individual practitioner, but has some general rules of thumb:
- During the striking of a punch, it is being restrained/held back by the one who is doing the testing. By applying this resistance, a boundary of the practitioner's capabilities is sought; however, the resistance should not be so great as to unbalance the practitioner in posture and stance. (Although occasionally greater resistance is applied for other reasons, this is how the intention in force should normally be). The resistance can be achieved, for instance, by pressing a hand against the knuckles of the executor and restraining the punch, or by holding onto the elbow of the executor's punching arm and pulling it backward, (almost) preventing the arm from extending. In this way, the Sanchin practitioner gets a reasonable indication as to how and with what intensity he or she must apply force during the execution or maintaining of techniques. This applies also to the fixing of techniques or stances. Even during a standstill, forces are applied from all angles, as previously discussed.
- The respiration and muscle tension during the final moment, or kimé, have the highest intensity in energy. During this climax everything within the indicated boundaries is brought to a maximum. This is for a very brief moment and should not be extensively maintained.
- The abdominal respiration muscles are directly involved in both muscle tension and breathing. During inhalation, the abdomen fills itself (one tries to relax the abdominal muscles, although some tension remains in order to maintain a slightly upturned position of the pelvis). During this process, the flanks expand (without conscious muscle tension), and the belly and even the lower back expand (there is no conscious tension in the back except that which is needed to stand up straight). The abdomen expands. After a brief moment, the abdominal muscles are consciously tensed. This tension is brought to a maximum during exhalation. After the climax, the muscles "relax" again from the conscious tension after which a new cycle can begin.

Respiration/breathing

During the practice of Sanchin kata, one uses abdominal respiration or deep breathing. This deep breathing ensures that the oxygenation of the entire body, including the brain, is as complete as possible. This creates the optimal conditions for the exchange of signals between the brain and the nervous system to come about. Parts of the body, such as the organs, are oxygenized with a more optimal

_____ *Kata*

Young Lex Opdam performing Sanchin kata. The muscles reach a maximum focus.

Young Lex Opdam performing Sanchin kata. Inhaling through the nose and exhaling through the mouth.

dose of oxygen, and the carbon dioxide can be expelled more optimally, as well.

In addition, the internal organs are being "massaged" by the abdominal breathing. Because of the more complete up and down movement of the diaphragm, "new" blood can enter the organs and purify them, carrying away waste products. The organs become more active and stronger which, if carried out correctly, has a positive effect on general health.

Sanchin has many aspects on a physical, but certainly also on a mental level. These writings concerning Sanchin kata are far from complete, but only attempt to express the importance of this unique kata upon the reader. So far, the "outward core" of Sanchin kata has been addressed in such a way that it is comprehensible for the average Western reader. However, there is more to Sanchin, and in fact, its great strength lies in its deeply-anchored Eastern viewpoint. Sanchin has evolved from an Eastern culture that, even thousands of years ago, viewed nature in a way unknown to the West, although there are many resemblances with ancient Greek culture. Sanchin is the product of this Eastern culture in which the "great fire," the force of life/soul, expresses the core of existence.

The bio-energetic aspect

There are more meanings to the posture of the human body combined with respiration and the form of muscle tension in Sanchin kata than have thus far been discussed. Sanchin kata is a form of moving in which various elements of the Eastern Martial Arts are expressed. Linked to the Eastern ways of viewing the world around us and the associated "forces of nature," Sanchin kata is a creation of a hard and external form of Qi Gong (exercise) that has a direct and actively intertwined combat meaning. Prior to continuing, it is useful to expand a little on the term Qi.

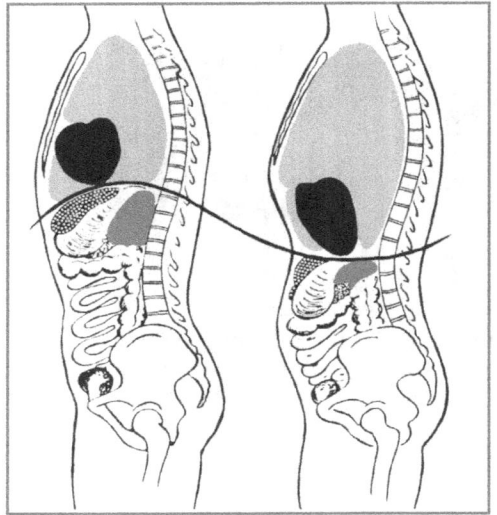

Movement of diaphragm and massage of the organs.

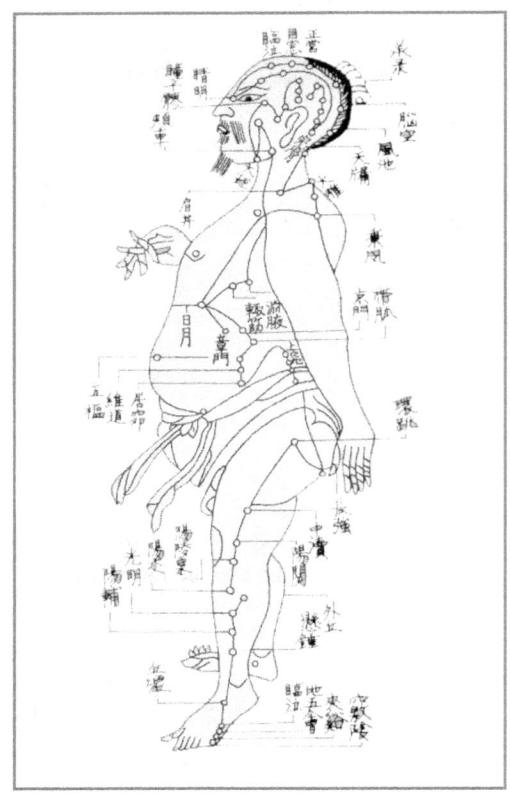

Meridians.

Ki/Qi

Ki is the Japanese term for "energy-forms" that are present throughout the universe. In China, it is called Qi (Chi). These energy forms, sometimes referred to as "life-force," can manifest themselves as, for example, heat, electricity, magnetic fields, and so on. But thoughts also are considered to be forms of energy; therefore, Qi. Qi is present in all beings and things, in what is usually separated as living or dead matter, i.e., an animal, a stone, a planet, and so on.

From scientific research during recent years, it appears that Qi as a form of energy has many resemblances to electricity. An example of this is the human body and bioelectricity.

In Sanchin kata, much emphasis is placed on posture, respiration, and muscle tension. During the practice of Sanchin, we encounter a Qi-form that manifests itself (partly) as bioelectricity. Through deep breathing or abdominal respiration, a movement of abdominal muscles is created by moving the diaphragm. This movement, together with breathing and nutrients present in the body (fuel), enable biochemical reactions that generate electromagnetic energy. During the practice of Sanchin, there is one central point on which one focuses. This point is called Dan Tien in Chinese or Tanden in Japanese. It is located between the internal organs, where the gravitational center of the body is situated. Put more simply, it is located between the front of the abdomen, the sides of the hipbones, the navel, and the crotch. In Eastern medicine and Martial Arts, the Dan Tien is thought to be the most important center for the generation of bio-electricity: the central area for recharging energy. In simple terms, Sanchin in this context can be viewed as a means to raise the bioelectricity to a higher level.

Hard Qi exercise

Sanchin is a hard or external way of Qi generation. When the brain sends signals to the targeted muscles, they respond by contracting and relaxing. The better one controls this mentally, the better signals will reach the body, and the better or more fully the desired effect can be brought about. The fitter the body, the better this process can take place. The guidance of signals through the body is carried out along nerves. Signals are passed between different nerve cells or to the cells of muscles or glands through synapses. The conductance of signals takes place through electrical and chemical reactions.

Heightened tension through muscle focus

During the practice of Sanchin, one has a consciously manipulated muscle focus. This is achieved by sending signals from the brain to the muscles involved, in order to assume and maintain postures and execute techniques. The tension in the muscles in question can be said to be very high. During the moving of limbs, there is an increased tension (higher than is necessary to keep the limbs of the body at the desired position or move them into the preferred situation), with strongly increased tension during moments of kimé (simultaneous with the breathing focus during exhalation). During this process, considerable focus or kimé is applied around the tendon and muscle areas. Subsequently, there is increased activity within the tendons and muscles, including the attachment sites between tendon and bone, as well as tendon and muscle.

During this increased activity, locally present Qi is released and local Qi is created. Anyone contracting his or her muscles releases energy at the site of tension. This energy, spoken of here as Qi, is not only generated, but also is present latently and can be drawn upon as if it were a small battery. Virtually everyone can directly release and create Qi in this fashion. This also holds true during the first practice of Sanchin kata. However, the advanced practitioner of Sanchin kata not only will use local Qi, but also will be able to make better use of the Qi originating from the Dan Tien. The Dan Tien, like a large battery, is the largest source of Qi, or energy, in the body. The Qi stemming from the Dan Tien flows through the body along paths and channels called meridians. Its flow can be both strong and weak (see the chapter "the mental aspect"). Among other things, this is dependent on possible blockages/restrictions of the meridians and on mental control.

The location of the Dan Tian is about four fingers beneath the navel and in the middle between the front and back of the body.

Qi flow

In order for Qi to flow freely through the body, certain conditions must be met. As a consequence of muscle contraction, some bones are pulled together, resulting in a reduced flow of Qi. Here, the passage of Qi is constricted, blocked, and stagnated. In part, this also happens during Sanchin kata. In fact Sanchin kata is a hard (Go) energy "Qi" exercise "Gong" (Qi Gong). The extreme muscle contraction and, therefore, the local energy within the muscles is very important because the aspect of combat, originating from the stylistic fighting system, has a very prominent role. Within the more general Qi Gong exercises that lack a martial focus, the tension in the muscles is very minimal. Other conditions, such as heavy kimé contractions and strict mental control of breathing, also are formulated differently. Because of the lack of extreme muscle focus, in general Qi Gong exercises, the Qi from the Dan Tien can flow through the body more freely during the practice of "pure" Qi Gong than during Sanchin kata.

The main goal of Sanchin kata is to direct the focus toward the hard, external side of the martial art, because the technical basis is to assert mainly the Go principles during a fight. In Sanchin kata, there is a strong emphasis on Qi-maintenance, especially within and around the tendons and muscles, which, seen from the specific fighting point of view of Goju-ryu Karate-do, is of great importance (one can think of a protective armor, strong contraction during explosive movements, maintaining muscle tension during wrestling, pushing through, etc.). Had this not been so, another viewpoint would have been taken. (The Go principle here should not be seen as just being pure hardness and external extremity. The Ju principle also is present in Sanchin kata. Both are interdependent and constantly connected with each other). The Ju principle is expressed through the full abdominal breathing; however, its range is limited by the hard nature of muscle tension. Within the Kaishu kata, the Ju aspects are expressed more fully, because of the softer nature of these katas. Especially during kimé moments, the hard aspect takes over. Thus, the Goju-ryu system knows different energy flows that can be both hard and soft and are present alternatively during practice.

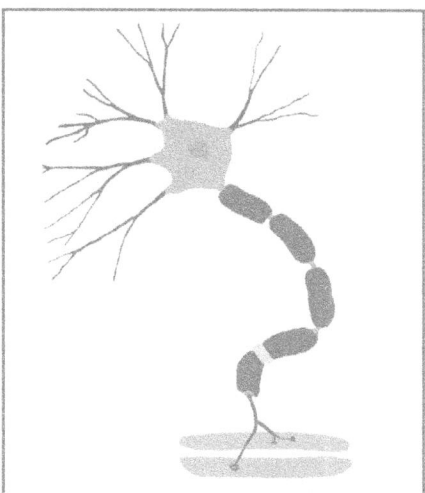

Synaps. Signals are passed on between different nerve cells or on to the cells of muscles or glands through synapses.

Internal and external Qi practice

A rough distinction can be made between internal (Neidan Qi Gong) and external (Wai Dan Qi Gong) Qi practice. The external methods, or hard exercises, such as the Shaolin Kung Fu methods, use exercises that aim to send Qi to the limbs and to train the body for absorbing an impact by sending Qi to the muscles and the skin ("Iron Shirt" exercises). Also, hardening exercises ("Iron Palm") in which one kicks or strikes against resistances and Qi lead to those parts of the body that make contact with the object, often are part of the external fighting arts.

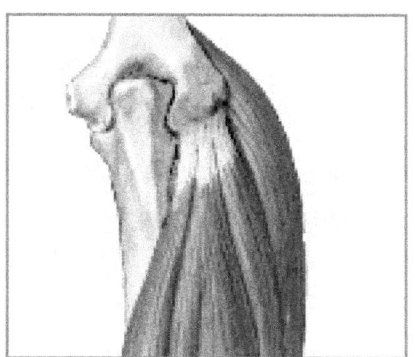

Conditioning and tension of this area, where the tendon meets the bone and the muscle, will keep the tissue strong.

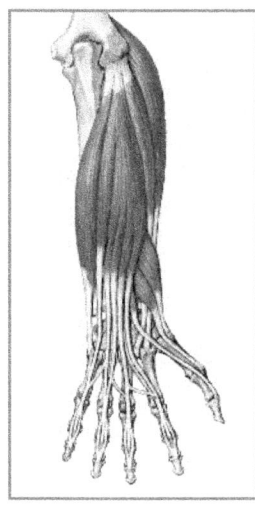

The bone of the forearm and upper arm and the attached tendon/muscles.

External fighting arts, from which Goju-ryu karate mainly stems, have forms and exercises that aim to raise the specific energy level of the muscular system, and to enlarge its capacity. All of this is aimed to make effective use of the body during fighting situations. Prerequisite is that the Qi flowing from the brain to the muscles is pure and powerful. In order to achieve this pure concentration, one needs a calm mind and a strong force of will. The soft martial arts, such as Tai Chi, for example, require the same pure concentration during practice. This core element is universal and inextricable from each form of art, whether martial or not. It is the essence of practice. The outward features of hard and soft martial arts, however, can be called rather dissimilar. During the practice of the external martial arts, there is a great emphasis/focus on the surface (muscles/tendons/skin), whereas within the internal martial arts, the focus is aimed more inwardly.

The internal Qi Gong emphasizes the completely free flow of Qi through the body without focusing, during which the harmony of the complete body takes on a different proportion than with the external martial arts. In both cases, there is harmony between mind and body. During a fight, both principles can be needed in order to go with the flow of action. Hard needs soft and vice versa.

The mental aspect

The mental training of Sanchin kata often is underestimated. The mental focus, the flow of thoughts, can be enormous during the practice of Sanchin. Sanchin kata is very strong in mental focus and ultimately a powerful and energy rich mental activity.

Much is written about the heavy muscular activity and the possible negative consequences this may have for high blood pressure, cramps, etc. (albeit often written by people of different styles, people not correctly instructed, or people who haven't taken their practice and studies seriously enough). However it is especially the mental aspects of Sanchin that enrich it and are of main importance in order to practice it correctly. For this book, it would lead too far to elaborate extensively on the spiritual side of Sanchin kata, or karate-do, as well as the psychological processes that emerge during the practice of karate-do. However, the mental strength that needs to be employed in Sanchin kata, as well as other katas, in order to focus physical and mental energy, is of great value. If the focus leads the practitioner to rise above the form of the kata, its value is inexpressible. Then, practice is not only valuable but becomes sensible.

During the practice of karate-do, the practitioner tries, through utmost concentration, to lose him or herself in the technique, the movement. This state of mind, the true spirit of karate as "empty hand," is called "Mushin" in Japanese. There are no distractions. There is only concentration. We lose ourselves to come into contact with the world. Often, the largest obstacles in our lives are those raised by our emotions, which determine our spiritual state/state of mind. By controlling our emotions, we are able to act effectively, and in the event of a fight, to respond adequately. In the same way, our strength of spirit during the practice of Sanchin kata is of the utmost importance. Any distraction from controlling our thoughts in order to move our body will dupe the body (this is of great importance in "reading" an opponent during a fight). Therefore, the first prerequisite for a correct flow of Qi is the strength of spirit with which signals are sent through the body. Our Qi reflects this spiritual strength. Although some blockades may be present in the body (due to accidents, injury, etc.), most blockades can be found in the mind. In the mind, we find our greatest enemies and, through karate-do as a martial art, we try to free ourselves from these enemies by training our force of will and by persevering in our practice in a disciplined way. We engage in a fight with ourselves. We attempt to evolve spiritually through karate-do.

One visualises that the energy expands in all directions from the Dan Tian.

Sanchin is of pivotal importance in Goju-ryu Karate-do in various ways. Sanchin has an amazing amount of various aspects that merit investigation in both a theoretical and a practical sense.

To a large extent, Sanchin teaches the correct posture and attitude, as well as movements needed for the practice and mastering of the Goju-ryu Karate-do system. Sanchin teaches the basics of breathing in accordance with movement (technique), along with coordination and focus.

Sanchin is preeminently the Kihon kata for Goju-ryu, because of the basic principles that are effective during its practice, such as physical conditioning and the development of the meditative state.

During Sanchin kata, different forms of visualization are active. These support breathing, posture, the adjustment of muscle tension, and the fighting applications.

The most important basic visualizations for novices and semi-advanced practitioners are included in this book. They are meant as a support and are to be used until the visualization has become a new "reality" for the practitioner.

Visualization of breathing

Several visualization processes play a role in breathing during Sanchin kata. In the Kanryo Higaonna Sanchin kata, as is it meant in full strength, one should focus mainly on the Dan Tien during breathing. One inhales through the nose and imagines the breath following a route to the Dan Tien, where it merges with several other elements. These elements (energy from food, water, chemical compounds, etc.) are present as potential energy. Together with thought control, breathing, and movement, they are converted into or contribute to the charging of a continuously growing "balloon" of energy.

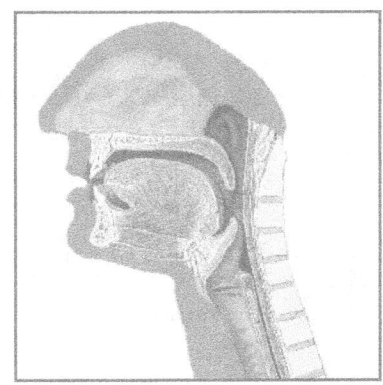

The tongue and the palate have to come into contact with each other.

As a means of visualization of the inhalation, one imagines the central point of this balloon to be expanding. Since the balloon has a round form, it "expands" within the belly in all directions. Thus, during the visualization process, as a way to control thoughts, one focuses on the path traveled by the breath (via the nose, through the throat, larynx, etc.), which doesn't stop at the lungs, but continues on its (imaginary) path towards the Dan Tien. Through this visualization, the practitioner can achieve a more fixed focus on moving the diaphragm and achieving a stronger expansion of the muscles around the Dan Tien (abdomen, back, and loins). During exhalation, breath is sent from the Dan Tien to the mouth, where it is expelled from the body. Even though there is also some "emission" of Qi during exhalation, the total amount of Qi within the body increases through this process. Therefore, if practiced correctly, the amount of (active) Qi before Sanchin kata is less than after. As oxygen and other compounds are inhaled, they are exhaled as well. However, the composition of the exhaled breath is different (for example the proportion of oxygen breathed in is 21 percent; breathed out, it has diminished to 17 percent).

It is important for the visualization process that there is a correct balance between inhalation and exhalation. No "preference" should dominate, since this would mean that more air is breathed in than out or vice versa, resulting in associated harmful consequences. In principle, the basic visualization during inhalation is the same as during exhalation. At the "final moment" of exhalation, the tongue is pressed against the palate and the inside of the front teeth while the exhalation is accelerated. This acceleration takes place just prior to the (controlled) "passing away" of the exhalation. (The way of cutting off of exhalation has to do with the fact that the tongue and the palate come into contact with each other to connect two important meridians, namely the Conception Vessel and the Governor Vessel).

Kata

Visualization of stance, movement and fighting applications

The most important and frequently reappearing stance within the Kanryo Higaonna Sanchin kata is the Sanchin Dachi with a Chudan Morote Soto Uke (see photo). Apart from the limbs, we must first consider the spine.

Imagine that there is a thread connected to the crown of the head pulling toward the heavens above, while a thread connected to the sacrum is pulling the body toward the center of the earth. The tension needed in the body is addressed on page 40 ('Muscle tension'). When one is in Sanchin Dachi, imagine the legs to have roots that attach to the ground below the body. Another often used visualization is that of the feet having suckers like an octopus or claws like an eagle's, clasping a prey.

The back should be straight and one should visualize a thread connected to the crown of the head pulling towards the heavens above, while a thread connected to the sacrum is pulling the body towards the center of the earth.

The tree root visualization is very easy because our language calls forth a strong image, due to the fact that trees are commonplace objects in nature. The visualization of suckers mostly resembles the clinging/sticking function of the toes. The toes spread prior to being placed on the ground, after which they draw together toward the ball of the foot, creating the "sucking effect." These visualizations in part ensure that a person stands well rooted. Together with the posture and the muscle tension in the legs and around the pelvis, the tree is rooted solidly, with roots (legs), trunk (torso), and branches (arms). A more abstract visualization also is available. As soon as one is rooted, imagine forces being applied on the legs simultaneously from all sides: left, right, front, back, above, and below. In this way, one strains all possible muscles in order to resist these forces and to guarantee stability. To stimulate this process (among other things) there also is "testing" (see "Sanchin Testing"), during which another person checks if the correct muscle focus is present by connecting with the legs of the practitioner (i.e., by pushing).

As far as the arms are concerned, which in principle includes most of the (visible) movement in the kata, several other visualization models are involved. As well as within the legs, in the arms there should be continuous tension (the amount depending on the position and situation); imaginary force is applied from all angles. During the movements of techniques, one not only imagines reaching a visual "endpoint" (such as the anatomical end position of a punch technically reaching its goal), but one tries to extend the technique somewhat further than physically necessary. Imagine sending the technique endlessly through the universe without physical boundaries. Using the punching technique (Chudan Gyaku Tsuki) as an example, one imagines the axial rotation of a bullet (the arm is the bullet), which again sends the right signals to the muscles, enabling the optimal execution of the technique.

If these techniques are carried out, one imagines a virtual opponent against whom they are directed. However, the path toward the contact (physical contact with the actual goal) is one with resistance. This resistance is comprised of forces that act on the body and thus influence the execution of the technique. Mentally, this is a very strong point in training.

Due to the nature of this book, it is not meant as a written means to teach Goju-ryu Karate-do and thus Sanchin kata. Examples and basic concepts are explained, and are meant to be used as tools and as an introduction to Sanchin kata. The visualization forms strengthen the execution of the kata and support the main issues.

Sanchin Testing

Like all the other aspects of Karate-do, Sanchin kata is observed by the Sensei. This observation takes place both passively and actively. The active part is closely interwoven with the instructions the student receives concerning Sanchin kata. These can be instructions such as the intensity of muscle power, as discussed previously, and instructions concerning various other aspects of the practice of Sanchin kata. Although the mental testing (which is done partly through the active observation) is of great importance, this book will not address the issue for various reasons (among other things, to protect the psychological process occurring inside the practitioner). The physical testing always is carried out by the Sensei, or by assistants who are knowledgeable enough about the main issues in Sanchin kata. The physical testing consists of checking if posture, breathing, and muscle tension are correct. Practically speaking, physical contact

Lex Opdam is checked for proper execution (shimé) of Sanchin Kata by Renshi Peter Andritsakis.

is made with various parts of the body by feeling if there is tension or relaxation, and to what extent. Corrections are carried out and resistances are raised to continuously check and help the practitioner. The raising of resistance by the person who tests the Sanchin practitioner, helps the practitioner to strengthen his or her visualization process. A practical example is pushing against an arm; the practitioner feels this resistance and tries to preserve this feeling the next time, even though the tester does not apply resistance through physical contact this time. In this way, the practitioner can call upon the previous experience and thus better signal his muscles in order to achieve the same goal.

Another type of testing is performed on the eyes. Naturally, there are no actual thrusts into the eyes, but still, when at unforeseen moments a thrust is made in the direction of the eyes of the Sanchin practitioner, the eyelids will blink reflexively, in order to prevent damage to the eyes. The reflex must be controlled by not moving the eyelids. The practitioner must keep the eye open and prevent blinking as a response. This testing has a lot to do with the fighting spirit, but also with the meditative side of Sanchin. Furthermore, it is a form of keeping bodily reflexes (including emotions) under control. At more advanced levels, Sanchin testing can involve punches and kicks that are placed at the right moment with the correct intention on the right spot. If this is not done properly, it can lead to damage to the practitioner's body. Therefore, leave testing to the Sensei or to people appointed by him or her (as well as the tutoring of nearly all aspects of Sanchin kata). The teaching of the embusen and the techniques without the special muscle tension and respiration is harmless, but keep in mind to respect your body and to be careful.

Example of Sanchin testing.

Execution of the Kanryo Higaonna Sanchin kata

The Kanryo Higaonna Sanchin kata is the only Sanchin kata that has officially been taken up in the Meibukan school of Dai Sensei Meitoku Yagi. For this reason, practical explanations are given only for the Kanryo Higaonna Sanchin kata.

> *"Sanchin is the kihon kata, the basic kata of Okinawan Goju-ryu.*
>
> *"In my opinion, the Sanchin kata is of utmost importance for a karateka in order to master Goju-ryu karate. The education of Goju-ryu is based on the Sanchin principles of correct inhalation and exhalation, and the expansion and contraction of the abdomen. If a person refrains from training Sanchin, this will affect the whole Goju-ryu karate training."*
>
> —Hanshi Anthony Mirakian

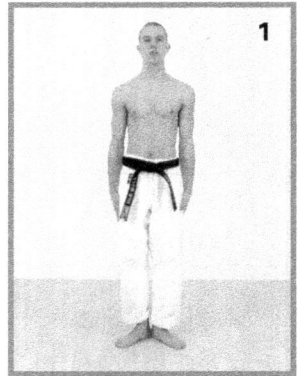

Formal attention in Musubi Dachi.

Preparation in Musubi Dachi to start the form.

Transition to Yoi position in Musubi Dachi.

Kata

Yoi position in Heiko Dachi.

Migi Sanchin Dachi with Chudan Morote Soto Uke.

Migi Sanchin Dachi with Hikite.

Migi Sanchin Dachi with Chudan Gyaku Tsuki.

Migi Sanchin Dachi back in Chudan Morote Soto Uke.

Hidari Sanchin Dachi.

Hidari Sanchin Dachi with Hikite.

Hidari Sanchin Dachi with Chudan Gyaku Tsuki.

Hidari Sanchin Dachi back in Chudan Morote Soto Uke.

Migi Sanchin Dachi.

Migi Sanchin Dachi with Hikite.

Migi Sanchin Dachi with Chudan Gyaku Tsuki.

Migi Sanchin Dachi with Hikite.

Migi Sanchin Dachi with Kaki Chudan Ura Tsuki.

Migi Benzoku Dachi.

Hidari Sanchin Dachi with Chudan Soto Uke and Hikite.

Hidari Sanchin Dachi with Chudan Gyaku Tsuki.

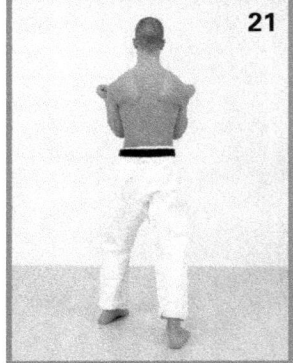
Hidari Sanchin Dachi back in Chudan Morote Soto Uke.

Kata

Migi Sanchin Dachi.

Migi Sanchin Dachi with Hikite.

Migi Sanchin Dachi with Chudan Gyaku Tsuki.

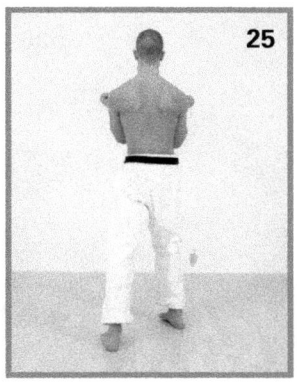
Migi Sanchin Dachi back in Chudan Morote Soto Uke.

Hidari Sanchin Dachi.

Hidari Sanchin Dachi with Hikite.

Hidari Sanchin Dachi with Chudan Gyaku Tsuki.

Hidari Sanchin Dachi back in Chudan Morote Soto Uke.

Migi Sanchin Dachi.

Migi Sanchin Dachi with Hikite.

Migi Sanchin Dachi with Chudan Gyaku Tsuki.

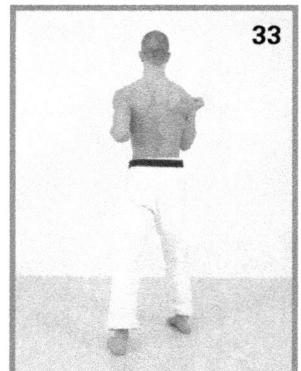
Migi Sanchin Dachi with Hikite.

Migi Sanchin Dachi with Chudan Kaki Ura Tsuki.

Migi Benzoku Dachi.

Hidari Sanchin Dachi with Chudan Soto Uke and Hikite.

Hidari Sanchin Dachi with Chudan Gyaku Tsuki.

Hidari Sanchin Dachi with Chudan Morote Soto Uke.

Migi Sanchin Dachi.

Kata

Migi Sanchin Dachi with Chudan Gyaku Tsuki (repeat in the same position a total of four more Tsuki's with on turns the left and right)

Migi Sanchin Dachi Hikite.

Migi Sanchin Dachi with Chudan Morote Soto Uke.

Migi Sanchin Dachi bringing the arms to the front with hands at floating rib level.

Migi Sanchin Dachi with Morote Hikite.

Migi Sanchin Dachi bringing the arms to the front with hands at floating rib level.

Migi Sanchin Dachi with Morote Hikite.

Migi Sanchin Dachi bringing the arms to the front with hands at floating rib level.

Migi Sanchin Dachi with Morote Hikite.

Migi Sanchin Dachi bringing the arms to the front with hands at floating rib level.

Hidari Sanchin Dachi with preparation for block.

Hidari Sanchin Dachi with Mawashi Uke and finishing with Hikite.

Hidari Sanchin Dachi with Morote Shotei Oshi and Tora Guchi.

Step back in Musubi Dachi in preparation to finish the form.

Musubi Dachi and finishing the form.

Formal attention in Musubi Dachi.

Kata

Embusen of the Kanryo Higaonna Sanchin Kata

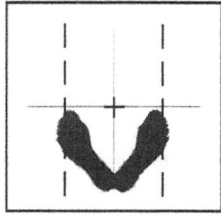 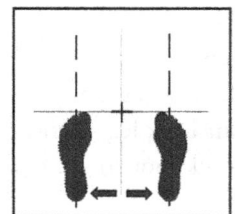 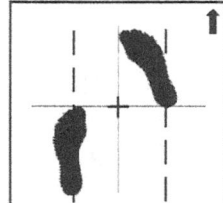

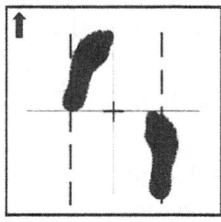 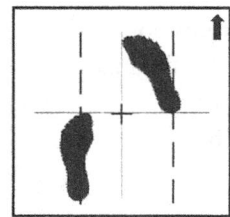 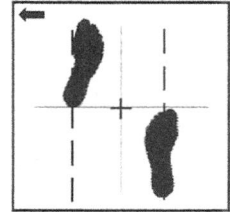

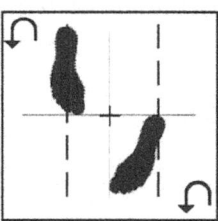 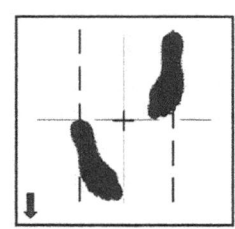 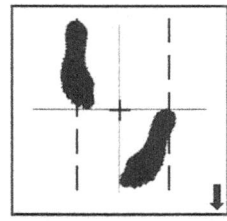

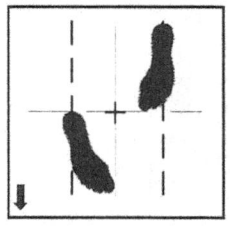 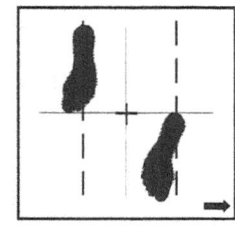 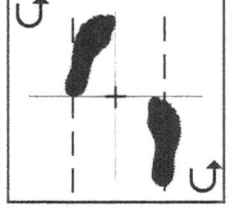

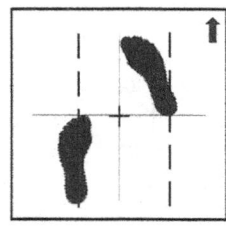 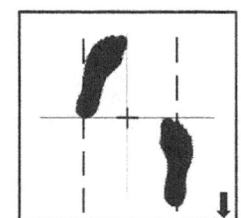 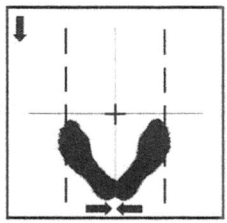

Attentions concerning general posture
This book does not address movements

A	1.	Straight back.
A	1a.	Retracted chin.
A	1b.	Turn up the pelvis slightly.
B	2.	Extend your back leg almost completely.
B	2a	Keep the back foot straight (with the toes directed) to the front.
B	3.	Slightly bend the front leg and push the knee lightly inward (between the ball of the foot and the heel inwardly).
B	3a.	Turn the front foot (with the toes) inwardly between 30 and 45 degrees (individually).
B	4.	Line distance remains between the front foot (heel) and the back foot (ball/toes). (This applies to people up to approximately 1,75m. Larger people can adjust proportionally by stepping further forward). To measure the distance, bend the back foot/back leg toward the front foot. If the back knee can just reach the inside of the heel of the front foot, the stance is correct; otherwise adjust.
B	4a.	The feet are at approximately shoulder width.

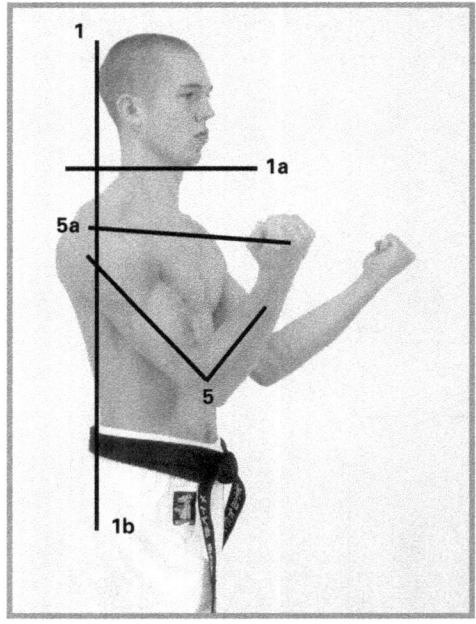 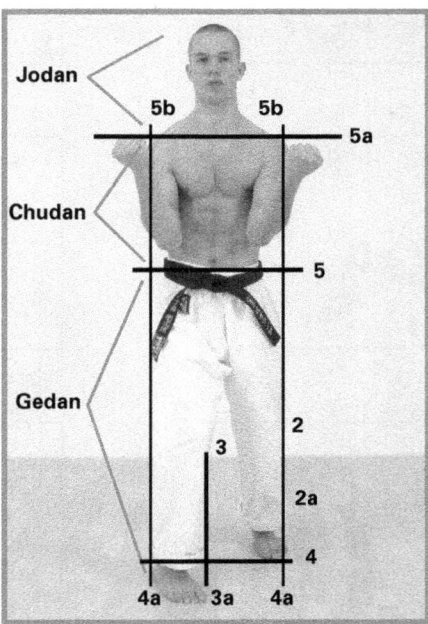

Figure A.   Figure B.

Kata

A	5.	Elbows should be about a fist's distance away from the body and turned inwardly (in front of the body).
A	5a.	The fists should be below the shoulder line.
B	5b.	The shoulder blades should be in a neutral position (keep the upper body straight and don't push the chest inward or overly outward).
C	6.	Keep the arm horizontal while retracting the fist backwards at least beyond the line of the chest into the sides (Hikite).
D	6a.	Aim the fist straight forward and keep it horizontal while pulling downward and fixing the shoulder blade by contracting the latissimus dorsi (large back muscle).
E	7.	Although the actual movements generally are not addressed here, the following is too important not to mention: As soon as the (extending) elbow sets out forward beside the body, the forearm is physically rotated until it has perfected its extension and rotation to the final arm position. Until this time, the palm of the fist remains upward.
F	7a.	The final position of the punch, and thus the arm/fist position, should be about a fist inward and two fists downward in relation to the shoulder blade. The retracting of the fist occurs in the exact same, but inverted, order.

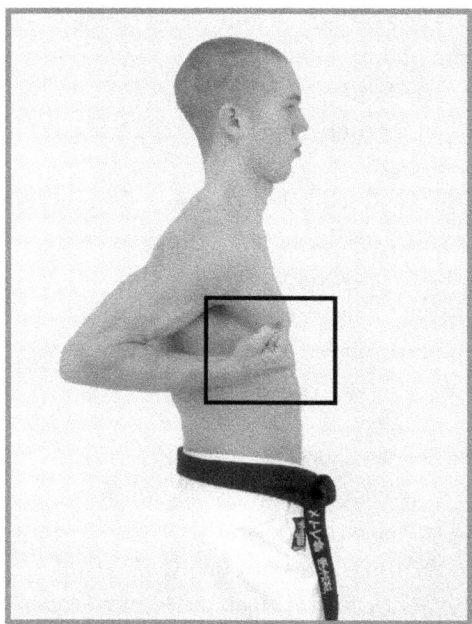

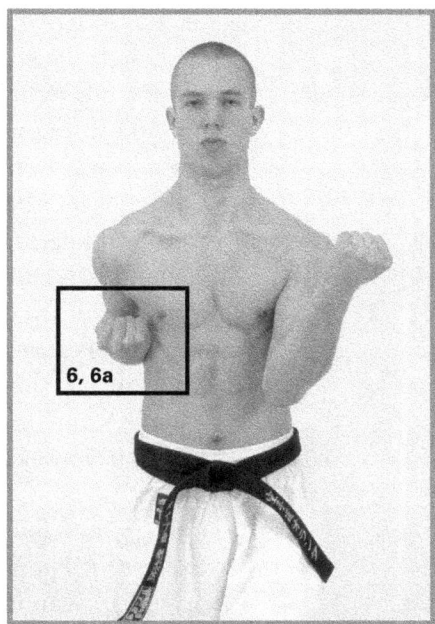

Figure C.   Figure D.

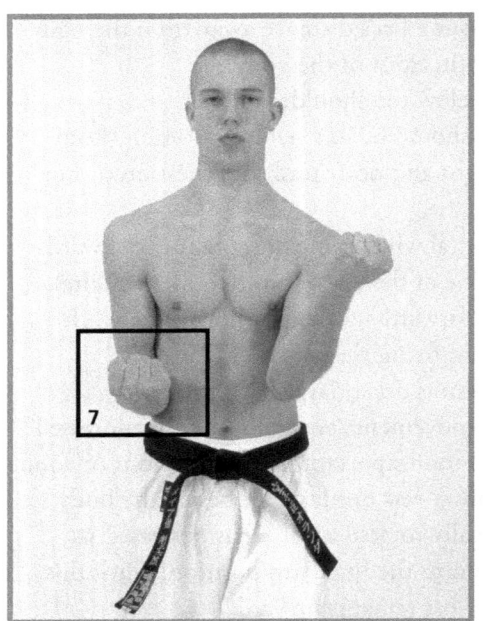
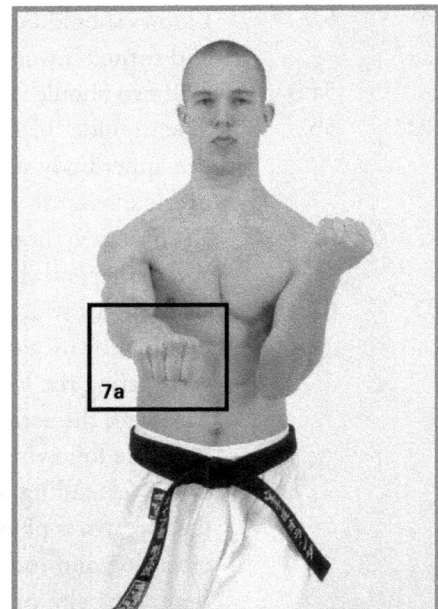

Figure E.   Figure F.

G	8.	At the moment of impact, the technique Kaki Tsuki is located slightly further than the elbow, after which it should retract naturally until below the elbow joint. This last position is shown in the photograph.
G	8a.	During this technique, the head is turned toward the opposite direction so that the line of sight is to the left (180 degrees away from the punch).
G	9.	One steps into Benzoku dachi while letting down the body with bent knees (afterwhich one comes back up spirally). The previous end position is maintained during this step.
H	10.	The knuckles of the opened hand are at shoulder level with the fingers extending slightly above. The positions of the joints are the same as with the previously described Chudan Morote Soto Uke.
I	10a.	The arms form an oval shape in which the shoulder is the highest point of the arm as seen from the earth, followed by the elbow, followed by the wrist.
I	10b.	In their final position, the fingers of both hands are at an inward angle of roughly 45 degrees to each other, at a level just below the lower ribs.

_____ *Kata*

J   10c.   Both fists are retracted into the sides with a final position (and movements in the joints) identical to the previously described Hikite (see 6).

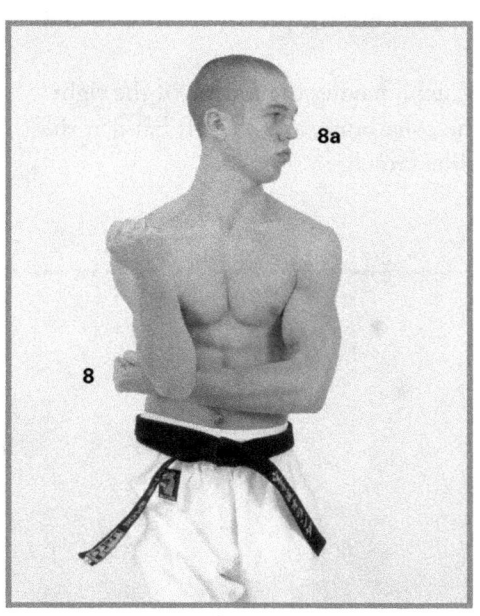

Figure G.

Figure H.

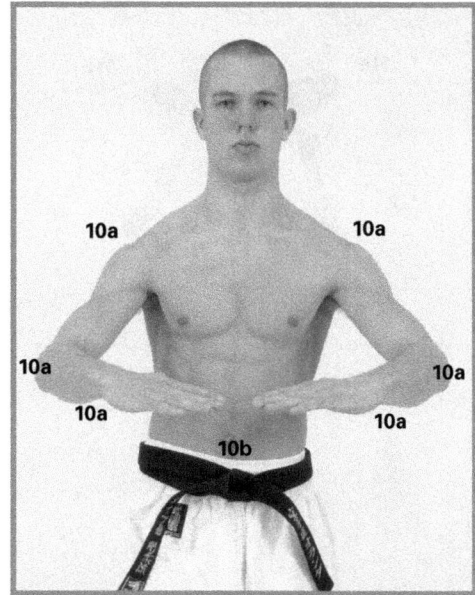

Figure I.

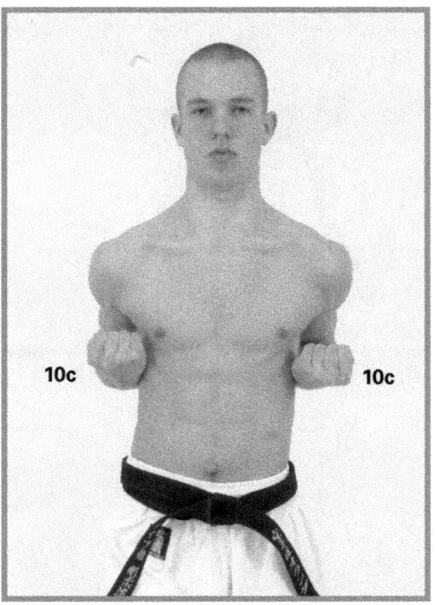

Figure J.

K	11.	From the last position, one steps back, drawing back the right hand opened like Hikite and having the left hand right under the right hand with the palm side down.
L	11a.	After Mawashi Uke, both forearms and elbow joints are in the same position as Hikite, but the probes are rotated and the hands are opened.
M	11b.	End technique Tora Guchi, having the fingers of the right hand at the level of the collarbone, and the left hand at the level of the left groin/the crotch.

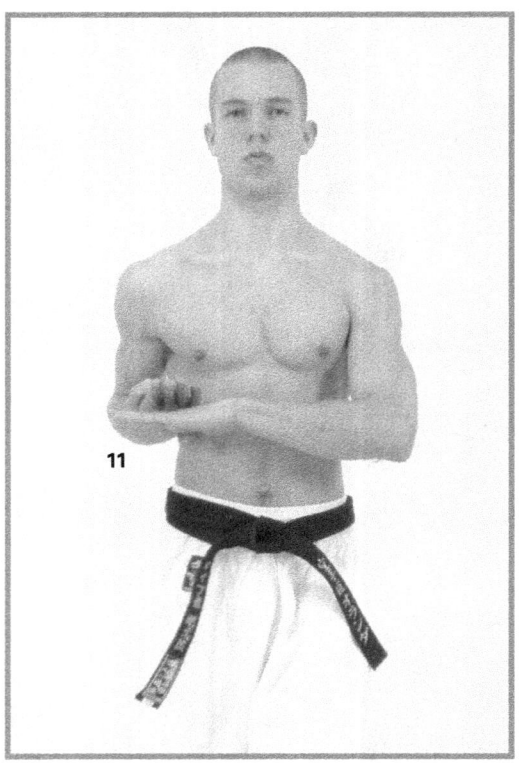

Figure K.

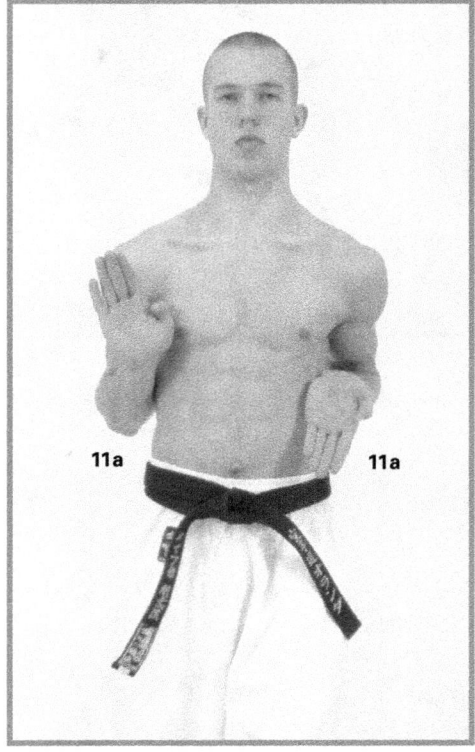

Figure L.

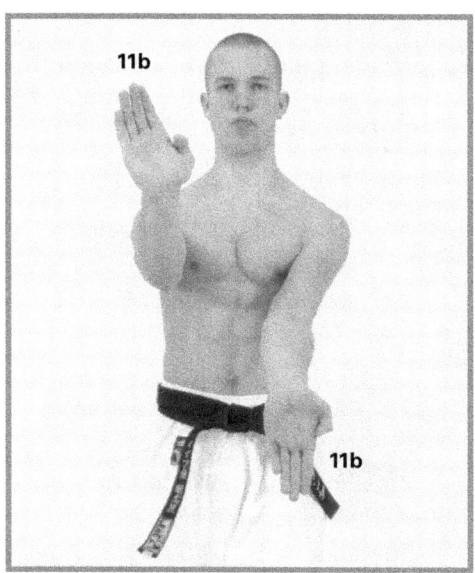

Figure M.

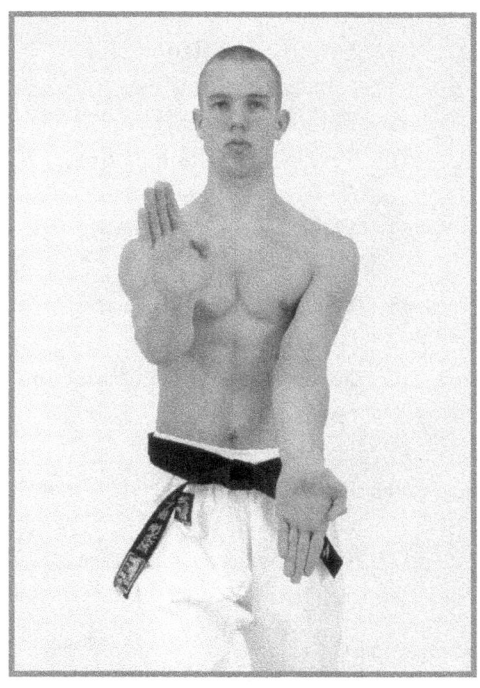 

Specific to the Meibukan school is the visible execution of the Tora Guchi (Tiger mouth) before and after performing the Morote Shotei Oshi (push with the palm of the hands).

Execution of breathing

Schematic overview of the execution of breathing during Sanchin kata in reference to the photo series

Photo	Way of breathing	Photo	Way of breathing
1	Natural breathing	21	Powerful inhalation and exhalation (brief)
2	Natural breathing	22	Release breathing
3	Natural breathing	23	Very powerful inhalation (lengthy)
4	Powerful inhalation and exhalation	24	Very powerful exhalation (lengthy)
5	Powerful inhalation while stepping forward and exhalation during rooting	25	Powerful inhalation and exhalation (brief)
6	Very powerful inhalation (lengthy)	26	Release breathing
7	Very powerful exhalation (lengthy)	27	Very powerful inhalation (lengthy)
8	Powerful inhalation and exhalation (brief)	28	Very powerful exhalation (lengthy)
9	Release breathing	29	Powerful inhalation and exhalation (brief)
10	Very powerful inhalation (lengthy)	30	Release breathing
11	Very powerful exhalation (lengthy)	31	Very powerful inhalation (lengthy)
12	Powerful inhalation and exhalation (brief)	32	Very powerful exhalation (lengthy)
13	Release breathing	33	Very powerful inhalation (lengthy)
14	Very powerful inhalation (lengthy)	34	Powerful exhalation (brief and fast/explosive)
15	Very powerful exhalation (lengthy)	35	Fix breathing
16	Very powerful inhalation (lengthy)	36	Powerful inhalation (brief and fast/explosive)
17	Powerful exhalation (brief and fast/explosive)	37	Very powerful exhalation (lengthy)
18	Fix breathing	38	Powerful inhalation and exhalation (brief)
19	Powerful inhalation (brief and fast/explosive)	39	Release breathing
20	Very powerful exhalation (lengthy)	40	Very powerful inhalation (lengthy)

Photo	Way of breathing	Photo	Way of breathing
41	Very powerful exhalation (lengthy)	48	Very powerful inhalation (lengthy)
42	Powerful inhalation (brief and fast/explosive)	49	Very powerful exhalation (lengthy)
43	Powerful exhalation (brief)	50	Release breathing (connected to following inhalation)
44	Very powerful inhalation (lengthy)	51	Very powerful inhalation (lengthy with medium speed)
45	Very powerful exhalation (lengthy)	52	Very powerful exhalation (lengthy)
46	Very powerful inhalation (lengthy)	53	Slightly focused inhalation
47	Very powerful exhalation (lengthy)	54	Declining focus of exhalation
		55	Natural breathing

Important key points in the training method of Sanchin kata

- Body and spirit are one. The body does not act without the spirit steering it. Take care of an optimal concentration and use forms of visualization.
- Take practice of Sanchin kata seriously, out of respect and integrity for your own person. Before practicing Sanchin kata, be aware of your physical condition and possible limiting circumstances, and inform your Sensei about it.
- Motion and breathing are geared to each other. Bring them together in harmony. Be aware of the proportions of oxygen and carbon dioxide, and of signs of dizziness, headache, sickness, "additional breathing," and other unpleasant signals.
- The rhythm of the motion should be equal to the rhythm of the breathing. Do not use muscles that do not have to be used—for example, the facial muscles.
- See to it that the breathing, when exhaling, is not held too long. Only hold it on the moment of focus or kimé. Breathe by abdominal respiration.
- See to it that your posture is correct and do not force it by intense tightening, except for the moments of kimé.
- Warm up before practicing Sanchin kata, or start practicing the kata twice with reduced muscle tension—once without any muscle tension and once with minimal muscle tension and a light kimé.
- Become conscious and be aware of all parts of your body. Practice regularly (6).

Afterword Sanchin kata

In this book, we paid a lot of attention to Sanchin kata, compared to other kata, the reason being the importance of Sanchin kata.

To obtain a better understanding of Goju-ryu Karate-do and the profundity that traditional karate can have, Sanchin kata is an outstanding example of Okinawan/Chinese martial art.

Sanchin kata and Fukyu kata Jodan, together with the beginner kata Gekisai Ichi, are integrated as a series of photos in this book, to support the beginning karatedoka. With the additional information, it can serve as a reference book, supporting the practice of Goju-ryu Karate-do. As a base, this is adequate. In my opinion, additional suggestions should be transferred from teacher to student in direct and personal communication.

TENSHO KATA

Tensho kata is the second Haishu kata from Okinawan Karate-do. The principles of Tensho kata are inherent to those of Sanchin kata.

The name Tensho means "rotating hand palms" and "changing grips." The purpose of exercising Tensho kata is, like Sanchin kata, to activate the tendons and muscles that are located around the joints, to load up bioelectricity, harmonize breath, motion, and posture, and to construct body armor against external attacks.

Although Chojun Miyagi officially created Tensho kata, its techniques and principles had been in existence earlier. Most probably Chojun Miyagi formulated Tensho kata from Rokkishi kata (7).

Tensho kata has many open-hand movements. In this respect, it differs from Sanchin kata, with its mainly closed-fist techniques. In Tensho kata, the direction in which the movements of the arms are executed is eye-catching. All existing directions are present: up and down, inside and outside, diagonal, pushing and pulling, away from the body and toward the body. The movements are executed singularly and doubly by one and two arms, respectively.

Breathing

Although in some places in the Meibukan Sanchin kata one inhales (incompletely) during a block-technique, full inhalation is used when retracting or preparing the next technique. In Tensho kata, however, inhalation is used continuously while practicing attacking techniques and defensive techniques. All exhalations are comparable to those in Sanchin kata, although not all "end-techniques" are finished with kimé. This affects breathing directly.

Motion

Although the basic concepts recur, as described in the explanation of Sanchin kata, the sequence of techniques is more fluid in Tensho. The "rotating hand palms" are clearly present, and the flowing transition from one technique to another is typical for this kata. In the Meibukan School, it is the Sensei who decides at which time he trains and instructs a kata to his students. It is common in Meibukan training, however, to start the training (after a possible warm-up) with Sanchin kata and to end it with Tensho kata. Between these two katas, the other exercises and forms take place, like Kaishu kata and kumite.

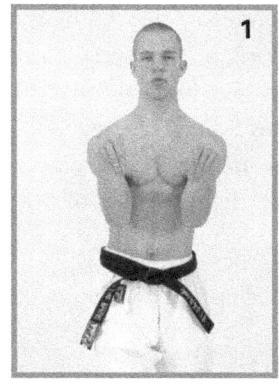

Specific movements of the kata Tensho concerning the rotation of the wrists and palms of the hand.

NAIHANCHI KATA

Sensei Mirakian performing Naihanchi Kata.

Although Chojun Miyagi passed on Naihanchi kata to his student Meitoku Yagi, who in turn passed it on to Sensei Anthony Mirakian, this kata was never integrated in the Goju-ryu Karate-do syllabus. It has, therefore, no official position within active practice in the Meibukan. The branch of Hanshi Anthony Mirakian, nevertheless, continues to practice this kata, although it is not officially a part of the Goju-ryu system.

The origins of Naihanchi kata are unknown, although the history can be traced back to the so-called Shuri and Tomari schools. Naihanchi kata officially belongs to the Shorin-ryu syllabus. There are three variations: Shodan, Nidan and Sandan. The Shodan version is practiced by the branch of Sensei

Mirakian. The kata is characterized by movements to the left and to the right, the low Kiba Dachi position, also known as horse ride position, and the heavy movements of legs and hips. Maximal force is used to execute the movements. One has to take root with his legs to make possible stable techniques and the heavy use of the hips. This kata often is used as base-kata for beginners, as well as base-kata to develop and exercise the principles of power, position, and breathing.

Kata

Notes

(1) There are certain indications that the roots of the martial art of Liu Liu Ko are to be found in the Shaolin monastery, in the Chinese province of Fujian. Physical exercises were practiced in this Buddhist monastery to strengthen the body. Apart from traditions, some wall paintings found in the Shaolin monastery make clear that early self-defense methods were taught there, and that those methods were subservient to Zen (Ch'an) from the Zen Buddhist base and as active practice. Together with the knowledge of human spirit and body in the monastery culture, some specific existing martial exercises probably were partially copied, while new ones were composed and introduced. Although many indications point in the direction of the Shaolin monastery as the source of Sanchin, it also is reasonable to assume that Sanchin may have other origins in the Chinese culture (medical and martial) as a muscular cultivation activity.

Wall paintings of the Shaolin monastery.

(2) Again, there is no absolute certainty about this because some traditions state that not Chojun Miyagi but other persons, mainly martial artists, took the Bubishi to Okinawa.

(3) In Chinese arts, open-hand techniques appear more often than closed hands as fists, which appear more often in karate. During the first years that Kanryo Higaonna taught Sanchin kata, it was practiced by him using open hands.

(4) According to some Goju-ryu masters, including Morio Higaonna, Chojun Miyagi created a second kind of Sanchin kata, better known as Chojun Miyagi Sanchin kata. The story tells that Chojun Miyagi created in his Sanchin kata another pattern of stepping, and put another emphasis on breath regulation. The most important difference between the two katas

Photograph of Grandmaster Chojun Miyagi taken in his younger years.

should relate to the breathing technique. Where the original "Kanryo Higaonna version" has a powerful expression in breathing, the Chojun Miyagi Sanchin kata has more quiet breathing. Additionally, the "embusen," or chorographical pattern of stepping, was changed.

The "embusen": In the Chojun Miyagi Sanchin kata, one does not rotate his body, and walks three times forward and three times backward, with the front of the body continuously directed to the start position. In the Kanryo Higaonna Sanchin kata, one steps backward only once (see personal addition under note 6). Some Goju-ryu karate masters suggest that Chojun Miyagi mainly introduced this change—step backward twice instead of once—to develop a stronger physical sensitivity in the processes that take place, especially when stepping backward.

The breathing: Although the breathing is identical concerning inhalation through the nose and exhalation through the mouth, there is a difference in intensity. The Kanryo Higaonna kata has powerful and direct breathing, while the breathing of the Chojun Miyagi kata is quieter and longer. A different process of visualization to accompany the breathing is used, as well. The method of breathing is related to the activity of the muscles, which adapts itself to the breathing, and vice versa. The spirit guides the whole in the sense of creating, controlling, conducting, and coordinating.

Some Goju masters consider the Kanryo Higaonna kata as a kata whose intention is directed more towards "fight qualities," and consider the later Sanchin version of Chojun Miyagi as a kata whose intention is directed more toward the aspect of "health." However, both have the same kernel in relation to the Qi-circulation, and these differences should be considered minor.

Sensei Toguchi, one of Chojun Miyagi's senior students, gives an explanation for the genesis of this second Sanchin kata. In his book *Okinawa Goju-ryu 2 – Advanced Techniques of Shoreikan Karate,* Toguchi states that before the World War II, Sanchin kata was taught in only one way: the form in which one rotates twice over 180 degrees. After the war, Toguchi tells us, Miyagi only taught his students while sitting in a chair. His students were not allowed to turn their back on him—for that would demonstrate a lack of respect. So the rotations were eliminated and the form was reduced to a pattern of three steps forward and three steps backward, without rotation. Toguchi also points to the fact that everybody who joined Miyagi's dojo

around 1950 was taught only this version of Sanchin. Additionally, he emphasizes that this change caused a lot of obscurity in Goju-ryu karate in Okinawa and elsewhere, and that it is of great importance that one continues practicing the original version, in which the rotation is made. This rotation is essential and without it, the practice of Sanchin doesn't match its goals for advanced training, and it loses one of its keystones. Toguchi, however, does not endorse the view that Chojun Miyagi explicitly designed a new kata for special purposes.

(5) Key points: When Sanchin kata is practiced the right way, the body is conditioned well for mastering the Goju-ryu system. The same expressions and techniques appear in other techniques and kata of the Goju-ryu system. Especially, the positions of joints reappear in the Heishu kata, open-hand kata, and the tightening of the muscles in question that Sanchin teaches the practitioner by practicing continuously. The answers that their practitioner seeks in relation to finding "the correct body posture," executing the technique, and the technique itself, are given by the active practice of Sanchin. This relates to the general body posture, to the balance in breathing, to the motion, and to the harmony among these three within the kata practice.

(6) Interesting is the possibility that the practitioner of Kanryo Higaonna Sanchin kata can adapt the execution of this kata. Dependent on age, physical condition, and personality or character of the practitioner, the execution can differ in the way the aspects of the kata are emphasized. For training purposes, one can adopt individually the "embusen" of Kanryo Higaonna Sanchin kata. Instead of the standard pattern, a very strong person could take twelve steps instead of three, or push five times instead of three. The embusen was designed as a starting-point, but can be adapted, depending on the needs of body and spirit. This could be valid for the Chojun Miyagi kata as well. Considering the reasons for this kata to exist, one could deduce that karatedokas "of a high level"—those who have mastered the key physical and spiritual principles—can adopt this kata to their own individual needs. Eventually, this is what one should do: take the liberty in technical and physical respects to achieve physical development as strong as possible. "Mastering" implies that, from a certain level, one should listen to his/her own body. The individual application exceeds the dogma on the technical level as well, because body and spirit cannot exist separately. As a kata used by the Goju-ryu system, however, the "official" embusen remains the starting-point, as taught by Kanryo Higaonna and Chojun Miyagi.

(7) According to Kogyu Takashi (born June 6, 1912), a student of Juhatsu Kiyoda and Chojun Miyagi, a kata by the name of Rokkishi was practiced during the trainings period in the Kenkyu Club. In this kata, the "embusen" was equal to that in Sanchin kata. Later on, according to Takashi, this kata was called Tensho. One of the most outstanding masters in the Kenkyu Club was Go Ken Ki (White Crane Kung Fu), who taught the kata Happoren. This kata, and the clues that can be found in the Bubushi about the kata Happoren and the eclectic transfer of knowledge by Go Ken Ki's distinguished teacher Kanryo Higaonna, form the ingredients that made Chojun Miyagi decide to add Tensho kata with his own view to his Goju-ryu syllabus.

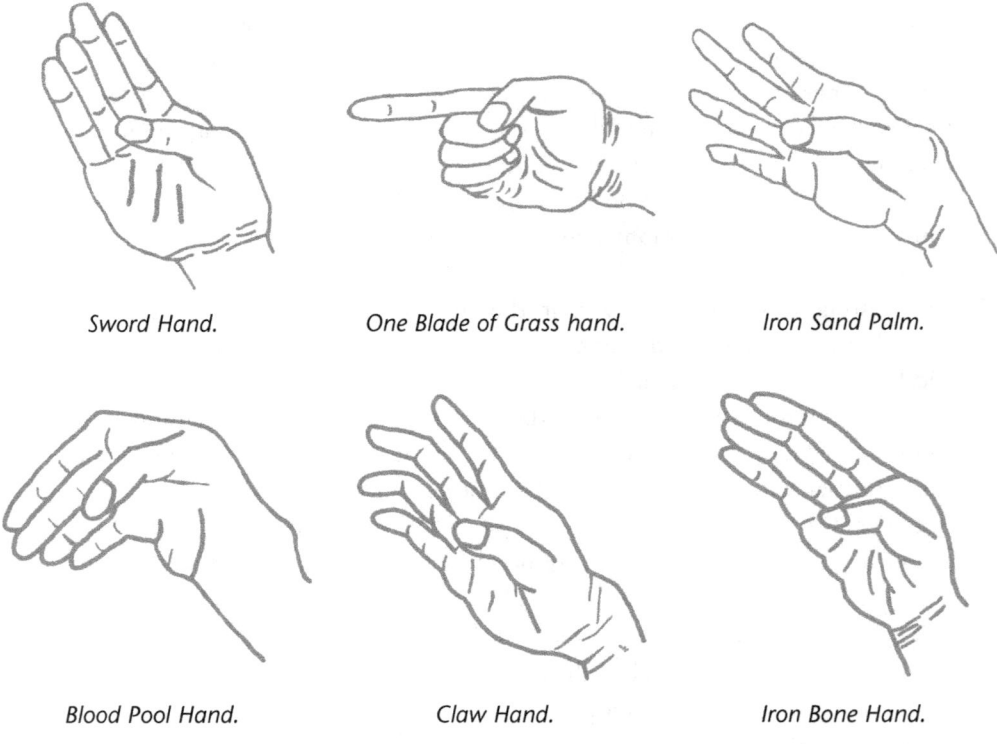

Sword Hand.   One Blade of Grass hand.   Iron Sand Palm.

Blood Pool Hand.   Claw Hand.   Iron Bone Hand.

Drawings from the Bubishi.

Kaishu Kata

> *Nowadays, there are twenty to thirty Kaishu kata. Many of these exercises have been named after their creators. Adapted to each other, the kata in different models consist of combined defensive and offensive techniques that are observed while practicing. By practicing these forms and understanding their goal, one gains a deeper insight into the relation between body and spirit. In this way, the principles of the chaotic mind and rational understanding are cultivated to reach spirituality.*
>
> —Chojun Miyagi, 1934

FUKYU KATA
Origin and development

Fukyu kata is a training kata that develops a basic pattern through which mainly reflexes and techniques can be trained in a powerful way. In general, most of the primary techniques are trained this way.

Originally, the Fukyu kata were known as Tai Chi Ken (Tai Chi Ken Jodan, Chudan, Gedan and variations). Later, in Japan, they became known as Taikyoku. Finally, they were named Fukyu kata (basic kata).

According to Sensei Mirakian, the different styles of karate were divided into two categories known as Naha-te and Shuri-te, by the Perfector, Bushi Sokon Matsumara in 1790 (in those days responsible for perfecting Ryukyu Karate) and the use of the Fukyu kata spread within these two roughly divided training systems. Until some 50 to 80 years ago, these kata remained popular; however, they were practiced mostly within the Shorin system. Since these kata teach the basics, Dai Sensei Meitoku Yagi decided to include these kata in his Meibukan School. Nowadays, the Fukyu kata is even practiced in Korean systems because of the same reason. Each system took what was useful for that particular way for training and adapted the Fukyu kata to suit its needs. Although there is no hard evidence, the Fukyu kata of nowadays probably was reshaped from Shorin-ryu by

Anko Itosu. Since then, the Fukyu kata has evolved and changes to its original form have been applied, so the original has been lost in history. The only part of the original form that still remains is the embusen (pattern), which is the most important part of the kata.

Many Goju-ryu organizations and schools changed their educational system during the 1960s and 70s, partly due to the influence of powerful Japanese karate organizations. For several reasons, the kata techniques were fragmented after analysis. On the spot (standing still with the feel next to each other at shoulder's width), many repetitions of the same technique were made. Also in movement, during which every separate technique is coupled to a changing stance while moving, the techniques dissected from the kata were practiced at length. Combinations from kata, but also newly-designed consecutive techniques, were created and applied. As a drill exercise, this form of training was and is practiced mainly in a straight line, forward and backward. Although the word "kihon" means nothing more than "basic," it is used to indicate this type of exercise in many karate organizations. Officially, this form of kihon is not recognized by the Meibukan School, so it is not included in this syllabus. However, there are situations in training during which the previously described concept is practiced in a natural, individual way, in order to strengthen the practice of the kata and the related technique. The Meibukan School does include the practice of the most common techniques of the Goju-ryu system, by combining them with the embusen of the Fukyu kata. In principle, a number of appointed Fukyu kata are included in the educational system, which serves mainly to teach novices an easy, recurring pattern. Apart from these appointed techniques, several other techniques also are practiced, using the embusen of the Fukyu kata. The principle of kihon exercises being repetitive technique exercises in the Meibukan is found mainly in the practice of the Fukyu kata.

> *Fukyu kata, based on the Taikyoku pattern, teaches the beginner simple basic movements and techniques in particular, and can function as a physical and mental warm-up for any practitioner.*
> —Anthony Mirakian

Basic Meibukan Goju-ryu Fukyu kata survey

Even though nearly all existing Goju-ryu techniques can occur in the Fukyu kata, and indeed are trained and practiced, the following have been included into the standard Meibukan curriculum for the Netherlands:

FUKYU KATA JODAN
Defensive technique: Jodan Age Uke in Migi or Hidari Heiko Dachi
Offensive technique: Jodan Tsuki in Migi or Hidari Heiko Dachi

FUKYU KATA CHUDAN
Defensive technique: Chudan Uke in Migi or Hidari Heiko Dachi
Offensive technique: Chudan Tsuki in Migi or Hidari Heiko Dachi

FUKYU KATA GEDAN
Defensive technique: Gedan Uke in Migi or Hidari Shiko Dachi
Offensive technique: Gedan Tsuki in Migi or Hidari Shiko Dachi

FUKYU KATA MAE GERI
Defensive technique: Gedan Osae Uke in Migi or Hidari Heiko Dachi
Offensive technique: Migi or Hidari Gedan Mae Geri

FUKYU KATA CHU GERI GE
Defensive technique: Chudan Uke in Migi or Hidari Heiko Dachi
Offensive technique: Migi or Hidari Jodan Mae Geri
Defensive technique: Gedan Uke in Migi or Hidari Shiko Dachi

FUKYU KATA KO CHU GE
Defensive technique: Jodan Ko Uke in Migi or Hidari Kokutsu Dachi
Offensive technique: Chudan Gyaku Tsuki in Migi or Hidari Heiko Dachi
Defensive technique: Gedan Uke in Migi or Hidari Shiko Dachi

FUKYU KATA GE SHUTO CHU
Defensive technique: Gedan Uke in Migi or Hidari Shiko Dachi
Offensive technique: Jodan Shuto Uchi in Migi or Hidari Heiko Dachi
Defensive technique: Chudan Uke in Migi or Hidari Heiko Dachi

The first Fukyu kata that one learns is the Fukyu kata Jodan, which has been included in this book both as a photo series and in embusen form. Although the Fukyu kata Jodan, Chudan, and Gedan are similar, and the three techniques (Jodan Tsuki/Chudan Tsuki/Gedan Tsuki and Jodan Age Uke/Chudan

Uke/Gedan Uke) within these kata can be combined, there are some differences in steps/movements among them. The embusen in the form of the capital I is maintained for each kata and forms the core. Within the kumite section, two kumite forms derived from the Fukyu kata are explained.

The embusen of the Fukyu kata practiced in the Meibukan School has the form of the capital I. It is important to note that the starting point of the kata is also the endpoint.

Kata

Execution of the Fukyu kata Jodan

Formal attention in Musubi Dachi.

Preparation in Musubi Dachi to start the form.

Transition to Yoi position in Musubi Dachi.

Yoi position in Heiko Dachi.

Hidari Heiko Dachi with Jodan Age Uke.

Migi Heiko Dachi with Jodan Oi Tsuki.

Hidari Heiko Dachi with Jodan Age Uke.

Migi Heiko Dachi with Jodan Age Uke.

Hidari Heiko Dachi with Jodan Oi Tsuki.

Migi Heiko Dachi with Jodan Age Uke.

Hidari Heiko Dachi with Jodan Age Uke.

Migi Heiko Dachi with Jodan Oi Tsuki.

Hidari Heiko Dachi with Jodan Oi Tsuki.

Migi Heiko Dachi with Jodan Oi Tsuki.

Hidari Heiko Dachi with Jodan Age Uke.

Migi Heiko Dachi with Jodan Oi Tsuki.

Hidari Heiko Dachi with Jodan Age Uke.

Migi Heiko Dachi with Jodan Age Uke.

Kata

Hidari Heiko Dachi with Jodan Oi Tsuki.

Migi Heiko Dachi with Jodan Age Uke.

Hidari Heiko Dachi with Jodan Age Uke.

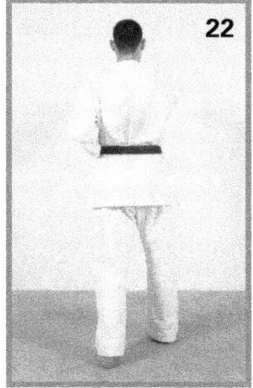

Migi Heiko Dachi with Jodan Oi Tsuki.

Hidari Heiko Dachi with Jodan Oi Tsuki.

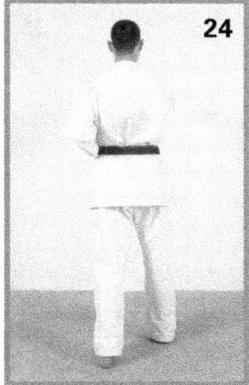

Migi Heiko Dachi with Jodan Oi Tsuki.

Hidari Heiko Dachi with Jodan Age Uke.

Migi Heiko Dachi with Jodan Oi Tsuki.

Hidari Heiko Dachi with Jodan Age Uke.

Migi Heiko Dachi with Jodan Age Uke.

Hidari Heiko Dachi with Jodan Oi Tsuki.

Migi Heiko Dachi with Jodan Age Uke.

Turn and step back facing the front in Musubi Dachi in preparation to finish the form.

Musubi Dachi and finishing the form.

Formal attention in Musubi Dachi.

Kata

Embusen of the Fukyu kata Jodan

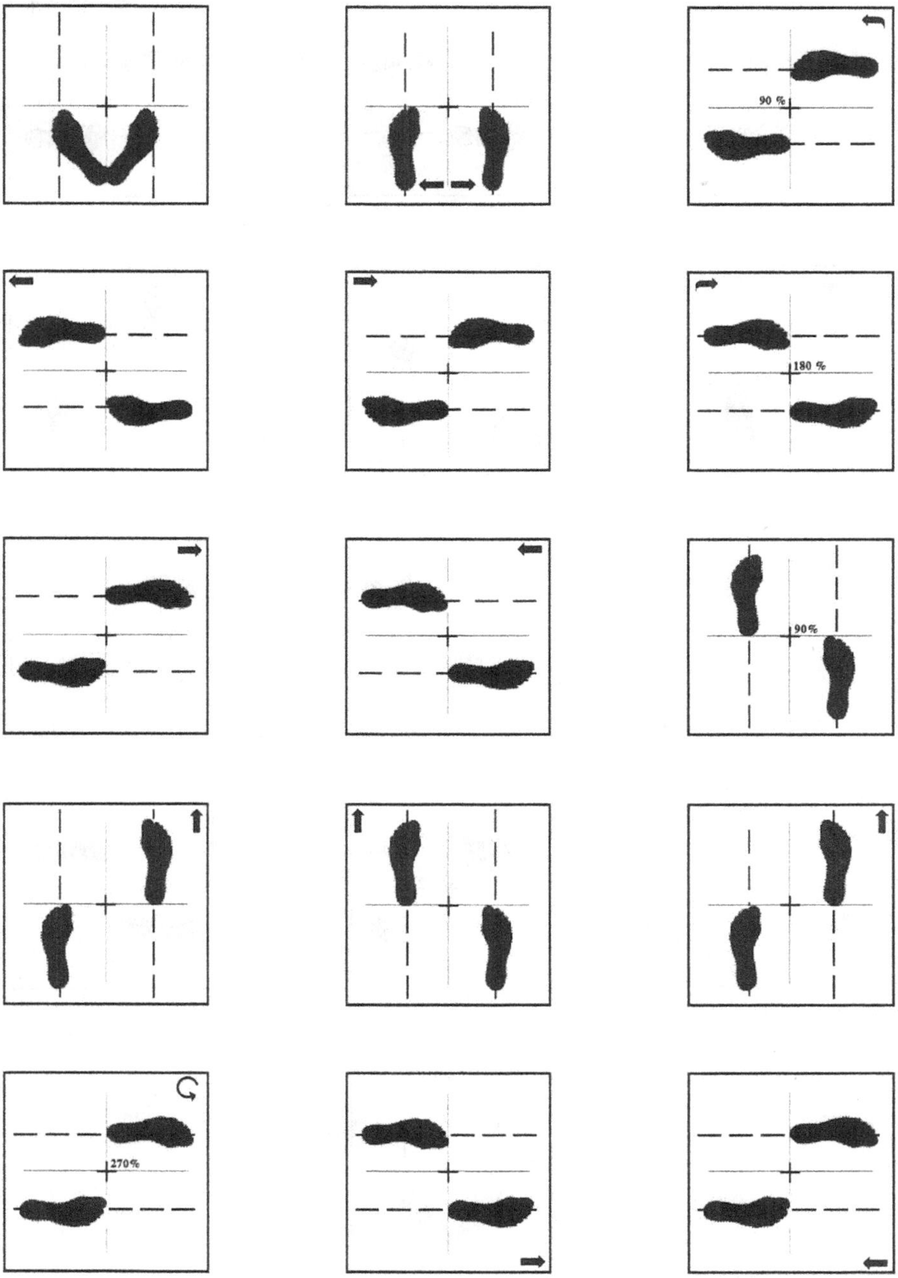

Embusen Fukyu kata Part 1.

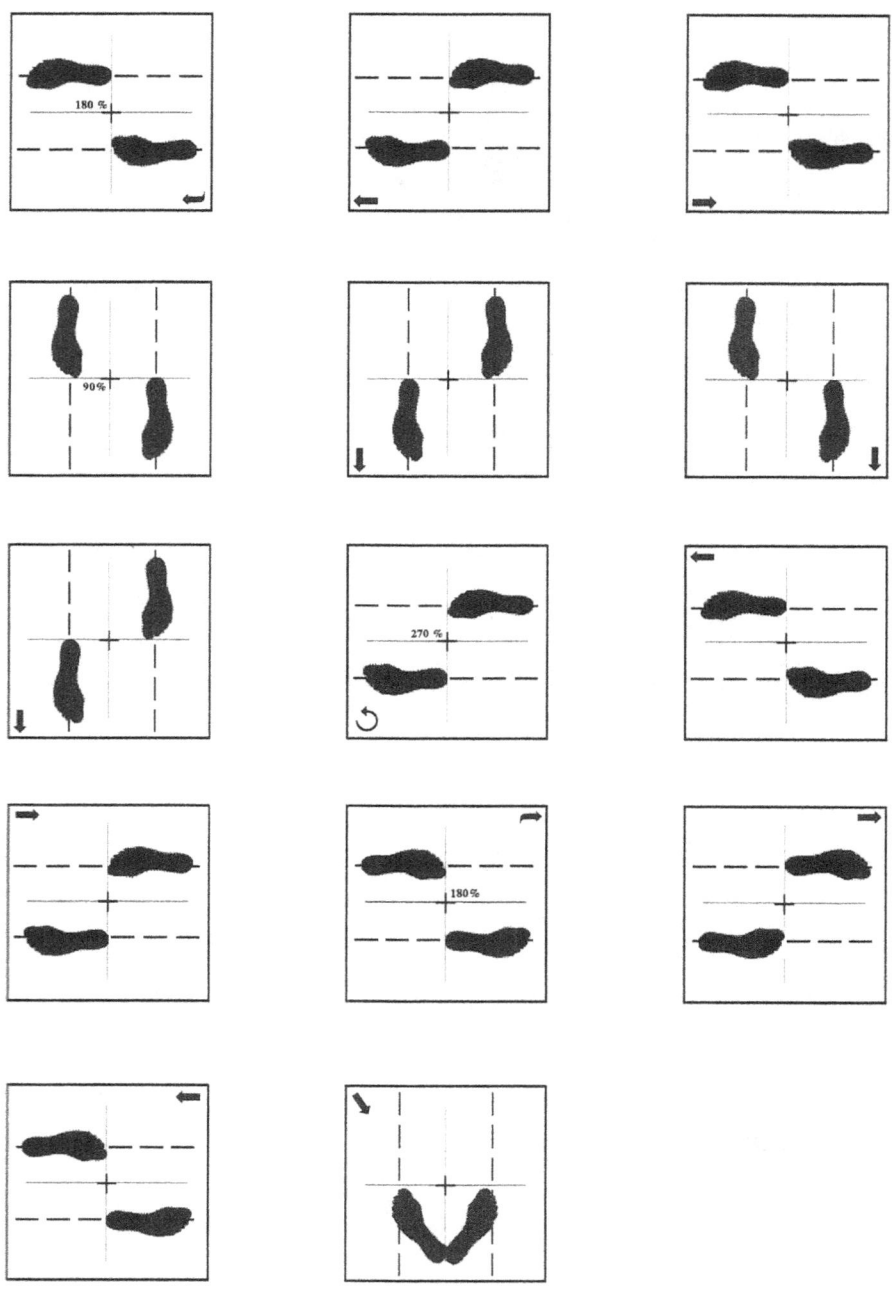

Embusen Fukyu kata Part 2.

THE ORIGINS OF THE GOJU-RYU KATA

In his paper, "An Outline of karate-do," published in 1934, Chojun Miyagi himself has pronounced "the only detail of which we can be sure is that a "style" from Fuzhou has been introduced on Okinawa in 1828. This style formed the basis from which Goju-ryu karate kempo originated." Here, Chojun Miyagi himself indicates that the kata/fighting techniques of Goju-ryu already existed prior to the birth of Liu Liu Ko.

In many of the Chinese Kung Fu (Chinese boxing) styles, the names of kata can be found that are also known in Goju-ryu: Sanchin, "Saamchin" in Chinese, can be found in the Styles of the Lion, the Crane, the Tiger, the Dog, the Dragon, the Monk and others. Other classical Goju-ryu kata also can be found within these styles.

In all probability, Kanryo Higaonna has studied several Chinese Kung Fu "styles" under different masters, among whom Liu Liu Ko has been the most important. His course of life in the martial arts started on Okinawa and led him to China. After his return, he passed on his knowledge and skill, and his personalized kata and techniques, to (among others) Chojun Miyagi, who in turn familiarized himself with the kata and techniques and passed them on in "his" way. The names of the kata have remained as "proof" of transfer, but the way they arose cannot be retraced. Only a sparkle of the kanji and demonstration of the kata refer to a long history.

GEKISAI KATA

In the mid-1930s, Chojun Miyagi gave a lecture asking for more unity within the martial arts and pleading for greater accessibility, in order to attract more people to karate (1). He also announced that with only the classical form of teaching karate, it was stagnating and, for this reason, it was important that new kata were being developed.

A few years later, around 1940, Chojun Miyagi, together with some other masters, developed the Gekisai kata and accomplished his goal to make karate more accessible to a larger target group. The intensive and demanding Sanchin training, which usually dispirits most novices, was of such caliber that Miyagi wanted to create a transition phase that could be accomplished by anyone, regardless of age or physical constitution. In cooperation with various other masters (like Shoshin Nagamine), a series of newly developed kata was created. Ultimately, Chojun Miyagi designed two kata for Goju-ryu Karate-do—Gekisai dai ichi and

Gekisai dai ni. The prevailing explanation as to why only two kata were designed—since, according to Seikichi Toguchi, ten were planned initially—is the start of World War II. The circumstances that arose because of the war reduced the practice and development of karate-do on Okinawa.

'Geki' means "fighting" ("attack and seize") or "to confront" and "Sai" means "to hurl and break." Put together, it can mean "to destroy," but it is more often translated as "to seek out and destroy." The word "dai" often is added to the Gekisai kata. Depending on the placing of the kanji for "dai," it means a number, for example Gekisai dai ichi. In another context, such as in Dai Sensei Meitoku Yagi, it means "grand," "prominent," or "unique."

Seen against the background of World War II, the aggressive name probably was chosen to influence the morale and the intellectual substance of most youths, preparing them for the hardship still to come (2).

Since 1948, Chojun Miyagi has included the Gekisai kata in the official Goju-ryu Karate-do system and they are taught as such.

In part because of the reasonably taut, dynamic, and relatively easy techniques of this kata series, it became more attractive to practice karate-do, especially for juveniles in elementary schools.

As well as the classical Chinese kata, such as Saifa, Shisochin, Sesan, Seiunchin, Sepai, Kururunfa, Suparinpei, and later also Sanseru, the Gekisai kata belong to the Kaishu kata.

The embusen (3) of both Gekisai dai ichi and Gekisai dai ni are identical, as well as nearly all the techniques. The main difference between the two is the change from closed to open-hand techniques. The first Gekisai kata is executed almost completely with closed-hand techniques. In this way, the practitioner is not yet "burdened" with the open-hand techniques and the associated proportions of movement. Once the closed-fist techniques have been learned, within the embusen of the kata, a relative basis has been acquired, after which the time is ripe to concentrate on the open-hand techniques and a new stance (neko dachi). Now, one is not "distracted" by having to learn a new embusen, since it remains the same.

The application of the closed-hand techniques (bunkai) is not necessarily restricted to a single pattern. Practically, this means that a single movement in a kata can have more than one meaning.

Seizing during bunkai usually is more difficult than just blocking or averting in a kata. Starting with a basic response and an acquired locomotion of closed blocking techniques (hands in fist form), the foundation is laid for open-hand techniques. A distinct difference between Gekisai dai ichi and Gekisai dai ni is visible during the chudan uke, after the execution of the shuto uchi. Also, the mawashi uke and the tora guchi are technical differences between the two kata. In Gekisai dai ni also suri ashi and neko dachi are used.

Meibukan Gekisai dai ichi and Gekisai dai ni kata

Within the School of Dai Sensei Meitoku Yagi, during the execution of kaishu kata, the forward kicks (mae geri), from a physical training point of view, generally are given at jodan height. However, the fighting applications or interpretations (bunkai) can be given at different heights. During each forward kick in the kata, a kiai (4) is given.

A photo series of Gekisai dai ichi and its embusen have been included in this book.

Gyaku Tsuki in the deep Zenkutsu Dachi with focus on strong development of a punch.

Kiai is given with Shuto Uchi.

Kiai is given with Mae Geri.

Execution of the Gekisai dai ichi kata

Formal attention in Musubi Dachi.

Preparation in Musubi Dachi to start the form.

Transition to Yoi position in Musubi Dachi.

Yoi position in Heiko Dachi.

Hidari Heiko Dachi with Jodan Age Uke.

Migi Heiko Dachi with Chudan Oi Tsuki.

Hidari Shiko Dachi with Gedan Barai Uke.

Migi Heiko Dachi with Jodan Age Uke.

Hidari Heiko Dachi with Chudan Oi Tsuki.

Kata

Migi Shiko Dachi with Gedan Barai Uke.

Hidari Sanchin Dachi with Chudan Soto Uke.

Migi Sanchin Dachi with Chudan Soto Uke.

Jodan Mae Geri (Kiai!).

Hidari Zenkutsu Dachi with Chudan Age Hiji Ate.

Hidari Zenkutsu Dachi with Jodan Uraken Uchi.

Hidari Zenkutsu Dachi with Gedan Barai Uke.

Hidari Zenkutsu Dachi with Chudan Gyaku Tsuki.

Heiko Dachi (before execute Ashi Barai) with Jodan Shuto Uchi (Kiai!).

Hidari Sanchin Dachi with Chudan Soto Uke.

Jodan Mae Geri (Kiai!).

Migi Zenkutsu Dachi with Chudan Age Hiji Ate.

Migi Zenkutsu Dachi with Jodan Uraken Uchi.

Migi Zenkutsu Dachi with Gedan Barai Uke.

Migi Zenkutsu Dachi with Chudan Gyaku Tsuki.

Heiko Dachi (before execute Ashi Barai) with Jodan Shuto Uchi (Kiai!).

Migi Zenkutsu Dachi (before execute Uchi Uke) in preparation for Mawashi Uke.

Migi Zenkutsu Dachi with Mawashi Uke.

Kata

Migi Zenkutsu Dachi in preparation for Awase Tsuki.

Migi Zenkutsu Dachi with Awase Tsuki.

Musubi Dachi with Hikite as transition form.

Hidari Zenkutsu Dachi (before execute Uchi Uke) in preparation for Mawashi Uke.

Hidari Zenkutsu Dachi with Mawashi Uke.

Hidari Zenkutsu Dachi in preparation for Awase Tsuki.

Hidari Zenkutsu Dachi with Awase Tsuki.

Hidari Zenkutsu Dachi with preparation to pull back Awase Tsuki.

Hidari Zenkutsu Dachi with Hikite.

Goju Ryu Karate

Hidari Zenkutsu Dachi with Awase Tsuki.

Hidari Zenkutsu Dachi in preparation to step forward.

Step forward in Musubi Dachi in preparation to finish the form.

Musubi Dachi and finishing the form.

Formal attention in Musubi Dachi.

Kata

Embusen of the Gekisai dai ichi kata

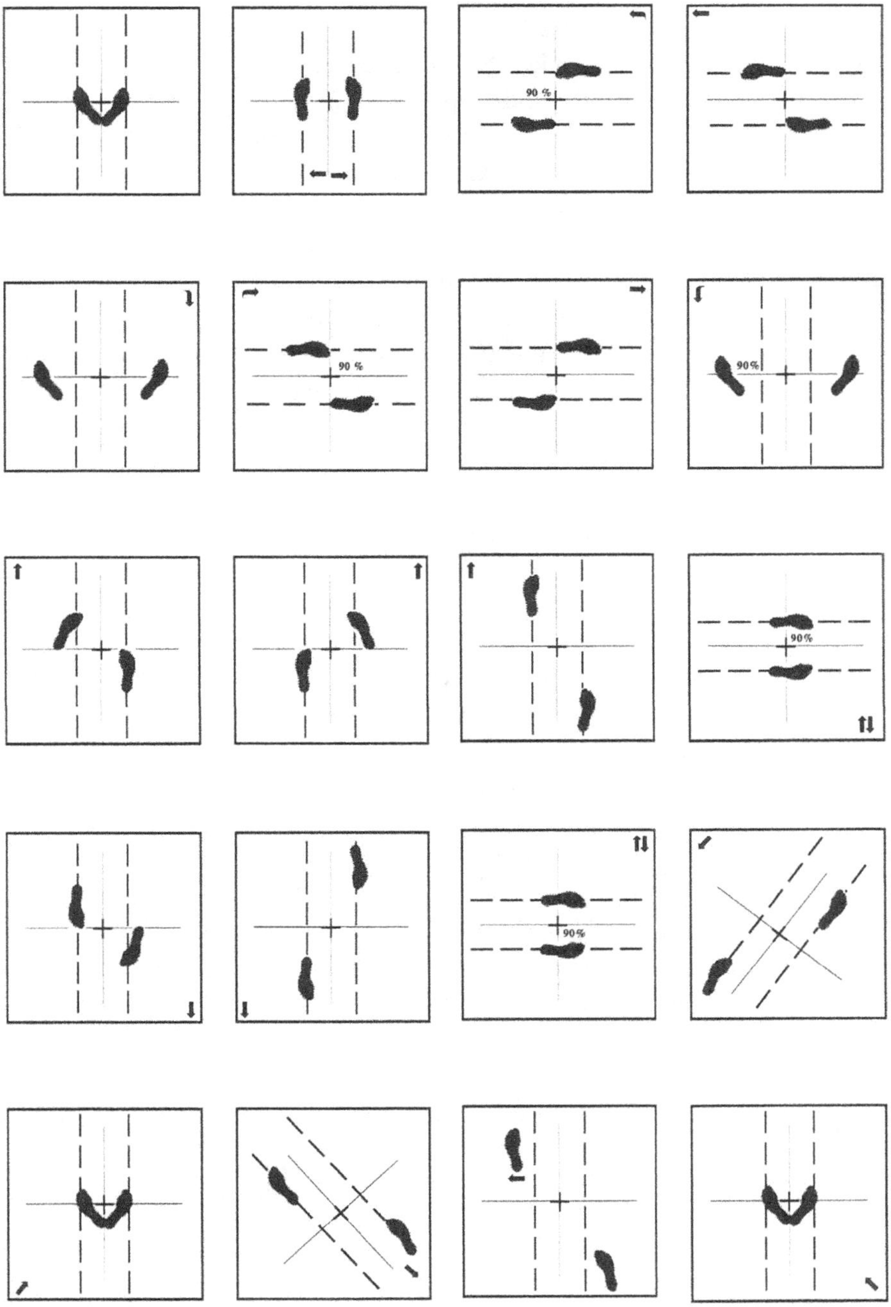

Embusen Gekisai dai ichi kata.

SAIFA KATA

Saifa kata is the first (5) kata in the Meibukan School that one learns after the Gekisai and Sanchin kata. As an original Chinese kata (6)—as well as the kata Shisochin, Sanseru, Sesan, Seiunchin, Sepai, Kururunfa, and Suparinpei that, among other things (7), were taught to Kanryo Higaonna in China—Chojun Miyagi made it a part of his Goju-ryu system.

Saifa or "Saifuwa" belongs to the classical kata of the Goju-ryu Karate-do system. Saifa means as much as "to hit and break," "to smash and break," or "devastating punches." Another interpretation is "to solve a certain physical conflict." Depending on the expression and the context in which the kanji is placed, it is difficult to give a single meaning for the names of kata. For some kata, it also is possible to give a certain philosophical interpretation that can place the name of a kata in a different light.

Posture from Saifa kata.

Supposedly, the Saifa kata was developed to meet the fighting tactics that occur in linear forward and backward fights. Partly because of standing on one leg during a specific technique in the kata, it is supposed that this signifies maintaining balance on an unstable footing. More important, however, in view of the bunkai's explaining this movement in the kata, is holding an opponent while standing on one leg and executing a fighting technique with the other leg.

Saifa kata is remarkable with regard to the aiming of the senses, such as hearing and seeing. There are strong hints to use the senses that one has, and also to train them for the fight. One always should be aware of all the surroundings and not be focused on a single subject or opponent. There could be more than one opponent, and situations that one perceives by hearing, seeing or touching. These stimuli are experienced separately or combined by the senses, and create an assessment or awareness of the situation. In the kata Saifa, there is a forwardly aimed technique during which one specifically looks sideways. Not only does one turn the head sideways, but one also aims one ear to the front and one to the back.

In Saifa kata, many techniques are aimed to grab an opponent and to strike subsequently.

SHISOCHIN KATA

Shisochin kata was one of the favorite (8) kata of Chojun Miyagi. Shisochin has more than one meaning, although all share a common central point. This point is the indication of the number four in combination with movements. Sometimes the kanji for Shisochin kata is translated as "four wind directions" or as "four gates" from which, seen from a technical fighting point of view, the attackers initiate their attack. The one executing the kata represses these attacks. Shisochin is also translated as "fight with the four Monks" and "fight from four directions." In Shisochin kata, one needs to be able to turn in a flexible way and to move swiftly. Characteristics are the nukite and shotei hands that are applied as key elements at several points in the kata in different techniques. Shisochin kata has many evasive and escaping techniques combined with an offensive technique. Shisochin kata, as well as Saifa kata, is seen as a "middle class kata" (concerning difficulty level) of the Goju-ryu curriculum.

Posture from Shisochin kata.

SANSERU KATA

Sanseru or "Sansedu" means "36," probably referring to the number of techniques occurring as exercises in the kata. It often is linked to a theory concerning Buddhism and Taoism, because the backgrounds of Chinese Fighting Arts have had a major role in the origination and development of Chinese culture, and thus Fighting Arts in general.

In the Buddhist numeral symbolism, the figure 36 is very important. It consists of two groups of 6 times 6. The first group contains spirit, body, ears, nose, tongue, and eyes. The second group is made up of justice, touch, sound, smell, taste, and color.

Sanseru kata is the only kata of the Goju-ryu Karate-do system that initially was not taught directly to Chojun Miyagi by Kanryo Higaonna. Juhatsu Kiyoda, sempai of Chojun Miyagi, was the first to be taught Sanseru kata by Kanryo Higaonna. At a later point in time, Chojun Miyagi also was instructed in this kata.

Posture from Sanseru kata.

Shortly after the death of Chojun Miyagi, two of his students, Meitoku Yagi and Seikichi Toguchi, visited Juhatsu Kiyoda (9) to increase their knowledge of Sanseru kata. (One of the few people who have mastered the Sanseru kata as instructed by Kanryo Higaonna to Juhatsu Kiyoda, the "Juhatsu Kiyoda" version, is Anthony Mirakian. Sensei Mirakian visited Juhatsu Kiyoda in Beppu, Japan in the late 1950s).

Within the Meibukan School, Sanseru kata is the first advanced kata in the syllabus. Technically, this is the first kata in which downwardly stamping kicks are employed, proportional to the number of forwardly aimed kicks. Elbows and punching techniques should follow up on each other in a single movement of the hip, during which a strong stance must be maintained.

SESAN KATA

Sesan means "13," probably a reference to the number of techniques occurring as exercises in the kata. Sesan kata is not exclusively a Goju-ryu kata. There are two forms of Sesan kata, divided roughly into the Naha-te form and the Shuri-te form (10). The Goju-ryu Sesan kata has been derived from the Naha-te form.

Sesan kata often was the kata of choice, demonstrated by Chojun Miyagi and some top students, during important events (11). Dai Sensei Meitoku Yagi has titled this kata, together with Seiunchin kata, as being the main kaishu training kata of the Meibukan Goju-ryu Karate-do system.

Posture from Sesan kata.

Sesan kata is exceptionally varied in techniques—contrasts between fast and slow movements and hard and soft techniques. The rhythm of the kata knows great variability.

Sesan kata is a kata that, partially because of its history, can be executed in several ways. Large differences can be seen between the Naha-te and Shuri-te forms and smaller ones within different Naha-te forms. A hallmark of the form practiced within the Meibukan School is the "washing cat" movement used as a circular block, and the weighing down "osae" of the lower arm (and in some bunkai intended as uke-tsuki) after a punching technique.

Posture from Seiunchin kata.

SEIUNCHIN KATA

Unfortunately, it has not been possible to retrace exactly what Seiunchin or Seenchin/ Seienchin means. Still, the most common translations reads "to remove while marching calmly" and "to control, pull, and suppress." Technically speaking, it can mean "to grab and pull into a fight." As is the case for the other classical kata, the origins of Seiunchin kata are not traceable.

In Seiunchin, the Shiko dachi is employed particularly often. This stance strengthens the leg muscles and is very suitable to direct the force during throwing techniques upwardly, and to remain standing stably while experiencing resistance. This kata also employs unique techniques in which one arm/hand supports the other.

In principle, one could say that Seiunchin kata is very suitable for someone who is physically small and less muscular, whereas Sesan kata is particularly suitable for the heavier and more muscular practitioner. This kata, compared with the other Goju-ryu kata, has a remarkable absence of kicking techniques.

Posture from Sepai kata.

SEPAI KATA

Sepai means "18," probably a reference to the number of techniques exercised in the kata. As in Sanseru, this number refers to the Buddhist numeral symbolism. The number 18 (3 x 6) refers to good, bad, and peace (3) and touch, color, taste, smell, voice, and justice (6).

Typical for Sepai kata is the general use of the body, coupled to fighting techniques being practiced by the limbs. Movements of the body are carried out simultaneously with fighting techniques, resulting in moments of very strong movement. Another hallmark is the cooperation of different techniques, having different structures of movement, that are executed at the same time.

KURURUNFA KATA

Kururunfa or "Kududunfuwa" means "to stand firm" and "to knock down forever and to keep under control with punches." Other translations are "to destroy with ancient techniques," "the calm before the storm," and "to take over."

Kururunfa, as well as the Meibukan Goju-ryu execution of Saifa kata, includes balancing on one leg, which gives the practitioner a stimulus to strengthen one's balance through practice. Fast sequences of different techniques, using many hooking and pulling techniques, are employed in this kata.

Posture from Kururunfa kata.

Posture from Suparinpei kata.

SUPARINPEI KATA

Suparinpei or "Suparinpe" means "108," possibly a reference to the number of techniques practiced in the kata. Some masters explain the name of Suparinpei kata as symbolic for the Buddhist way of thinking. The number 108 stands for the 108 (3 x 36) evil passions that influence a man.

Suparinpei kata often is the last classical (kaishu) kata that is taught to the student. In comparison with other Goju-ryu kata, Suparinpei kata is a very long kata in which previously executed techniques, seen in the other classical kata, are executed at a higher level with slight changes in accent.

THE MEIBUKEN KATA

"Ken," in "Meibuken kata," stands for specific Style kata or School kata. Dai Sensei Meitoku Yagi designed these as a contribution to the Goju-ryu Karate-do system.

At the request of the Okinawan government, Dai Sensei Meitoku Yagi has expressed his interpretation of Chojun Miyagi's Goju-ryu in new kata. The Okinawan government made this request because it sees karate as a cultural heritage, and wants to keep it alive and active. The status of Dai Sensei Meitoku Yagi as top student of Chojun Miyagi—the recognition as Goju-ryu style leader given to him by the Miyagi family in 1963 and the contributions and sacrifices he has made for the island of Okinawa and for karate-do in general—has led the Okinawan government to ask Dai Sensei Meitoku Yagi to create new kata.

Hikite of the Meibuken kata.

Dai Sensei Meitoku Yagi started developing these new kata around 1973 and introduced these as Fukyu kata 1 and Fukyu kata 2. Later, these were named "Ten-Chi." Tenchi is named after the

Taoist concept of Tai Chi. The techniques of Fukyu kata 1 and Fukyu kata 2 correspond to each other. It is a mirror kata during which, in the bunkai, two persons complete a continuous bunkai cycle very simular to Chinese two-man forms. The direct meaning of "Ten-Chi" is "heaven" and "earth," and it occupies the center of the Meibuken kata.

Later on, Dai Sensei Meitoku Yagi developed four more kata: "Seiryu" (blue dragon/East), "Byakko" (white tiger/West), "Shujakku" (red swallow/South) and "Genbu" (black turtle/North). These last two kata have Taoist Qigong exercises. These four kata also correspond to each other in their bunkai in opposite directions, both in offense and in defense. The kata Seiryu, Byakko, and Shujakku were introduced in the 1980s, and finally Genbu in 1990.

The Meibukan kata also are Fung Shui animals and can be divided as Yin or Yang. They are guardians of the four directions or gates.

Unique in these five Meibuken kata is that the hikite in the form of a fist is kept with the palm of the hand against the body (tateken). Also, the opening and the conclusion of the kata are done in the way of ancient Chinese Kempo. The right fist is pressed against the opened left hand. The fact that the hand is restraining the fist is a strong symbolic reference to the meaning of the true martial intention (12). During the preparation, "Yoi," prior to the opening of the fighting techniques within the kata, only the feet move from Musubi dachi to Heiko dachi. Likewise, the feet return to Musubi dachi at the end of the kata.

The official Meibukan presentation of the symbolic message derived from the Chinese martial arts.

The old Chinese way.

Notes

(1) On October 25, 1936, an important historical meeting was organized by Ota Chofu (employed by the newspaper Ryukyu Shimposha), and sponsored by the Ryukyu Shimposha, with important karate masters attending: Chomo Hanashiro, Chotoku Kyan, Choki Motobu, Juhatsu Kiyoda, Choshin Chibana, Chojun Miyagi, Shimpan Gusukuma, and Genwa Nakasone. Also present were several persons from the educational system, the army, the police, and the media. The important result of this meeting was the official recognition of the name karate-do, replacing the old name for Okinawan fighting arts, "Toudijutsu" (In Japan, the Okinawan fighting arts had already been named karate-do in December 1933, and taken up and ratified as such by the Dai Nippon Butoku-kai). But it also was decided at this meeting, led by Zensoku Yamaguchi (editor-in-chief of the Ryukyu Shimposha) to propose to the Bureau of Education to introduce karate-do to both primary and secondary schools. Through the recognition of the name karate-do, which already had great popularity in Japan, the road was cleared for unification on Okinawa. By adopting the name karate-do, it was intended (among other things) to familiarize a greater public, especially young people, with the Okinawan fighting arts. This also resulted in a standardization of the technical curriculum, which would lead to faster development and preservation of the Okinawan fighting arts as a cultural heritage.

Commemorating the establishment of the basic kata of karate-do (1937) (Front, from right) Chojun Miyagi, Chomo Hanashiro, Kentsu Yabu, Chotoku Kyan (Back, from right) Genwa Nakasone, Choshin Chibana, Choryo Maeshiro, Shinpan Shiroma.

(2) Remarkable are the two blocking techniques, indicated as "Jodan Age Uke," that, as a fighting technique, are not present in any other classical Goju-ryu kata. These techniques, as block/parry, are aimed upward and in a fighting technical sense have the most practical use when executed in response to an attack from someone larger/taller than oneself. (In view of the fact that Western mankind is larger in build and also was seen as a potential threat considering the time period and situation that Japan found itself in, one might speculate this was the reason for the introduction of this technique as part of the kata).

Jodan Age Uke from the kata Gekisai Dai Ichi.

(3) Embusen means "pre-programmed executing lines." It indicates the pattern to be followed comprising the contact between the ground and the body. This location where the feet contact the earth is similar to a choreographic pattern.

(4) In this context, "ki ai'" means the gathering of Qi (Chi) or energy, released through a shout. The willpower of the mind (through the mental impulse signals that are sent from the brain to the rest of the body) creates the vibrating capacity of the body (tone/sound) and sends this energy along with the respiration to exit via the mouth. The physical origin of the "ki ai" is the Dan Tian, the main energy center of the human body (see Sanchin; Dan Tian). "Ai," from "ki ai," embraces the meaning of "harmony," and it is this sound "ai" that ensures (during the practice of karate) that the breath can leave the body explosively in a short period of time. The expulsion of the breath should be in harmony with the intention of the technique being carried out. (Note: The expression in sound/vibration is dependent on the intention/execution of the technique, which can result in changes in sound.)

(5) Only at the introduction of the Gekisai kata did Chojun Miyagi determine a general division for the teaching of the kata. Previously, this was not the case. Depending on personal properties, each individual was taught certain kata by Chojun Miyagi. The results booked, and the individual suitability with which progress was made, determined if the person in question would be taught more kata. This also meant that some students were taught only a few kata by Chojun Miyagi, whereas others were taught the complete kata system.

After the introduction of the Gekisai kata, these were always instructed first before one could obtain instruction to other kata. After the death of Chojun Miyagi, his senior students started to develop karate education with a specific kata order in schools of their own. Since this time, virtually all kata are introduced in a certain order. Generally this order is the same within most Goju-ryu schools, although some differences do exist. Concerning the kata, the order of presentation in this book is the order used by the Meibukan School of Dai Sensei Meitoku Yagi at the present time. In the schematic overview (see Overview of Meibukan Goju-ryu Karate-do System), the general order of teaching of the classical Kaishu kata within the Meibukan School can be seen.

(6) It is still unclear where the kata of the Goju-ryu system originated, with the exception of the Gekisai kata and, to some extent, Tensho kata. There is no written evidence (reports, drawings, etc.) that can prove where, when, and by whom the other Goju-ryu kata, also indicated as classical kata, have been developed, whether these kata creations came directly from Liu Liu Ko or if he himself was taught them. Still, there are hints (sustained by drawings, manuscripts, and oral tradition) that techniques present in the kata of Goju-ryu Karate-do could be retraced to diverse systems of Chinese Kung Fu.

Tora Guchi technique demonstrated by Lex Opdam from the Gekisai Dai Ni Kata.

There also are many theories as to how the merging of techniques can lead to a pattern such as a kata. Although it is recognized that the techniques within the Goju-ryu kata originate from China and are thus identified as Chinese, the way in which the techniques are combined within a kata cannot really be called Chinese. The Chinese kata (quans) usually are very fluid in motion and are expressed less fragmented than is the case for the Goju-ryu kata.

(7) In 1867, during a demonstration in the village of Sakayama, Seisho Arakaki (see note 1 under the chapter Karate-do), the first martial arts teacher of Kanryo Higaonna, demonstrated the kata Suparinpei. Not until that same year, at the age of 15, did Kanryo Higaonna leave for China. Through research, it has come to light that Seisho Arakaki, prior to Higaonna's visit to China, studied the fighting arts in China under Wai Xinxian in the province of Fuzhou. It seems that the kata Sesan and Sanchin were already practiced on Okinawa before Kanryo Higaonna left for China in 1867. It is possible that Kanryo Higaonna had already been taught some of his Goju-ryu system kata on Okinawa, for example by Seisho Arakaki, before he visited China. During his stay in China, he could have had more instruction in these, including an expansion of techniques and kata.

(8) According to Anthony Mirakian, senior student of Meitoku Yagi, Chojun Miyagi felt a special preference for the practice of Shisochin.

(9) This important visit came about as a result of Chojun Miyagi's death. Meitoku Yagi and Seikichi Toguchi came to Juhatsu Kiyoda with the proposal that he, being the most senior student of Kanryo Higaonna, would lead the Goju-ryu system as chairman of the Goju-ryu Association. Juhatsu Kiyoda dismissed this proposal. During this visit, Meitoku Yagi and Seikichi Toguchi asked Juhatsu Kiyoda if he would correct their Sanseru kata. Juhatsu Kiyoda had learned Sanseru kata when Chojun Miyagi was in the military service. According to Juhatsu Kiyoda, the kata of Meitoku Yagi and Seikichi Toguchi was without fault and wouldn't need to be corrected.

Master Arakaki Chikudoun Pechin Seisho.

(10) Naha-te: indicative of the fighting arts/self-defense systems that were practiced within and around the area of Naha (city/population area). Likewise, Tomari-te and Shuri-te indicate the fighting arts/self-defense systems that were practiced within and around the areas of Tomari and Shuri. These fighting arts/self-defense systems came from China (introduced around 1850) and existed alongside the already "older" fighting art called "ti" ("ti" had been in use as self-defense and spiritual development for hundreds of years with the nobility of Okinawa). Later on, different styles (ryus) herein were given names, such as Goju-ryu, Uechi-ryu, Shorin-ryu, etc.

(11) Together with Sanchin, Sesan was demonstrated in 1930 by Jin'an Shinzato to the crown prince Hirohito in Tokyo. Sesan was demonstrated publicly in 1935 by Chojun Miyagi.

(12) The threatening closed fist is being restrained by the open hand; the symbolic message is to show that the martial arts serve a higher goal than entering a physical confrontation with someone else. It means, with the help of practice, to confront oneself in order to realize harmony. Through this greeting, one also indicates to one's surroundings not to have negative intentions, but rather that one is honorably striving for fraternization.

KUMITE

Kumite Kata

Kumite renshu embraces the applications of defensive and offensive activities within the kaishu kata and presents the actual fight. Through kumite renshu, one can recognize the practical meaning and purpose of the kata. The practice of Kaishu kata and Kumite renshu will lead to understanding and ripening of the true Budo spirit.

—Chojun Miyagi, 1934

ABOUT KUMITE

Kumite, in karate terms, means the practice of the actual physical confrontation between two or more persons. Within the Meibukan School in Goju-ryu Karate-do several specific kumite forms (kumite kata) exist.

These kumite kata originate from the kata (as a solo form) that comprise its fighting system. The Meibukan Goju-ryu kumite kata will be named and illuminated and the most important ones for beginners and half advanced practitioners will be shown in the form of a photo-series. Before clarifying the different kumite kata, the general concept of attack and defense first will be explained.

Calligraphy by Meitoku Yagi saying "The secret is to train one's heart."

Attack and defense

Within the Meibukan School, there are one or more so called attacker(s) (semete or tori) and defenders (ukete or uke) who confront each other in a physical (simulated) confrontation further mentioned as kumite kata. The attacker is the one who displays his of hers aggression first in a conflict by starting a physical action in relation to a victim in this case the defender. The defender (ukete) is the one were upon the attack is aimed and, therefore, is forced to take a defensive action. Although the defender has the possibility to attack after being attacked, he or she attacks for self-defense purposes. The attacker (semete), in the role of the aggressor, doesn't start his or her attack from the point of self-defense but rather out of malicious intentions. This is an important difference and in the dojo students will be explained by ritual, postures and eye contact, how this concept, which has its foundation in philosophical and moral grounds, transforms in practice.

With the above having been said, it is important to explain the role of semete in the kumite kata practice. Semete functions, ethically, as a tool for ukete. In randori or jiyu kumite (free-sparring), both "potential" opponents have the same purpose—to win and score. In randori, one should start a fight as soon as there is an opening, with or without the other attacking first. This is a contradiction compared to the kata, where the first move is always defensive to propagate karate-dos nature in a technical defensive sense, but more important, it is a reflection of

Grandmaster Chojun Miyagi teaching Goju-ryu kumites in his dojo in Okinawa in 1950 (standing in the rear). Students are from the left to right: Mr. Meitoku Yagi, Mr. Eiichi Miyazato, Mr. Seikichi Toguchi and Mr. Eiko Miyazato.

As a 7th kyu Lex Opdam started doing kumite fighting in regional and national championships. He stopped before his Nidan (IOGKF) examination with competition kumite.

philosophical and introspective aims—one of the reasons why the Meibukan School does not compete in sport competition karate as free-fighting.

But except for being a tool for the practice of the physical confrontation for ukete, there is an important task for semete, and semete also trains his or her mind in doing so.

Within the first period of training, the emphasis in the way of attacking ukete will be of a soft approach, however, on higher levels of practice this shifts to full force attacks from the side of semete. After the initial period, semete learns to attack another person with full force without having the emotional intention to hurt the person, which could be a negative by product, but to help ukete to prepare for a real fight. For many people it is very hard to hit someone when asked to do so in a simulated physical confrontation. However, this task that should be performed by semete is very important for ukete in practising realistic kumite kata. Otherwise, ukete would handle the training of kumite kata as a game, without confronting fear (for possible damage to ones body) and controlling emotions raised by this sort of danger.

Through full force applied attacks upon ukete, the semete also will train his or her mind. Since both partners, as opponents in the simulated confrontation, have agreed upon (prearranged) physical confrontations, and are aware of the consequences, semete should fulfill his or her task without hesitation or holding back—an important but often neglected task. If one hesitates in a fight, this could have serious consequences. Also, one should train oneself in protecting oneself and should not only have a thought in defending oneself but also act accordingly. If one does not dare (for advanced students) to

Hanshi Meitatsu Yagi performing Ippon Kumite.

attack full force in training, one should not expect to do so when really needed in life. From this point of view of self-defense, we should try to come as close as possible to real fighting situations. More important than style and techniques is learning to deal with danger and fear. If the mind is not focused, the technique will lose its use and even could become dangerous, since one should not expect the opponent to give you a second chance.

Grandmaster Chojun Miyagi in the far left teaching at the Commercial High School, Naha City, Okinawa, in 1927.

Alertness

Partner forms should be practiced seriously. For all partner forms, in particular kumite kata, one should remain highly focused and alert (Zanchin). Almost ceaselessly, one should look in the eyes of the opponent and be trying to discover the other's breathing and emotions, so one could use this within the confrontation. Kumite kata, in particular those forms that one masters and doesn't need to rationalize anymore, is of great value for the spirit. The visible confrontation on the physical level, if seriously practiced by both semete and ukete, has a less visible but very strong influence upon one's psyche and state of mind. Every mistake, indolence, arrogance, or other distraction could have enormous consequences, bringing direct damage towards the body and direct and indirect damage upon the developing spiritual path karate-do should bring.

Close-in fighting

It is very important to stay very close to the opponent when executing Goju-ryu kumites to fully deliver effective fighting techniques. Close-in fighting is characteristic of the Goju-ryu fighting system, meaning that one wants to stay within reach of the other's body range since decisions on ending a fight are made mostly within this short distance (often opposite to competition fighting). Often, many Japanese karate styles emphasize their training on deep stances (especially Zenkutsu dachi), not only for leg conditioning but also as one of the most important stances within the practice of kumite. Within Meibukan Goju-ryu, the most important stance is the high stance of Sanchin dachi. Combined and often executed in explosive high speed movements, this Sanchin dachi externally will often be visible as a Heiko dachi. With these two stances (with the left or right foot in front), one focuses on a realistic fighting aspect. One can quickly respond, is mobile, and has a short-range possibility to the opponent's head (the most important target in a serious life-threatening situation).

Misunderstanding of body contact

Chojun Miyagi and Juhatsu Kyoda performing Chudan Soto Uke.

It often is said that karate techniques, especially punches, are stopped before the target. This is a misconception. In Goju-ryu karate, one punches through the target! As a Goju-ryu master once told me: "They can scratch me on my skin, but I will break their bones!"

A good reflection on Goju-ryu's technical power characteristic is the use of the makiwara. When punching the makiwara, the purpose is not to stop before the target is hit but to punch with full force as far as possible (within the right motoric movement and finishing posture), through the "skin" of the target. Punches of Goju-ryu on the makiwara are mostly meant, especially on chudan level, to hold the resistance of the makiwara for a moment when the highest resistance is met (through the recoiling effect of the wood). This resembles the impact of a punch on one's body. One should not forget that a human body exposed to punches on the chudan level can take quite an impact without it resulting directly into damage. On the street, a person has clothes on (which dim the impact) and possess muscle tissues and a bone structure that further play a role in lowering possible impact and protecting the organs. So, compared with the head area (and, of course, some other vital areas, like the groin, etc.) one should give more focus on power to the chudan area than the jodan area to have a result that could influence the end of a fight. This certainly does not mean that both power and speed are not involved when punching to other areas than on the chudan level.

The same is true, for example, concerning striking with nukite to the eyes. Speed here is much more important than power. The soft tissues of the eyes are easily damaged, and to hit this target full force and, therefore, with excessive power is of no use. It only slows down the attacking movement and, therefore, has a greater risk to be intercepted or deflected. In this concept, one should keep in mind that the tuning of power and speed depends on the tactic, target, and possibilities. An angry person often will be led by his emotions and, without control over his mental state, that person often will move full force with any technique and, therefore, can create harmful situations for him/herself.

Coming back to the concept of "stopping before the target," which does exist but should be properly addressed, too, I will try to explain the idea behind it relating to the kumite forms. As one can read in the section on Yakusoku Ippon and Nippon Kumite; "Upon this counterattack of ukete, semete will not respond but remains (as frozen) for a moment in their last position." Here, the ukete will stop his or her technique before hitting the semete. The reason is clear: the semete is not allowed (prearranged) to react to the ukete's counterattack. In this sense, one could say that, indeed, the attack of the ukete is controlled and stopped just before the target.

High-level practitioners should train upon "knockdown" in the role of the semete. This does not account for the ukete's last technique, as described before.

Renshi Lex Opdam and Renshi Hing-Poon Chan demonstrating Ippon Kumite.

Renshi Hing-Poon Chan and Renshi Lex Opdam demonstrating Ippon Kumite.

YAKUSOKU KUMITE

Yakusoku Ippon Kumite

Prearranged (yakusoku) confrontation (kumite) concentrated on a single (ippon) attack.

This form of physical confrontation means simply that semete attacks ukete with a single technique.

The attack of semete consists of a form of body displacement combined with an attacking technique, supported by the possibilities (speed, power, coordination, flexibility, etc.) that the body has at its disposal. In the case of Yakusoku Ippon Kumite, one limits oneself to execute a single (attacking) technique that usually consists of an arm or leg technique. The answer of ukete upon this action will follow in a block/deflection and possible movement of the body, and thereafter a counterattack. Also possible for ukete is to counterattack simultaneously upon the attack of semete, with or without a block/deflection. Although ukete has more freedom in the way the counterattack can be utilized, only one counterattack should be used. Upon this counterattack of ukete, semete will not respond but remain (as if frozen) for a moment in his/her last position.

Although the explanation above is the general technical base of Yakusoku Ippon Kumite, ritualized etiquette in bowing, focusing, preparation, finishing, and ending the action all are integrated parts of all karate-do forms, including kumite kata. This chapter about kumite kata will explain some of these correlating parts but will not focus on them.

Yakusoku Nippon Kumite

Prearranged (yakusoku) confrontation (kumite) concentrated on a twofold (nippon) attack. This form of physical confrontation is similar to the previous Yakusoku Ippon Kumite, with the difference that semete is attacking ukete with two consecutive attacks. Ukete will respond to these attacks by blocking/deflecting, using the right body movement and a counterattack, which can be executed simultaneously on or after the second attack of semete.

The two Yakusoku kumites are standard within the Meibukan School, although more kumite forms are trained, consisting of three (sanbon) or more attacks performed by semete and answered by ukete. Dai Sensei Meitoku Yagi did not officially put them into his Meibukan Goju-ryu Karate-do curriculum.

In an advanced stage, the Yakusoku kumites can be changed into kumite forms that are not prearranged. Yakusoku Ippon and/or Nippon kumites become Ippon and/or Nippon kumite. Without a prearranged attack initiated from semete, semete can attack on every height level (jodan/chudan/gedan, see Chapter on Sanchin kata, "Attentions concerning general posture") with a free choice in the (one or two) executing technique(s). Ukete responds with a suitable defense and counterattacks in free choice.

The deeper grounds of the ritualized fighting stances and etiquette

In all civilized countries, there is a certain morality and system of values that, although there are some differences, have a common core. Generally speaking, each individual collectively (by culture) knows what one should do or not do, and by placing criteria with approval and disapproval, we strengthen and support our collective values and moral goals. The law is a tool for strengthening and supporting collective values and moral goals.

One of our basic civilized thoughts is to have respect for human life. Within this context, we can point toward physical conflicts. In the appendices, under "Law and Self-defense," you can read about how the law in general looks upon physical conflicts concerning self-defense. An important reason for this part of the appendix concerns not only the fact that one should know in which way the law, and therefore the authorities, looks upon legal justice concerning the subject of self-defense, but also to open the eyes of martial arts practitioners in raising questions about why the Law exists and how the above-named postures and rituals are related.

Within the trained fighting postures and etiquette of the Meibukan School, you will find morality and values that people, as human beings, should globally have in common. Within the ritualized forms, etiquette, and the directions of the Sensei, whose goal is to guide the process of the practitioner, the practitioner should be stimulated to interact, bringing the dojo-practice into one's life. Every bow, movement, word, look, breath, or thought should have a direct practical goal in our practice in the dojo, but also be used as a reflection of our daily life. Throughout the years, the practice of these (etiquettes of the Meibukan School) will build rituals with strong moral and philosophical backgrounds. It should become second nature and build up one's character. So, postures should be seen not merely as technical applications but also moral tools to give a positive blueprint to one's personality, insight, and connection with others.

To paraphrase Sensei Mirakian's words: "If you take the morality away from karate training, then you're left with something dangerously close to brutality."

The fighting postures of the Yakusoku kumite's
Neko Ashi No Kamae

The fighting postures (kamaes), of the Meibukan School are very specific and have different names. The first one is called Neko Ashi No Kamae (sometimes also refered as Kake Uke No Kamae). The stance of the kamae is in Neko dachi, freely translated as "cat-stance." In this stance, both hands are pointed towards the opponent. There are two ways of holding the hands in front of the body in this posture:

– The first hand position consists of an opened frontline hand (the hand that is closest to the opponent) and a closed hand, a fist, behind the frontline hand. This last hand, in the form of a vertical fist (tateken), is not clearly seen from the viewpoint of the opponent, since the frontline

(Left) Semete (attacker)
(Right) Ukete (defender).

hand is blocking the opponent's sight (see picture). Like all defensive/protective hand positions in the area in front of the solaris plexus this tateken position has a space the thickness of a fist between the solar plexus and its hand (in the form of the fist as tateken).

– The second hand position is almost identical to the first, with the difference

The hand closest to the body is open.

The hand closest to the body is a fist.

The hand closest to the body is not visible to the opponent.

that the hand position closest to the body is open. So, like the frontline hand, both hands now are opened, with the palms directed at the opponent (shotei).

Morote Gedan Heiko No Kamae

Except for this Neko Ashi No Kamae, there are two other kamaes used in most of the Meibukan schools. Next to the Neko Ashi No Kamae is the Morote Gedan Heiko No Kamae. This kamae is as important as the first one. The stance of this kamae is in Heiko dachi, meaning that the feet are shoulder width with slightly bent knees and the toes pointing parallel to the front. In this stance, the fists are in front of the upper legs with the elbows slightly bent (see picture). It is mostly used by ukete as a "ready" ("yoi'") stance before action is taken by ukete. (Also semete uses this kamae in certain forms. As an example, see the performance of the Fukyu kata Jodan Renzoku Kumite, in which semete directly attacks ukete in the first action.) A (potential) attacker does not always give aggressive body signals before attacking. On the street, a person could attack very suddenly, without prior notice. Within the Meibukan, this kamae and its "forced" short distance is used especially to give a greater risk and stress level (adjustment of distance, power, and speed, and don't forget emotions in relation to the feeling of unease in connection with fear and danger) to ukete. Although a minimal preparation and focus is present the posture itself (in which the muscles are slightly tensed and knees and elbows are slightly bent) comes very close to a representation of a potential "street situation" in which an attack, without any visible motive, can occur.

Saifa No Kamae

The third kamae is called Saifa No Kamae. This is a posture taken from the Saifa kata (and the Meibuken kata Seiryu). This Saifa No Kamae is used for ukete as a possible defensive posture. Without being too aggressive (this posture is taken after the aggressor takes a position in Neko Ashi No Kamae), it is a preparation for the possible attack of the semete, who takes the first aggressive initiative going into the fighting posture Neko Ashi No Kamae. At higher levels of kumite practice, one could make feinting movements within the postures mentioned here to feel and sense the

Neko Ashi No Kamae.   Saifa No Kamae.

other's intentions (moving from a left side posture to a right side posture and vise versa). The attacker could suddenly attack from a left or right posture, or in the midst of changing the posture. The stance of this kamae is also in Neko dachi. The hands are in a position in which the arm in front of the body can easily perform a block or strike, and the back hand (open hikite) can perform a strike or punch (see picture).

Measuring and movement regarding Yakusoku kumite

Before semete begins taking his fighting posture in Neko Ashi No Kamae, he or she prepares oneself to bring his or her body into the right position in relation to the ukete. There are two important positions concerning the distance and, therefore, measuring within the kumite forms that are practiced:

Short distance:

From the position of "Yoi," the attacker takes a small step back, about one foot length, with the right foot. The left foot stays. Drop the body in Neko dachi and form the posture of Neko Ashi No Kamae (see picture).

From this position, semete will attack ukete with the chosen technique, and supporting his or her technique, come one step forward with the right foot. The left foot will stay in its place (if no shifting of support is used) although rotation and strong(er) surface contact with the sole of the foot is possible and presumable (depending on the technique executed). This final stance is called Migi Heiko dachi.

All fighting postures in action in an exercise to 'scan' each other for a possible attack.

Long distance:

From the position of "Yoi," the attacker takes a long shifting step back (zenkutsu distance, approximately four times one's own foot length) with the right foot and takes along the left leg. While moving in position, drop the body in Neko dachi and form the posture Hidari (left) Neko Ashi No Kamae (see picture).

From this position, semete will attack ukete with the chosen technique and, supporting his or her technique, move one big step forward with the right foot. The left foot will slide (Suri Ashi) explosively forward, but stays behind the right leg, and both form the stance Migi Heiko dachi.

If a punch is executed by semete, it relates to the left leg/foot movement and repositioning. This means that the punch departs (after the right leg/foot is initially moved to the front) together with the left leg/foot that follows the left leg/foot in an explosive manner. So the movement of the right punch starts with the movement of the left leg.

One should keep in mind that when attacking, the punching fist does not retreat to the chamber first. The attacking hand, which has its starting position in front of the solar plexus, will directly follow its path from this position to the target without building up more power (by retracting the arm). Speed in attacking from this hand position, especially from a long distance, is more important than focusing on more arm power. Also, by first retracting the arm, the visibility of the coming attack will be clearer for the ukete; therefore, the ukete will be better prepared to ward off the coming attack.

Remarks upon the execution of Yakusoku kumite.

Before the actual performance of the fighting techniques, one bows to the partner and prepares to transition in the Yoi position. Thereafter the attacker will execute a kamae position.

Kumite

Yoi position.

Neko Ashi Dachi No Kamae short distance.

Yoi position.

Neko Ashi No Kamae long distance.

After execution of the Yakusoku kumite techniques, one should remain alert and position oneself in kamae. Semete is the first one who will transition to the Yoi position to show the aggression has ended. Thereafter, ukete will return in Yoi position.

The attacks of both semete and ukete can be supported with a shout (kiai), but this is not a rule. In general, within the Meibukan School, one does not focus on the kiai within kumite kata.

Goju Ryu Karate

The Yakusoku Ippon and Nippon kumites, originated from the Kaishu katas, are the most trained kumite forms within the Meibukan School.

Although several Yakusoku kumites exist, in this book some fixed/settled Ippon and Nippon Yakusoku kumites are depicted. The given examples are intended to be used as a mnemonic, given the impossibility and to some extent my desire not to explain and reflect on all aspects connected to these kumites. The transferring movements from one posture to the next are not presented in this book.

Rei (bow).

Yoi (ready) position.

Neko Ashi No Kamae (position preparing for attack).

Example from Ippon Kumite. The attacker has executed his attack. The defender executes a counter attack.

Kumite

After the confrontation both Semete (attacker) and Ukete (defender) transit to Neko Ashi Dachi No Kamae.

Semete goes to the Yoi position while Ukete remains in Neko Ashi No Kamae until Semete has returned to the Yoi position.

Ukete also returns to the Yoi position.

Both Semete and Ukete finish the exercise with a repectful bow to each other.

Execution of the Yakusoku Ippon Kumite

Semete: Migi Heiko Dachi with Jodan Oi. Tsuki Ukete: Hidari Heiko Dachi with Jodan Age Uke.

Ukete: Hidari Heiko Dachi with Chudan Ura Tsuki.

Semete: Migi Heiko Dachi with Jodan Oi Tsuki. Ukete: Drop to the floor with Ura Tsuki.

Semete: Migi Heiko Dachi with Jodan Oi Tsuki. Ukete: Hidari Zenkutsu Dachi with Ashi Dori.

Ukete: Sokuto Geri.

Semete: Hidari Heiko Dachi with Jodan Oi Tsuki. Ukete: Migi Shiko Dachi with preparation to strike.

Kumite

Ukete: Migi Zenkutsu Dachi with Chudan Mawashi Hiji Ate.

Semete: Migi Heiko Dachi with Jodan Oi Tsuki. Ukete: Hidari Heiko Dachi with Chudan Osea Uke.

Ukete: Hidari Heiko Dachi with Jodan Uraken Uchi.

Semete: Hidari Heiko Dachi with Chudan Tsuki. Ukete: Migi Heiko Dachi with Chudan Uke Tsuki.

Semete: Migi Heiko Dachi with Chudan Oi Tsuki. Ukete: Migi Neko Ashi Dachi with Chudan Hiki Uke.

Ukete: Chudan Mae Geri.

Semete: Hidari Heiko Dachi with Chudan Oi Tsuki. Ukete: Migi Kokutsu Dachi with Chudan Nagashi Uke.

Ukete: Migi Kokutsu Dachi with Chudan Gyaku Tsuki.

Semete: Hidari Heiko Dachi with Chudan Oi Tsuki. Ukete: Hidaki Neko Ashi Dachi with Chudan Ura Uke.

Ukete: Hidari Heiko (or Sanchin) Dachi with Age Ura Tsuki.

Semete: Hidari Heiko Dachi with Chudan Oi Tsuki. Ukete: Hidari Kokutsu Dachi with Chudan Nagashi Uke and Chudan Barai Uke.

Ukete: Gedan Sokuto Geri.

Kumite

Semete: Migi Shiko Dachi with Gedan Oi Tsuki. Ukete: Hidari Shiko Dachi with Gedan Barai Uke.

Ukete: Migi Heiko Dachi with Ashi Barai and Jodan Shuto Uchi.

Semete: Migi Shiko Dachi with Gedan Oi Tsuki. Ukete: Hidari Shiko Dachi with Gedan Barai Uke.

Ukete: Migi Heiko Dachi with Jodan Tetsui Uchi.

Semete: Hidari Shiko Dachi with Gedan Oi Tsuki. Ukete: Hidari Shiko Dachi with Chudan Oi Tsuki.

Semete: Migi Shiko Dachi with Gedan Oi Tsuki. Ukete: Hidari Kokutsu Dachi with Gedan Barai Uke.

Goju Ryu Karate

Ukete: Chudan Soto Geri.

Semete: Migi Shiko Dachi with Gedan Oi Tsuki. Ukete: Migi Shiko Dachi with Gedan Shuto Uke.

Ukete: Migi Zenkutsu Dachi with Haito Age Uke.

Ukete: Migi Heiko Dachi with Jodan Age Shuto Uchi.

Ukete: Hidari Zenkutsu Dachi with Chudan Mawashi Hiji Ate.

Semete: Lower Chudan Mae Geri. Ukete: Naname Heiko Dachi with Gedan Sukui Uke.

Kumite

Ukete: Migi Kokutsu Dachi with Gedan Uchi Hiji Ate.

Semete: Lower Chudan Mae Geri
Ukete: Naname Heiko Dachi with Gedan Sukui Uke.

Ukete: Gedan Mae Geri.

Execution of the Yakusoku Nippon Kumite

Semete: Migi Heiko Dachi with Jodan Oi Tsuki. Ukete: Hidari Heiko Dachi with Jodan Age Uke.

Semete: Migi Heiko Dachi with Jodan Gyaku Tsuki. Ukete: Hidari Heiko Dachi with Jodan Age Uke.

Ukete: Hidari Heiko Dachi with Jodan Uraken Uchi.

Semete: Migi Heiko Dachi with Jodan Oi Tsuki. Ukete: Hidari Heiko Dachi with Jodan Age Uke.

Semete: Migi Heiko Dachi with Chudan Gyaku Tsuki. Ukete: Hidari Heiko Dachi with Chudan Barai Uke.

Ukete: Hidari Heiko Dachi with Jodan Oi Tsuki.

Kumite

Semete: Migi Heiko Dachi with Jodan Oi Tsuki.
Ukete: Hidari Heiko Dachi with Jodan Age Uke.

Semete: Hidari Shiko Dachi with Gedan
Oi Tsuki. Ukete: Migi Shiko Dachi
with Chudan Uke Tsuki.

Semete: Migi Heiko Dachi with Chudan
Oi Tsuki. Ukete: Hidari Heiko Dachi
with Chudan Barai Uke.

Semete: Migi Heiko Dachi with Jodan
Gyaku Tsuki. Ukete: Hidari Heiko Dachi
with Jodan Age Uke.

Ukete: Hidari Heiko Dachi with
Chudan Oi Tsuki.

Semete: Migi Heiko Dachi with
Chudan Oi Tsuki. Ukete: Hidari Heiko
Dachi with Chudan Barai Uke.

Semete: Migi Heiko Dachi with Chudan Gyaku Tsuki. Ukete: Hidari Heiko Dachi with Chudan Uke Tsuki.

Semete: Migi Heiko Dachi with Chudan Oi Tsuki. Ukete: Hidari Heiko Dachi with Chudan Barai Uke.

Semete: Hidari Shiko dachi with Gedan Oi Tsuki. Ukete: Migi Shiko Dachi with Gedan Barai Uke.

Ukete: Hidari Heiko Dachi with Ashi Barai and Jodan Shuto Uchi.

Semete: Migi Shiko Dachi with Gedan Oi Tsuki. Ukete: Hidari Shiko Dachi with Gedan Barai Uke.

Semete: Migi Heiko Dachi with Jodan Gyaku Tsuki. Ukete: Hidari Heiko Dachi with Jodan Age Uke.

Kumite

Ukete: Migi Shiko Dachi with Mawashi/Otoshi Hiji Ate.

Semete: Migi Shiko Dachi with Gedan Oi Tsuki. Ukete: Hidari Shiko Dachi with Gedan Barai Uke.

Semete: Migi Heiko Dachi with Chudan Gyaku Tsuki. Ukete: Hidari Heiko Dachi with Chudan Barai Uke.

Ukete: Gedan Mae Geri.

Semete: Migi Shiko Dachi with Gedan Oi Tsuki. Ukete: Hidari Shiko Dachi with Gedan Barai Uke.

Semete: Hidari Shiko Dachi with Gedan Oi Tsuki. Ukete: Migi Shiko Dachi with Gedan Barai Uke.

Ukete: Hidari Shiko Dachi with Gedan Shotei Uchi.

RENZOKU KUMITE

Chojun Miyagi and Juhatsu Kyoda performing kumite.

General
Continuous (renzoku) confrontation (kumite)

Continuous confrontation as a kumite form of karate practice means that during a certain time, multiple techniques are executed by two or more persons. This can be freely executed, like randori kumite, or more or less programmed (yakusoku) like the Meibukan School does.

In general, with renzoku kumite, a relatively great number of punches/strikes/ kicks and their defensive counterparts are executed in a high-speed frequency, and sometimes are followed by breaking/strangling/throwing techniques.

The potential "first" attacker in this confrontation also becomes a temporary defender, and the same applies to the person who is defending at first and, therefore, can become an attacker. It is important to keep in mind that the person who attacks first is the "assailant," as explained in the part of "semete and ukete"; however, the first attack (and other attacks) will be deflected/blocked and the attack, technically seen, will be taken over. This principle can continue forever if the opponent reacts to every new attack with a takeover. In the practice of renzoku kumite, the actions of both (or more) opponents will stop (if there isn't a prearranged agreement when the confrontation stops) if there is no longer an adequate answer upon an attack within a certain frame or sense of fighting reality.

Characteristic of renzoku kumite is the complete performance of the fighting techniques that possess certain locomotion and stylistic value that, as a drill exercise, trains the mind and body in flexibility—in relation to the fast succession of technique changes and adequate answers.

Within the Meibukan School, mainly two kinds of renzoku kumite (Taikyoko and Kakomi) are practiced. These are basically prearranged (yakusoku), although the prearranged dogma is somewhat released at advanced levels.

Yakusoku Renzoku Fukyu kumite

Prearranged (yakusoku) continuous (renzoku) exercise from the Fukyu kata existing originated techniques, frequency of movement and pattern in a straightforward physical confrontation (kumite).

The renzoku forms within the Meibukan School originated from the Fukyu kata. The first renzoku form came from a confrontation between two persons who perform the Fukyu (Taikyoko) kata as a partner form. The kata, which in the solo form has many directions, in the partner form is executed in a straight line in which both opponents step back and forth. The one who performs the first defense is the one who demonstrates the solo kata as a partner form. This form within the Meibukan is simply specified as Fukyu renzoku kumite—practically pronounced as Fukyu (rather than the name/techniques of a specified Fukyu kata) kumite.

As an example, the performance of one of the Fukyu katas (Fukyu kata Jodan) as a renzoku kumite is demonstrated as a photo-series.

Execution of the Yakusoku Renzoku Fukyu kumite

The general ritual has already taken place and the Yoi position is formed.

Kumite

The Yoi position is executed before the final ritual is performed.

Yakusoku Renzoku Fukyu Kakomi kumite

Prearranged (yakusoku) continuous (renzoku) exercise from the Fukyu kata existing originated techniques, frequency of movement and pattern in a surrounded (kakomi) physical confrontation (kumite).

The second renzoku form consists of a confrontation among five persons. One person is performing the solo form of the Fukyu (Taikyoko) kata as a multiple partner form without imaginary opponents, but with four real opponents surrounding him or her from four directions. This form within the Meibukan is simply specified as Fukyu Kakomi kumite—practically pronounced as Fukyu (the name/techniques of a specified Fukyu kata) Kakomi kumite.

Other than these official renzoku kumites, there are many training exercises one can think of and train in—for example, renzoku kumites consisting of bunkai of the kaishu kata. Because Dai Sensei Meitoku Yagi did not include other renzoku kumites in his Meibukan Goju-ryu Karate-do curriculum, these are not addressed to in this book.

Kakomi Kumite.

BUNKAI KUMITE

Bunkai is the Japanese term for "analysis" of the techniques and applications of the martial arts. Bunkai kumite, in karate terms, has a special meaning that addresses the analysis of applied fighting techniques originating from the solo form named kata. In other words, the fighting applications of the kata are analyzed, if applied in real combat against one or multiple opponents.

Bunkai consists of specific practical physical possibilities as answers to one or more specific attacks, possibly followed up with or without one or more combining defenses explained in renzoku kumites.

These answers or bunkai can be traced back from the kata as a solo form and practiced as prearranged (yakusoku) physical confrontation (kumite) forms. The techniques and execution in the solo form will adjust to the circumstances in Bunkai kumite practice when a real physical confrontation takes place (one should think of adjustments in details of the bunkai, depending on the opponent and situation: body size, body weight, vital points, gender, position, stance, etc.).

Analyzing the kata as a solo form in training by making it a partner form, one obtains direct understanding in the practical applicability. Through this understanding, one can practice the kata as a ritualized form of Bunkai kumite, projecting the meaning of the techniques upon an imaginary opponent, strengthening kata performance and, therefore, one's spirit.

Ippon and Nippon kumites, together with the renzoku kumites, which reflect the principles of movements in attack and defense, will, among other things, give the practitioner a strong base in technical fighting motion and in developing reflexes through continuous repetition.

Bunkai kumite remains the principle of attack and defense, but gives more complex and detailed analyses of a variety of physical confrontations. So, Bunkai kumite, compared to the often fixed Ippon and Nippon kumites, contains a far

Example of Bunkai Kumite from Sanseru kata.

greater range of techniques and targets, and, to some extent a more profound working of defenses and attacks.

It is possible that more than one movement in the kata as a solo form is identical to the amount of movements/locomotion performed in Bunkai kumite. Within the kata, it also is possible that one single movement/motion has more than one meaning and, therefore, could contain multiple attacks and/or defenses. This will be reflected in Bunkai kumite.

In principle, one should maintain the same postures and ritualized actions as used within the other kumite forms during general training. For didactical and methodical reasons, these fighting postures and connected actions should be executed before and after the attacks/defenses. From the

Master Choki Motobu performing bunkai of Naihanchi Kata.

point of self-defense, one should keep in mind that real "street situations" have an unpredictable nature without ritualizations, buildup of actions and precise techniques. From the point of self-defense, one could train, once a strong base is founded, unpredictable movements, like feinting movements, especially made by semete, the assailant, and move in a more natural and intuitive way that belongs to your own body and mind. This way of training also is applicable to other kumite forms.

In recent decades, schools and organizations often have promoted Bunkai kumite in a very detailed way in books and films. Every movement is analyzed, fragmented, split, combined, rebuilt, and newly arranged. Although, in my opinion, there is nothing wrong with analyzing the kata, rather the opposite, giving direction to the karate-do practitioner, means that it should be done in a way that serves the practitioner's self-realization. Giving only pre-chewed fabricated answers does not do this. Of course, one needs direction in proper techniques and movements related to the bunkai, but this should be done mainly (not only) in a way that serves the student/practitioner for further development/identification of the bunkai. The basic principles of movement in a defense and/or offense are given by the kata itself, and further guidance should be obtained by the teacher. As Chojun Miyagi said, "Budo should have its transmission through a teacher, a Sensei (literally meaning 'the one who has been before'), whose mission is to provide physical, mental, and spiritual direction." If one, as a teacher, provides too much detail and

Chojun Miyagi watches his students demonstrate kumite.

only wants the student to copy things instead of creating his or her own, there is an obstruction in the path of Budo.

An important thought in the oral Budo transmission from teacher to student is that the student should deserve knowledge. By deserving, I mean that a person has shown perseverance, willpower, dedication, and positive attitude toward the surroundings before he or she is given knowledge that has been carefully built and cherished for generations. By judging the student in this manner, the teacher knows that the information and instruction are received with respect. Depending on his opinion, the teacher judges if the information, any information, is suitable for the student to receive. This also is the case in instructing Bunkai kumite. Bunkais, compared to the general strikes and punches of Ippon and Nippon kumite, show a lot of lethal techniques and, therefore, could become dangerous in the hands of a malicious individual or group. It is the teacher's responsibility that the knowledge he transfers is not only technically judged (which information is suitable for the student at a particular moment is his/her process) but also morally.

At present, in most of the karate dojos around the world, one enters, signs in, pays a fee and starts training. In traditional karate-do dojos, however, one will be judged first or receive a sort of probationary time. This all has to do with the elements mentioned above. Every teacher has his/her own criteria in judgment, but if one calls oneself a Sensei, he or she is responsible for the way and things he or she teaches. The teacher should only give the student tools if they will be used properly—in the case of karate-do, to follow a path that leads to harmony within the person and with his or her surroundings.

KAKE UKE KUMITE

Kake Uke Kumite, also called "Kakie," "Koki," or "Kakete," can be described as "sticky hands." Kake Uke Kumite is an exercise that, by means of physical contact through the arms, develops sensitivity and stability. The origin of this "sticky," and sometimes called "pushing hands exercise," is found in the Chinese martial arts.

Sensitivity

Developing sensitivity means to sense and therefore "read" the intentions of the opponent. Within Kake Uke Kumite, developing sensitivity is done through sight and touch. Through arm/skin contact with the opponent, often the most important contact in the beginning of a close combat fight, one can sense the amount of power/energy the opponent uses, and in which direction or at which location it is aimed, returned, or focused.

When a large distance exists between two opponents, visual signals of movements are of great importance. However, within a short distance, the sense of touch can become more important. Also, when situations occur in which there is almost no light or a lack of light to see what is happening, touch is of the utmost importance.

By enlarging the surface contact one has with the opponent's body, the sensitivity in "reading" the opponents body and, therefore, intentions, will be increased, and the possibility to use multiple parts of ones own body, for an attack or defense, will be extended.

Stability

Stability is defined as the way the body remains focused and balanced while undergoing punches, kicks, pushes, pulling, etc., executed by the opponent but also performed upon the opponent. In all cases, the body should remain as stable as possible without loss of balance. Remaining in the right posture and contracting or relaxing the right muscle groups at the right time in conjunction with proper breathing are key components of balance and stability.

Proper breathing combined with the speed and power of one's movements also is very important to one's balance. Therefore, "reading" the opponent's breathing also is important. If one is able to interpret the opponent's breathing pattern, one can use this information to make critical decisions in the tactics of a fight. With every breath, there are moments of weakness and strength that one can use to advantage to undermine the opponent's action. For example, when the opponent inhales, his or her body is generally more vulnerable to impact, and usually the opponent can't react as quickly as when exhaling. Depending on the situation, this moment of inhaling by the opponent could be crucial for making the decision to attack.

Basic exercise

Initially, the first drill in Kake Uke Kumite consists of an exercise in which partners push each other's arm (contact point on the wrists and knife hand) in a straight forward line toward each other's body (without pushing the body away). The arm is stretched out when pushing and bent when being pushed. At the end of the momentum of a push, one focuses shortly through means of a light muscle contraction (kime). After this contraction, the fluid motion of pushing restarts. Semete starts stepping to the front and pushes for the first time. After the first push, ukete will take over the push and this will continue alternately.

In the next phase, this exercise will continue; but, without a fixed frequency, at the end of the forward fluid motion (seen from the perspective of semete) a fighting technique by semete is placed. This attack can be parried by ukete by all kinds of different defenses. Both exercises (pushing with and without further fighting techniques) are performed stationary in Sanchin dachi.

As a training form, the pushes are repeated ten times, after which the foot position is changed (left to right or right to left) and the opposite arm takes over the drill.

This exercise is a basic drill within the Meibukan School. To some extent, supporting this basic drill, but more focused upon being a part of a power exercise or part of a warming-up, there are resistance exercises that outwardly look similar to the basic exercise. See "Kake Uke power exercises."

Advanced exercise

After the initial phase of the basic exercise, more advanced exercises will be taught. These include not only linear pushing motions, but also circular pushing motions. Slight knee bends and stretches, for using body weight, will be made to support the arm techniques. Once understood and controlled, more attention could be paid towards body shifting motions to use the body mass in motion, again to support pushing or receiving motions/techniques. The most used stances within these exercises are Sanchin/Heiko dachi and Neko dachi.

In principle, all Goju-ryu fighting applications can be used in Kake Uke Kumite.

Power exercise

Combined with warm-up, or being part of a supplemental training that focuses on muscle development and stamina, the above explained basic exercise has led to a similar power exercise performed with a heavy muscular focus during the whole motion. So, not only at the end of the motion are the muscles contracted; during the whole motion, the muscles are tensed in both eccentric and concentric ways (see explanation in the chapter Hojo undo). Although the outward appearance of the exercise resembles the basic exercise, there are differences in arm postures and movements. The power exercises are performed in two ways:

– Standing in Sanchin dachi, both partners place the same leg (right leg of semete in front, right leg of ukete in front) pointed toward each other, with only a little space between (see picture). The right elbow is fixed against the side of the body and will not move. The arms of both partners make contact with each other at the wrist area. From this position, the pushing starts with both right arms. The focus should be on the muscles of the biceps and triceps. By pushing the forearms down and up in a sideward motion, with continuous resistance from both partners at every stage of the motion, one strengthens the upper arm muscles.

Power exercise for biceps and triceps with elbow fixation.

Power exercise for shoulders with straight elbows.

– Standing in Sanchin dachi, both partners place the same leg (right leg of semete in front, right leg ukete in front) pointed toward each other with only a little space between (see picture). The arms of both partners are stretched and contact is made around the wrist area. From this position, the pushing starts with both right arms. The focus should be on the shoulder muscles. By pushing the arms down and up in a sideward motion, with continuous resistance from both partners at every stage of the motion, one strengthens the shoulder muscles and, to some extent, muscles attached to the shoulder (back and chest). Keep in mind, especially with this last exercise with stretched arms, that the shoulder top to the neck (m.trapezius) stays low, the rest of the body stays immobile, and the legs and feet are rooted.

Besides the two described power exercises, there are more variations possible (with leg movement, instead of a sideward arm motion, a frontal motion or downward and upward arm motions) and even specialized traditional and modern training equipment for this purpose exists, but these are not addressed in this book.

To learn how many repetitions or sets of each training of these power exercises one should practice, please refer to the chapter of Hojo undo.

UDE TANREN KUMITE

Ude (forearm) Tanren (to connect to a discipline) Kumite (confrontation), or Kote (forearm) Kitae (method), is a method for conditioning the arms for battle.

Although more Okinawan karate schools and organizations include methods of conditioning the limbs in their curriculum, the Ude Tanren kumite trained in the Meibukan School is contributed by Meitoku Yagi. He integrated limb conditioning in his curriculum in the 1960s, mainly from his martial arts experiences in Taiwan.

Grandmaster Meitoku Yagi, 10th Degree, Hanshisai, the top student and successor to Grandmaster Chojun Miyagi. Born on March 6, 1912.

The method of Ude Tanren kumite consists of making hard contact upon each other's forearms by means of different kinds of attack and defense techniques.

While conditioning, one is meant to undergo and experience pressure, sensitivity, pain stimulus, and push and pull forces, and to be able to bear it both physically and mentally. (Even on the physical level, by training Ude Tanren kumite on a regular and consistent basis, some cell structures will change and become stronger. This also is the case with other contact training like the use of makiwara).

The point of using this method is to be acquainted with the violence that should be expected in a physical confrontation. The arms, regarding the Goju-ryu Karate-do system as a self-defense system, are preeminently suited to make contact with the opponent.

Through conditioning of the limbs and, therefore, getting used to the stimuli, one shall, relatively speaking, not be distracted unnecessarily in a real fight.

Secondly, the hard contact made by Ude Tanren kumite, which is performed through combined drilling movements of basic defense and offense techniques against each other, gives a realistic insight in the body forces that are used in a physical confrontation. By this is meant the explosive and combining pressing force that is pursued by moving the arms toward the target that are resisted/guided by the arms of the opponent.

If there is no training with physical contact, one does not experience the realism of a fight. One does not properly estimate the dangers and consequences of the incoming attacks and with which intention (power and speed) these techniques should be stopped, or where outgoing techniques should be used. Without having contact on objects like makiwara, a punching/kicking bag, etc., but also without physical contact with a partner, one receives wrongly assumed insights and reflexes. This means that negative outcomes in the mental steering of the body and wrongly trained reflexes are developed that are not usable for self-defense.

Although more than one exercise and many variations of Ude Tanren Kumite are trained within the Meibukan School of Dai Sensei Meitoku Yagi, one central exercise is always practiced and should be focused upon.

Examples of conditioning the body.

The basic exercise

One stands across from each other in Heiko dachi and both perform together a single midlevel block/push/strike (haito ude uke/uchi) against each other's forearms. After this, one follows with a single low-level block/push/strike (gedan shuto ude uke/uchi). This will be repeated two more times, alternately with the right and left arm; starting with the third time, one steps with the right foot next to each other. Together with the right foot, the right arm makes the midlevel block/push/strike, followed by the low-level block/push/strike in this closely resembling stance, but much smaller, of Migi Heiko dachi. After this step and technique is performed, one turns around with the left foot in front (Hidari Heiko dachi) and, for the fourth time, performs the arm techniques. The left foot is pulled back into a Heiko dachi, together with a new frequency like that explained before. This complete exercise is clearly seen on the next page demonstrated in a photo-series.

Meitatsu Yagi demonstrating a Kote Kitae drill.

Conditioning of the body by so called "hardening exercises" can be very diverse. Also, within the Meibukan School, multiple ways of conditioning are applied. From school to school and Sensei to Sensei, these exercises differ. As an example, concerning the diversity of hardenings exercises, look at some exercises for abdominal training: One lies down on the floor on the back and drops a chi'shi or medicine ball to one's abdomen, or one punches upon the abdomen while standing, and by contracting the abdominal area, one stops deeper penetration. As the example clarifies, there is more than one way for an area of the body to be conditioned by hardening through contact.

Important, especially with hardening exercises: keep in mind that the body should stay in good health! When the conditioning is too soft, it does not carry the name and principles of "hardening," but if it's too hard, it could lead to injuries. The body, being the vessel of the karatedoka, should be kept in good health so as to be useful for the mind and, thus, the mind can lead a meaningful existence.

Execution of the basic Ude Tanren kumite exercise

Kumite

UNDO

Hojo Undo

Complementary exercises are helpful in supporting and enriching the overall performance of karate techniques and give a better understanding of the Kaishu kata. These drills, performed with various kinds of equipment, give a general proficiency towards locomotion and strengthen specific skills.

Chojun Miyagi, 1934

GENERAL

Hojo undo, or complementary exercises, strengthen the practitioner's performance of karate techniques and general kinetic locomotion. This means that the practitioner becomes more skilful in speed, power, and coordination, and, to some degree, increases muscle stamina, through the practice of distinct exercises linked to varied equipment.

Chojun Miyagi (fifth from the left) watches the performance of Hojo undo, 1926.

In principle, all training methods that have as the objective to develop and keep the physical competence at an adequate level with the use of equipment, as a support for the main practice (kata and kumite), could be called Hojo undo.

The physical resistance within the practice of Hojo undo is one of the main points. By means of weights and/or through materials, apparatuses, and their specific working, body movements will be made heavier to perform.

By working with opposition forces, one increases muscular strength and becomes conscious of the realistic resistance one encounters during a fight (for example, working with punching objects like the makiwara, or pulling a heavy object toward the body like a barbell). With resistance training, especially dynamically performed, the nervous system and reflexes will be trained in accordance with the locomotion principles of Goju-ryu's fighting system.

CLARIFICATIONS OF TERMS AND CONCEPTS

Before elaborating on the most important and used apparatus and exercises, some clarification of terms and concepts belonging to Hojo undo is offered:

Isolating

Isolation of movement is realized by contracting one specific muscle (group). Often the main muscle that contracts is supported by so called synergists. These are muscles that establish the movement. Whenever these "synergists" play a supporting role to accomplish a movement, we speak of the isolating and working of the main muscle.

Muscle chain/collaborating

A muscle chain is a series of different muscle groups working collaboratively to establish a movement. When a movement (exercise) is realized through one specific muscle (with little cooperation from other muscles), as explained before, this is isolation. When a movement (exercise) is not realized by one specific muscle alone, and there are other muscles groups needed to accomplish a movement, then this is called a muscle chain.

Concentric

The term concentric describes when a muscle contracts and becomes shorter because the attaching points of the muscle upon the bone come closer. For example, this is applied to the biceps muscle (the front upper arm muscle) when the arm goes from the stretched position to a bent position.

Eccentric

The term eccentric is used when a muscle extends and becomes longer because the attaching points of the muscle upon the bones are at a distance from each other. For example, it is applied to the biceps muscle (the front upper arm muscle) when the arm goes from a bent to a stretched position.

Static

When the muscle contracts but the length of the muscle remains the same, the muscle is called static. One should think of the contracted arm, for example, holding the tensed posture of Soto Uke in Sanchin kata. There is no visible movement, but yet the muscle is contracted.

Dynamic

The term dynamic, applied to Hojo undo, is used when movement is achieved without any difficulty. The movement is not obstructed and, depending on the direction intended, could fluidly go in all the different directions and angles performed with a relative speed. The more the resistance, the less the dynamic.

Percentage maximum force (or Repetition Percentage Maximum (RPM)

Percentage Maximum Force means maximum force (power) or absolute force (power). This is the greatest possible force executed by skeleton muscles within a maximum arbitrary contraction directed by the neuromuscular system. An example of this is weightlifting. (With weightlifting the visible speed is low but the actual speed within the muscle is tremendous.) The lift of the weight in the top performance only can be performed once (100 percent).

Knowing, or more accurately, estimating the maximum power by certain movements is important, because in the doctrine of weight training this is a point of departure in which outlines are set for the actual training.

Undo

Shinken Taira wearing kumite protection.

Body armor for the use of kumite shown by Master Kenwa Mabuni (left).

TRAINING
What is training?

Training means the intended increase of physical performance. Training is the undergoing of conscious, systematic, and, in heaviness, increasing functional loads with the goal to improve the physical performance capability. With training, one increases the locomotion qualities regarding power, speed, pliability, dexterity, and coordination.

With training one uses certain trainings methods. A trainings method is a way in which certain locomotion quality could be improved. These training methods are roughly divided:

— Repetition method is a method used during training in which complete motions are performed and repeated several times in succession, in compliance with a complete phase of recovery. (A complete phase of recovery means that after a certain rest period/time—in seconds—the total movement can be performed again with a negligible degree of tiredness.)

— Duration method is a method by which, during a longer period of time, motions are performed. No interruption takes place between the start and the end of the training. The motions are not performed with full intensity and no phase of recovery will be incorporated.

— Interval method is a method by which, during a certain time, a certain frequency of motions is performed with incomplete recovery between rest periods— in seconds and minutes—(where incomplete recovery means that renewed motions are fully performed but with an increasing degree of tiredness).

Power/weight training

Power training means that work is done that is focused to increase muscle power, with the intention and final goal to boost the actual sports performance. The increase of muscle power can be achieved in many ways. It is essential that specific muscle groups are more heavily aggravated than the actual sport performance without impairing the technique. One can divide weight training roughly in two ways: General power training and specific power training.

General power training

Isolating motions through specific muscles performed with a certain burden/load that has the aim to develop general or specific increase of muscle power—for example, a runner who squats with a weights to strengthen one's upper legs.

Specific (or functional) power training

Isolating and/or cooperating motions that fully or partly copy "top performance" movements executed through specific muscle groups with a specific burden, with the aim to develop specific muscle power and coordination for a specific motion—for example, a runner who sprints with a trail weight with the aim to activate and strengthen the cooperating muscle groups (muscle chain).

Important to both weight training methods is that the power is subordinated to the "top" performance, and both the general and specific weight training methods are often used in combinations.

APPEARANCE OF FORCE

There are two visible appearances of force:

Dynamic force

– Dynamic eccentric muscle power
– Dynamic concentric muscle power

Static force

– Static muscle power measured through isometric contraction (exercise of force without changing the muscle length). One speaks of static circumstances when the load is so heavy that only a very slow contraction (of the muscle) would be possible (by indulging of the muscle).

With dynamic forms, less force is developed compared to static forms, and with concentric, less than eccentric (about 23 percent). Thus, the next classification of increase of force appears:

- Dynamic concentric labor/training
- Dynamic eccentric labor/training
- Static labor/training
- Static concentric labor/training
- Static eccentric labor/training

The preceding text is to clarify and give some minimal direction and understanding for the practitioner of Hojo undo. The material in this book is mentioned only to point out some theoretical interpretations. This being said, I would advise the reader to purchase readings concerning power/weight training to further study its principles and mechanisms.

HOJO UNDO TRAINING APPARATUS

Hojo undo as complementary training of Goju-ryu Karate-do consists mainly out of the next parts:

(In the enumeration on the next pages regarding the exercises, only an indication is given of the body parts/muscle groups in connection to the weight training. Other purposes, that certainly are present, will not be addressed)

Chi'shi*

Power stone, stone/cement with stick

– a stick, different in size and thickness but usually with the length of a forearm, which is made heavier on one end.

– exercises are meant mainly for training the upper body, in particular for the muscles of the forearm, upper arm and shoulder, as well as the back, chest, and trunk. Because of the Chi'shi's structure (strong lever effect), exercises are very suitable to train muscles that are used for keeping the Chi'shi in balance.

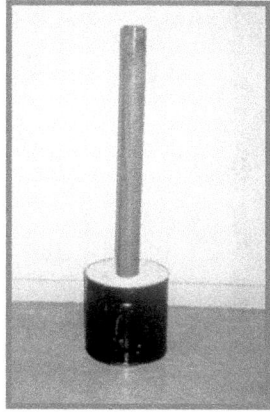

Chi'shi.

Practicing with the Chi'shi.

Nigiri game*
Gripping jar

– originally an oval/round baked clay jar that could be filled with water or sand, with the gripping part adjusted to one's hand.

– exercises are meant mainly for training the upper body, in particular for the shoulder muscles and, to some extent, the torso muscles.

Nigiri Game.

Practicing with the Nigiri.

Ishi sashi*
Stone padlock

– a ring of stone, iron, or a different kind of heavy material/weight that one can hang on the wrist or foot, or can hold with the hands.

– exercises are meant for upper and lower body, in particular for the muscles of arms, shoulders, and legs.

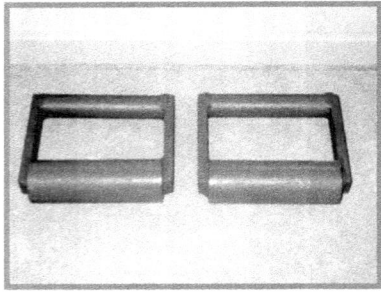
Ishi Sashi.

Practicing with the Ishi Sashi.

Tetsuarei*
Dumbbell

– a sort of handle adjusted for a single hand grip, usually made of iron in various weights, that is made heavier on both ends.

– exercises are meant mainly for the upper body, in particular for the forearms, upper arm, and shoulders.

Tetsuarei.

Practicing with the Tetsuarei.

Kogoken*
Iron oval weight

–a metal/iron oval-shaped barbell (in the form of a big paperclip), usually 150–200 cm long and weighing 25–50 kilos.

– exercises are meant mainly for the upper and lower body, and its focus, because of the weight, lies more on the bigger muscle groups.

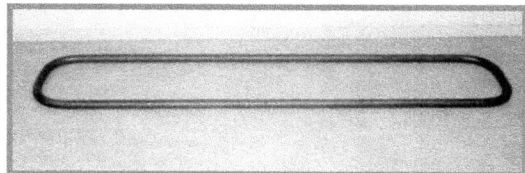

Kogoken.

Tan*
Barbell

– a modern barbell look-alike, with the exception that the traditional bar is made of an elastic part, like bamboo.

– except for the "usual" exercises, meant mainly for the upper body and, to some extent, the lower body, the flexible barbell also is used for throwing and receiving.

Practicing with the Tan.

Makiwara
Wooden striking post

– mostly a vertical wooden board that is fixed at the bottom so that one can hit the middle and top with punches and, to some extent, kicks without having too much resistance because of the board's flexible character.

– exercises are meant mainly for the muscle groups delivering the punch and absorbing the resistance, like the arms, shoulder, torso, hips, and legs.

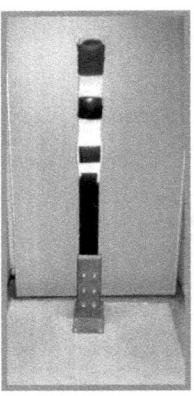

Makiwara.

Practicing with the makiwara.

Tetsu geta*
Iron shoes
— shoes or slippers made of iron of other heavy material suitable for a person to fit like a normal shoe or slipper.
— exercises are meant mainly for the legs.

Tetsu Geta (traditional).

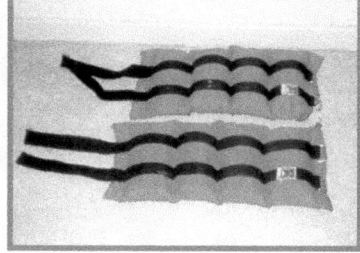

Tetsu Geta.

Practicing with the Tetsu Geta.

Tou
Bamboo bundle
— multiple bamboo stalks bound together in which one can perform finger thrusts. (Large bamboo bundles are suitable for kicks with the shin.)
— exercises are meant mainly for forearms/fingers.

Makiage Kigu*
Wrist roller
— a piece of stone or concrete with a stick through it, so that the outer ends are suitable to grasp.
— exercises are meant mainly for the wrists and forearms (and to some extent the shoulders).

Sashi Ishi
Atural stones
— stones the size of big pebbles pressed together through a net/gauze that one squeezes/throws.
— exercises are meant mainly for the wrists, forearms, and fingers.

Sari Bako
Sand box

– a bucket filled with stones, sand, beans, or other little objects suitable for the fingers to penetrate or squeeze in.

– exercises are mainly for the forearms and fingers.

Saki Bako.

The indicated enumerations form the traditional components of Hojo undo (the compound karate-system under the name Goju-ryu, as founded by Chojun Miyagi). With modern scientific knowledge and equipment, periodic shifts partially replace or improve old traditional exercises and accompanying equipment. Also new exercises and equipment, after experimenting, analyzing, improving, and deliberating, are added within the principles of Hojo undo.

Those components with a * refer to weight training (although other components/exercises also can be used for weight training as a secondary objective). This book will limit itself to the three most abundant and trained components of Hojo undo. Two of them refer to the weight training as done in the Meibukan School. These are Chi'shi and Nigiri game. The other, which includes qualities of weight training, also is a conditioning and general locomotion apparatus and is called the makiwara.

Undo

Training equipment for a variety of exercises.

The use of training equipment.

Heavy bags are very usefull since their size, mass and shape opens up for combinations of techniques to develop power, balance and focus.

Household material, such as rope, can also be useful in martial arts training in addition to specially developed equipment.

THE THREE MOST ABUNDANT AND TRAINED COMPONENTS
Employment of the Makiwara

Makiwara training is a very important part of karate training. Without resistance training, as experienced on the makiwara, punch, and/or kicking pads or other resistance objects/training, one could question the effectiveness of someone's techniques in an actual fight.

The makiwara, as a wooden striking post, has much in common with the resistance one meets when punching a human body. The makiwara is slightly flex-

A makiwara constructed with a metal shaft at the bottom and a board upon which the practitioner stands. These type of makiwara's can be placed anywhere since the have no solid connection to walls or floor/ground.

ible and, because of its construction and wooden nature, gives a certain resistance, depending on the force used when punched or kicked upon.

When punched or kicked upon, the makiwara's firmness of the wood (usually a sort of hard wood) or otherwise described as the linear line of the board's structure, is "broken," but because of the board's somewhat flexible character, through its material and construction, will readjust to its original linear shape. The resistance one meets depends on the force that is applied. The more force applied to the board to bend, the more the opposite force of resistance will be met (and therefore returning the board to its upright form).

Because of the makiwara's structure, there is no need for a partner to hold a striking object to punch or kick against, or to bring it back in position. Also, with the use of the makiwara, the practitioner gets used to hitting a hard object with one's bare hands (which occurs in a realistic fighting situation), and the concentration upon the practitioner's fist and performance of the punch is much more refined. The latter means that punching can be executed with exactly the two front knuckles, characteristic for Goju-ryu karate punches, and not sink into soft objects with the total surface of the front of the fist.

Because of the makiwara's heavy resistance, when hit, and the way Goju-ryu punches are mainly focused upon, the makiwara also is used as a specific way of weight training and reflects again some key points of the focus of energy that one holds at the maximum momentum of energy (kime)—a terrific supporting tool for the visualization of punching during the practice of Sanchin kata.

Except for all these advantages referring to the most commonly used makiwara, talked about, and visibly shown in this book, the makiwara has its limitations in being a static device.

The surface of the makiwara is very hard, with the exception of its striking target, which is slightly softened because of a protective casing. Many years ago, this protective casing, used as muffling, was composed of rope bound around the top of the makiwara, but nowadays, mostly for hygiene, it consists of leather, with some softening material like rubber sometimes underneath.

Within Goju-ryu practice, the makiwara is most often used for practicing punches, although kicks and strikes are trained upon this simple but effective device, as well.

The way Goju-ryu punches are executed on the makiwara can be described as hard and heavy. Like most Uechi-ryu punches, the majority of the Goju-ryu punches are executed and held for a moment when they reach their biggest resistance from the board. The total of the muscle chain, responsible for the performance of the punch and receiving the opposite force of the board, is tensed. For a moment, the board's resistance, to return to its original form and therefore pushing the fist back, is stopped/restrained. This momentum can be seen as the way the fist wants to completely deliver the punch until its end of focus without being externally interrupted.

Striking pads are a welcomed addition to the overall makiwara training regimen in that they allow the practitioner to focus executing proper techniques on a moving target, building speed and focus.

The components of the punch consist of moving the body's gravity point, rotating the hips, and executing the technique/punch, all jointly initiated, coordinated, and executed through the responsible muscles and muscle groups. From the moment the punch is explosively initiated, the muscles are dynamical concentric, contracting until the fist reaches its target. From the moment the target is hit, the muscles will continue from a dynamic to static concentric contraction through the heavy resistance from the board. (Here, a sort of weight training begins.) The moment the longest distance throughout the board is reached (from the point the board is hit and the arm has reached its destination x centimeters behind the original hitting location) and the fist is lightly pushed back, a static eccentric contraction is initiated. Directly, the muscles try to stop this counterforce from the board and focus in a static concentric and eccentric way, as in Sanchin kata.

We can speak of a light punch when the technique is pulled back before the counterforce from the board is fully met (short contact). Although there is a counterforce directly there at the moment of impact, because of the speed of the technique (especially the speed of retracting the punch after delivering it to the end position, without holding), it has a small role in terms of counterforce. Sometimes, light punches or other techniques can be executed even without bringing the body's gravity point toward the makiwara for a stronger/heavier technique.

Shotokan master Funakoshi is hitting a makiwara which has a bundle of rope in front of the hitting area.

Although, within Goju-ryu, punches with a lighter emphasis are trained on the makiwara (found more in the style of Shorin-ryu than Uechi-ryu and Goju-ryu), the accent remains on a strong and heavy punch supported by moving the body's gravity point, explosive muscle contraction, and holding the end momentum (long contact).

In general, one should see the makiwara as an expedient to develop a good and strong technique. This will help in focusing the body as well as the mind.

Often, linear and stretched out punching techniques are focused in kata practice, as one does within makiwara training. This is a gauge for the practitioner. When a person performs a straight punch on chudan level in the demonstration of a kata, he or she should punch with the same intensity, with the preservation of the right technique, as one does when punching on the makiwara. It would not be right if a person makes his punch more "extreme," more powerful than he or she could bear in reality. Generally speaking, the person's body couldn't match the resistance of the makiwara if he or she punched as hard as in the kata. The practitioner probably could not support and bear the recoiling effect of the makiwara from the punch, presumably leading to injury and ineffective technique (and, because of injury, this even would prevent making a consecutive technique).

If one is experienced in training upon the makiwara, one can align the power and speed of the technique with each other. Through resistance training, like makiwara training, one experiences speed, power, impact, resistance, etc., in a better and more realistic way. This would mean that the spiritual impulse corresponds with the ability of the body within the practice of the kata. So, makiwara training is not only useful from the point of view of self-defense, but is essential for the approach of executing the kata in which one should visualize an imaginary opponent.

Referring to the last paragraph, let me point out that in the display of kata and kumite, performed in competition, most of the so-called champions, who perform their kata with an incredible choreographic precision or have lightning-fast punching in kumite matches, never train makiwara, or simply do not insert makiwara experience in their performance. This is often because it's esthetically less beautiful, or only so-called "skin touch" is allowed in competition. The trained eye will see this, but for the spectator, it seems like the real thing, since karate as an art form has self-defense as its reference point. Resistance training in all its forms has a tremendous impact on the way karate techniques are approached. Makiwara training, weight training, and kumite in traditional Goju-ryu Karate-do, indicate that power and speed, combined with kimé, body movement, and rooting, have in mind and are based on one thing: Ending a real fight quickly and effective.

As mentioned in the kumite section, a punch usually is intended—however coarse it may sound—to knock someone down, not to dab someone. Many "modern" and Western karate schools only train their techniques in the air and do not, or hardly, make contact when training with a partner. Because of this, the practitioner will receive the wrong blueprint in realism and, therefore, in tactics. Techniques will be no more than extractions, the way of breathing, speed and power, and coordination; the whole biodynamic moving will become different from the intention of the traditional karate. It doesn't matter how many techniques one knows if one cannot even make one technique with the right intention. If one does not train in all the aspects, if one fragments, the ability to be effective will be stricken.

On a spiritual level, this is eminent. If one is sure of oneself; if one has experienced the abilities of one's own body and mind; if one has gained insight and, through self-activation, finds his or her own truth in the practice of karate-do; one could more effectively execute an attack or defense. The less the distraction, the greater the concentration will be. This will lead to spiritual growth.

Employment of the Chi'shi

The use of the Chi'shi is meant to develop power in the upper body, with the focus upon the hands, wrists, forearms, upper arms, and shoulders. The Chi'shi can be used for isolating exercises, but is generally used for "total" exercises (those where muscle chains are involved in the execution of locomotions). These "total" exercises serve the goal to make muscles and muscle chains collaborate with each other, to strengthen general locomotion and come as close as possible to imitate specific karate techniques under aggravated circumstances. Here, there is mention of specific muscle training.

A central posture that is often the starting point when practising with the Chi'shi.

In general, the Chi'ishi is used for dynamic concentric and eccentric training, but also static concentric and eccentric training (depending on the goal and exercise).

When using dynamic locomotion/training, the weight is negligible. The exercise should be performed in the right coordination, with relatively lengthy repetitions. Depending on the constitution of the practitioner, the exercise should be performed with less then 50 percent of the maximum force (as explained). Exhaustion or tiredness doesn't play an important role.

The correct way to perform is essential during the first period of practice, with attention on posture, breathing, the degree of speed, and coordination. After this period, one should start with the more static concentric and eccentric training. In this second period, the weight of the Chi'ishi is more important. The percentage of the maximum force should be raised above 50 percent (so a heavier Chi'ishi should be used). Exhaustion or tiredness becomes more important. The correct performance of the locomotion remains essential.

The correct performance requires choosing the maximum percentage/weight of the Chi'ishi. Again, if the performance is not correct, it could lead to damage to one's body. When using the wrong posture and/or locomotion, there could be tremendous pressure, for example, on the dorsal vertebra, which could lead to injury.

With this second, and "half advanced," period of training, the number of repetitions, the series, and the rest period become more important.

Moving in Shiko Dachi with the Nigiri Game is one of many exercises.

Employment of the Nigiri game

The use of the Nigiri game is meant to develop power in the upper body with the focus upon the shoulders. Also, the neck and back muscles are trained together—with the muscles responsible for the torso movements. The grip, which has a special posture, in holding the Nigiri game is meant to train the forearms, wrists, and hands. The tendons and muscles of the hand are strengthened through (as with the use of the Chi'shi) a continuous contraction (static) of its muscles during the exercises. Also, the posture of the hand is very specific, which also focuses upon specific weight training. When performing most Nigiri game exercises on the spot, there is a lesser degree of muscle chain contraction than with the use of, for example, the Chi'ishi. But, when moving from location to location as a part of an exercise, more focus will be upon using the totality of chain muscles. Think of the muscles involved that support keeping the gravity point of the body steady during movements.

When practicing with the Nigiri game, one can speak of dynamic eccentric and concentric contraction (locomotion, arm movements), and static concentric

Undo

Sanchin Kata is a special form of resistance training.

and eccentric contraction (rooting in Sanchin dachi, holding the Nigiri game).

As in using the Chi'shi, it is important to use the percentage of maximum force, depending upon the constitution of the practitioner. This rule is always applied within all parts of training. In every case, it is of utmost importance that, irrespective of the weight, the exercise should be performed without risk, so performing must be done with the correct locomotion, posture, and breathing.

GENERAL INDICATIONS FOR TRAINING

IT IS THE RESPONSIBILITY OF THE READER TO SEEK MEDICAL ADVICE AND A CHECKUP WITH ONE'S DOCTOR BEFORE ENGAGING IN ANY NEW PHYSICAL ACTIVITY OR THE EXCERISES OUTLINED BELOW.

THESE EXCERISES SHOULD BE DONE ONLY WITH PROPER SUPERVISION OF A SENSEI OR PERSON(S) EXPERIENCED IN THESE MATTERS.

It is important at the beginning to perform an exercise with a minimum of weight. If you are half advanced (referring to the general physical constitution of the practitioner and his or her experience in the performance of the exercise), you could raise the weight. If you're advanced and know what kind of maximum load you could handle, you should make specifications to the performance of the exercise depending on your goal, but within the possibilities and responsibilities of your own body. To give some indication:

1. Beginner
   – minimum weight
   – correct performance

2. Half-advanced
– slowly increase the weight between 50–85 percent (RPM)
– correct performance
– determine goal phase 3

3. Advanced
– Depending on goal
(for example, increase of muscle mass, muscle speed, muscle stamina, etc.)

Execute on:

– intensity
– number of repetitions
– duration of the series
– number of series per exercise
– duration of the pause (rest) between exercises
– the number of exercises per training
– duration of the pause (rest) between trainings

all in the correct performance of the exercise

4. Far advanced

– The use of additional modern training equipment is possible (as a beginner, already starting with this is optional).
– If one has enough experience and self-motivation, one could set a range of motion, apparatus, objects, and exercises geared to specific physical needs and specific karate performance. When starting with the training in Hojo Undo, especially from stage 2 on, one should think of the law of progressiveness: the training of the body progresses slowly and deliberately. Sudden increases of load or stamina demands on the body will lead to the body being "overtaxed," with poor results or even injury to the trainee. Not all body types will adapt to increasing loads equally. For example, muscle power is relatively easy to increase, but the strength of the tendons and their attachment points to the bones develops much slower. When the load used in the training increases too quickly, the muscles will become stronger, but this could lead to irritated attachment points of the tendons, possibly resulting in serious injuries, like the tearing, or even ripping, of a muscle.
The next schedule can be used as a guide to draw up a trainings program.

TARGET SCHEDULE WEIGHT TRAINING

Trainings form	% max. power	repetition	series	rest between series
Max. power	80–95	1–3	4–8	2–5 min.
Fast power	70–90	6–12	3–5	1.5–2 min.
Fast power/ Muscle stamina	50–70	10–20	3–5	45–90 sec.
Speed	less than 50	20+	3–4	less than 45 sec.

If one trains at least twice a week in all the muscle groups on an advanced level, one should change the program every six weeks in the percentage of weight and/or repetitions, series, rest, or exercises. Otherwise, the body gets too used to this training regimen. Research has shown that the body will gain more by changing the program every now and then (between five and seven weeks in general, depending on the individual).

> ## Yobi, Seiri and Junan Undo
>
> *Without further elaboration on specific preparatory exercises, one can say that these exercises help during warm-up or preparation to obtain an increased muscular flexibility, while at the same time creating an increase in power and stamina. Warm-up improves the preparation for training and exercise like the Kihon kata, such as Sanchin, Tensho and Naihanchi. After performing the Kihon kata, one repeats Yobi undo to allow the muscles to recover themselves, followed by breathing exercises and relaxation.*
>
> Chojun Miyagi, 1934

Yobi undo and Seiri undo

Yobi and Seiri undo, or "warm-up" and "cool-down" exercises, are meant to both prepare for and stimulate recovery after practicing kata, kumite and Hojo undo. Yobi and Seiri undo cause the supply and outflow of energy to change.

Warm-up exercises should foster better endurance, increased flexibility, and stimulation of blood circulation in muscles and tendons, helping to set up a power reservoir. They should cause a regulation of breathing and an increase and harmonization of the energy supply. Cool-down exercises are meant to relax the body, stimulate the flushing of waste, and decrease and harmonize the circulation of energy, resulting in rest, relaxation, and recovery.

In karate-do, the body and spirit cooperate closely, and Yobi and Seiri undo are as important for the spirit as they are for the body. Yobi and Seiri undo heighten body consciousness and facilitate better concentration. Body and spirit must align themselves when starting with training, as well as when breaking down the state of extreme preparedness after training is finished. Gradual transition from rest to exertion and vice versa is preferable to extreme and sudden transitions.

When warming up, Yobi undo exercises are characterized by gradually speeding up different kinds of movements, from small to larger and more intense movements. By combining these movements with dynamic, and to some extent static,

Undo

Knee rotation.

Hip rotation.

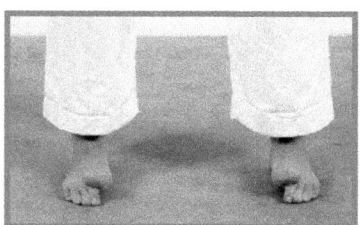
Toe exersises.

stretch (Junan undo) exercises, one prepares the body for the performance to come. These general and specific exercises—many of which imitate techniques—cause the heart rate to be increased gradually to a minimum of 120–130 beats per minute, so that the necessary blood circulation is initiated and the body temperature is raised.

When blood circulation is increased, more specific exercises are done, requiring in more effort. This intensifies warming up, but also represents a kind of training to build a minimum of general muscle power and endurance, and prepares the body for more powerful and explosive movements.

Breathing exercises, performed statically or in motion, are integral to building a good supply of oxygen, releasing the carbon dioxide, and correctly executing specific movements and techniques. Breathing exercises facilitate the use of the right kind of breathing, specifically abdominal respiration, in almost all circumstances, including those involving stress and physical exertion. Correct breathing brings

Shoulder rotation.

Wrist stetches and rotations.

Head movements.

Squats.   *Leg swings.*   *Stretching.*

about a better balance between tension and relaxation, and helps balance and control body and spirit.

Stretch exercises (just a few seconds static and a longer period dynamic) can be done as a very small part of a general warm-up, and to some extent interact between specific exercises during core training. Stetching also is done before the cool-down.

During the entire warm-up, one can engage in light breathing exercises and exercises to "loosen" the body (see examples). Sometimes, we can feel that something is not 'fitting well' in our body, and although we cannot tell what it is, there are signals that tell us that not everything is entirely in the right place—for example, a small bone or joint may be out of alignment. Pulling, rotating, or gently moving the dysfunctional area may possibly solve the problem. Some exercises, such as rotating the knees, are meant to stimulate the joints to produce "joint lubricant," enabling joints to move more easily and perform better.

Breathing and concentration

Breathing is extremely important in everything we do, physically and mentally, and breathing exercises should be incorporated into the training. Inhalation and exhalation have a great influence on the body. When exhaling, we are more able to relax, as we can see in some of the described stretches. You could stretch on "autopilot," but if you try to maximize your body awareness, you have to integrate concentration and breathing with the stretching exercises.

In every single exercise, there must be concentration. When you are stretching a muscle, you literally have to pull your attention toward the involved muscle

Sit ups.

Push ups.

and avoid distraction. If you exercise a punch, you must concentrate on making that punch. If you exercise a stretch, you must concentrate on making that stretch. By looking at your body, listening to it, and feeling it, you will get to know it. You will learn how it behaves under different circumstances, and become more familiar with its strengths and weaknesses. By studying your own body and that of others, you also will gain a much better understanding of human anatomy in general.

Junan undo

By stretching, or *Junan undo*, we mean the exercises by which muscles are stretched. In almost every branch of physical exercise or sport, some kind of stretching is applied, in some as an additional part of a warm-up or interacting within the main training, and often performed before the cool-down. Stretching can serve many purposes and, depending on the purpose, the sort of stretching and its execution can differ.

These are the purposes (effects) of stretching in the average practice of *karate*:
– Increase of movement effectness
– Increase of the blood flow to bones and muscles
– Reduction of acid as a waste product in the muscles (through better blood flow)
– Reduction of stress (by decreasing muscle tonus)

There are many ways of stretching, such as dynamic stretching, static stretching, and contract-relax-hold stretching. To learn more about these methods, one should consult specific literature on this matter. For this book, however, I want to give the reader some basic guidelines for static stretching and specific suggested stretches, together with some relaxation exercises. There are many other stretches and methods that can augment the following suggestions and practical stretching exercises.

Slight stretch

Go to the posture of the stretch, without springing, until you feel a slight tension. Maintain the stretch for 15 seconds while keeping your posture unchanged.

Then, relax yourself and breathe quietly. This slight stretch decreases the muscle tension and prepares the muscle for the so-called increasing stretch.

Increasing stretch

After doing the slight stretch (not going to your pain limit, only to the posture until you feel tension) for 15 seconds, repeat the same stretch for another 15 seconds, but this time stretch a bit further. Again, the tension must decrease during the stretch. If it does not, release the stretch so that the tension decreases. You can go a bit further by increasing the stretch when the tension decreases until you reach a new maximum level of stretch (in this way the pain stimulus is shifting and one can go further towards your stretching limit). Try to stretch a bit further every time you exhale. Do this in a quiet and relaxed fashion, while paying attention to the limits of the stretch. It is important to remember that the tension must decrease during every stretch. If not, return to your last position or even further back. Never start with a maximum stretch directly!

When you regularly practice this increasing stretch, you will become more focused and conscious of your body. However, you cannot stretch past the limits of your body without damaging muscles or tendons. Please recognize important influencing factors, such as age, heredity, overall physical condition, and current muscular tension, and adjust your regimen accordingly.

Breathing

During a stretch, the breathing, and all muscles that are not involved in the stretch, should be relaxed. Breathing and muscle tension interact, and many people must learn how to relax before they regain this natural kind of breathing. Do not hold your breath while stretching. In a more advanced stretch, in which you are trying to reach the limit of the stretch, you should stretch further on each breath. Do not allow anyone to disturb your attention while you are stretching, especially when executing an extreme stretch, as this could lead to a physical injury, such as a muscle tear.

Stretch reflex

Our muscles are protected against over-stretching by the so-called stretch reflex. This natural reflex causes the muscle to contract when it is overextended. By stretching to extreme, you damage the muscle by causing microscopic tears in the muscle tissue. This scar tissue makes the muscle increasingly less flexible. Pain, stiffness, damage to the tendons and bone attachments, and external stripe marks often result.

Note: Always stretch after a warm-up when the body temperature is raised, and not before!

Practical stretching exercises

It is never wrong to carry out some relaxation exercises prior to stretching, warming up or cool down. Lie down on the floor on your back and place the hand on the lower abdomen in a relaxed way. Try to take a calm deep breath three times, during which you imagine the abdomen expanding. The hands on the abdomen are meant to check for correct low (abdominal) breathing,

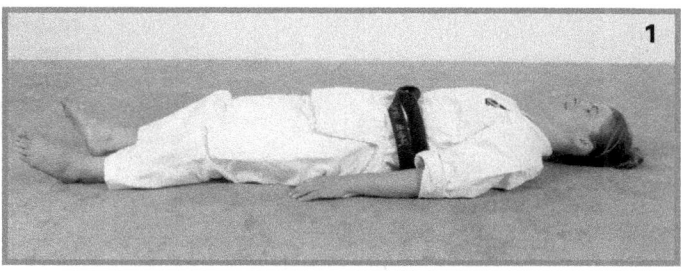

Exercise for the overall relaxation.

and will be pushed outward by the abdomen with each breath. It is easier for most people to relax and let the breathing flow freely while lying in this prone position. During each exhalation, try to release the tension in all of the muscles in your body and relax. After taking three 'big' breaths, continue on with shorter, normal breathes. Try to maintain the calm breathing obtained with this exercise with all subsequent stretching exercises.

Exercise for the back of the upper leg, buttocks and long back muscle.

Stand up and bend over while stretching the legs. Keep the head and shoulders relaxed. Place the feet closely together. Older people should be careful when doing this exercise, because it results in increased blood pressure to the brain with possible negative effects that can result in fainting or dizzy spells. As a general rule, whenever one feels dizzy, the exercise should be broken off. Not all exercises are appropriate for all individuals. This particular exercise can also be performed with the feet crossed over, leading to an increased stretch in the calves and other muscles. After the stretch is completed, first bend the knees slightly before calmly straightening the upper body (to help balance blood pressure).

Exercise for the buttocks and long back muscle.

Lie down while keeping the feet crossed over and bring the knees towards the chest. The tailbone remains on the floor. Embrace the lower legs with the hands grasping each other. The legs should be completely relaxed. Breathe while imagining the breath coming into the abdomen. During inhalation, press the lower back to the floor.

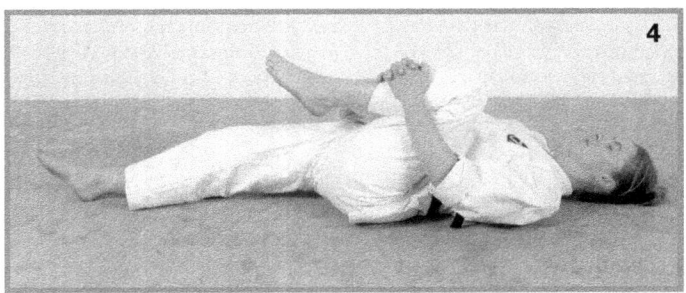

Exercise for the buttocks and long back muscle.

Grab the shin of one leg with both hands and pull the leg towards the belly/chest. The other leg remains stretched out and relaxed.

Exercise for the long back muscle.

Bring both arms between and below the legs and, grab the feet. Expand the back. The head follows this round movement and ends up facing between the legs (groin). Bring the elbows down towards the ground. When this position has been assumed, push the backbone backwards and upwards. Exercise pressure with the arms to force the body into this position. In case of breathing problems or discomfort, immediately reduce pressure or abort the exercise.

Undo

Make a hollow back and push the pelvis upward with the arms. In addition to the partial stretching of abdominal muscles, this exercise can provide health benefits to the backbone. (Individuals with back or other physical problems should take special care in performing any exercise involving the back or spine, including consulting with their doctor first before beginning any new excersize regimine). This particular stretch can be performed differently to yield a greater stretch range. Lie down stretched out on the belly, and using the arms, push the upper body upward while arching the back. This exercise resembles a push-up with the legs remaining on the floor.

Exercise for the abdomen and spine.

Exercise for the buttocks, upper leg/thighbone and lower back.

Lie down flat on your back. Bring the legs upward and bend the knees so that the upper and lower legs are roughly at an angle of 90 degrees (while keeping the feet on the ground). Keep the knees bent and bring the left leg across the right. This should result in relatively much contact between both legs. Allow the left leg to pull down the right towards the floor as far as possible. It is important the shoulder blades remain on the floor without following this motion. The best way to place the arms is stretched outwards on the floor. Once in position, the right leg should be relaxed completely. The left leg should also be relaxed as much as possible without losing control of the fixed position.

Exercise for the buttocks, upper leg/thighbone and lower back.

Assume the same starting position as with the previous exercise. Now, stretch out the left leg on the floor. Place the foot (instep) of the right leg behind the hollow of the left knee. Maintain this position of the legs during the whole exercise. Using the left hand, pull the right knee towards the left and to the ground. Once there, make sure the right knee doesn't lose contact with the floor. Now try to make contact with the floor with the right side of the upper body (roughly at an angle of 90 degrees). Keep pushing down the knee using the left hand/arm. At the same time, try to bring down the right arm and the right shoulder blade to the floor. During this exercise the respiration could be slightly hampered because of the anatomical position. If breathing becomes too difficult, reduce the stretch a little during each inhalation and increase it during exhalation again.

Exercise for the front of the upper leg.

A muscle that is often shortened through frequent karate practice is the m. Iliosoas, which is responsible for the raising of the upper leg. Stretching of this muscle is very important. Place the left foot forward. Make sure the left knee does not extend further than the toes of the left foot. Place the right foot, ball or instep, backward as far as possible while maintaining a straight back. If more stretch is needed, push the abdomen forward or place the right hand on the right buttocks and push forward a little.

Undo

Exercise for the back of the upper legs.

The hamstring stretch (back of the upper leg) is a well-known stretch popularized by its use in general sports such as gymnastics and football. This 'favored' exercise has a few variations: Sit on the floor with both legs stretched out. Bring the feet together and have the toes pointing towards the face a much as possible. Grab the toes and relax the legs. Once in this position, lean forward to stretch your back. Press the navel towards the toes and try to release the tension in the rest of the body (for example, in the elbow joints). If more stretch is required, then grab hold of the heels via the outside of the feet while resting the lower arms on the floor next to the legs. If this causes excessive discomfort, simply lean the upper body forward over the legs and grab the shins. If even more stretch is wanted, stretch your back forward further. Always keep the knees straight but without tension.

Exercise for the back of the upper leg.

In order to perform an extreme variation (only for advanced use) of this stretch, place the left leg across the stretched right leg in a relaxed, bent way as depicted in the photograph. Now use both hands to grab the right foot. Follow the same instructions as above. There are also pushing, rather than pulling, variations. It is possible to place the hands behind and next to the buttocks/hips, enabling one to use arm force to push the upper body forward. Or one can ask a partner to press the back gently forward from behind. This is preferable when the other exercises cause problems, or when there might be back or breathing problems.

Exercise for the inner side of the upper leg.

The area around the groin is important for sideward and circular kicks. Assume a reasonably wide position with the legs and with the feet parallel to each other. Bend the left knee forward and outward. Keep the body at the gravitational center between both legs (generally). Press with the left hand against the inner left knee joint and with the right hand press the outer right knee joint. The pressure should come only from the weight of the upper body (body weight). Be careful with this!

Exercise for the inner side of the upper leg.

Spread the legs as far as possible with the feet parallel to each other. Stretch the legs and come forward with the upper body. The stretched legs should roughly be at an angle of 90 degrees with the upper body (starting point). When coming forward with the upper body, lean on the hands to regulate counter pressure. If you want to go further with this stretch, try bringing the elbows to the floor (the body will automatically come forward more). Do not start with this stretch if the body is not warm yet. During or after an intensive warm-up one can work with motion to increase groin area blood flow to directly enhance performance. However, so-called springy stretches (moving stretches) can have different goals besides relaxing muscles or reducing muscle tension. Leave these kinds of exercises to a trainer who can judge their suitability correctly. Injuries to the groin can become serious and long term!

This exercise resembles the previous one, however now only the heels of both feet are touching the floor with the toes pointing upwards. The upper body is brought forward and the backbone is stretched (bringing the navel forward). First let the toes point toward the navel and have the heels press outward. When starting the stretch let the legs and the feet relax completely.

Exercise for the inner side and back of the upper legs.

Spread both legs wide while sitting on the floor. Using the left arm, reach for the right foot while keeping the arm above the head. Place the right shoulder on top of (or inside) the right upper leg and possibly the right hand towards the left foot. Try to keep both buttocks flat on the ground and bring the upper body in a position as if it were between two parallel walls ranging from the right buttocks to the right foot. In addition to the groin, this exercise also stretches muscles like the hamstrings and the side of the back muscle.

Exercise for the inner side of the upper leg and the side of the back.

Stand on your right leg. With your left hand (or both hands) grab the left shin where the instep starts while it is brought upward and behind towards the buttocks. Position the bent knee next to the stretched (right) knee. When this position is stable, push out the abdomen so that the stretch (in the front upper leg muscles) increases. This also stretches the important m. Iliopsoas muscle slightly.

Exercise for the front of the upper leg.

Bring the left leg forward while placing the right knee on the ground. Make sure the left knee is approximately above the left toes and the right knee is placed far to the back. If necessary, use something soft like a small cushion to place the right knee on. Grab the right lower leg with the right hand (or the left or both hands) and pull the foot towards the right buttocks. After this, push forward the abdomen again.

Exercise for the front of the upper leg.

Facing a wall, place both hands flat against the wall at roughly shoulder height with the arms at shoulder width. The backbone should be straight. Place the left foot forward so that the left knee is above the left toes. Place the stretching leg (calf) backward, so that the whole foot remains flat on the floor while keeping the right leg (knee) straight. This will require you to lower your upper body position. Placing the left knee further forward, while moving the upper body with it in a vertical position can increase the stretch. When you have been moving a lot with the legs (running, hopping etc.) or are about to begin this, it is sensible to do this stretch.

Exercise for the back of the lower leg.

Undo

Exercise for the side of the shoulder.

Stand at shoulder width and bring the right arm forward and stretched out. Now bring the left arm behind the right elbow to the left. Keep both shoulders at the same height. Do not let the right shoulder rise! The right arm should be completely relaxed (limp wrist, no tension in or around the elbow joint, no tension in or around the shoulder joint). This exercise appears quite difficult at first for most people because any deviation from the correct pose will not lead to the desired stretch. Some people, mainly women, are a little more flexible and have more suppleness around the shoulder joint often resulting in more loose muscles. In such cases, it could be that there is no 'stretch-feeling'. That doesn't always mean that the stretch is not taking place though.

Exercise for the chest and front of the shoulder.

Place the left hand, with a straight arm, diagonally upward and backward against a wall. This exercise can be done both standing and sitting. The left shoulder is next to the wall at a distance of about an arm's length. The feet are placed parallel to each other. When this position has been assumed, turn the hips in the opposite direction from the left arm. The stretch increases while turning further. This stretch can be varied by re-positioning the whole left lower arm, from the elbow up to the hand, so that it has contact with the wall. This slightly changes the emphasis of the stretch to a different region of the chest muscle. Chest muscles are used extensively in delivering both straight and hook punches. Practitioners often stretch the legs but neglect to stretch the muscles of the upper body.

Exercise for the chest and front of the shoulder.

Another exercise involving the chest muscle, as well as back and rump muscles, can be seen on the photograph. Sit in seiza (on the instep, the shins and the knees, keeping roughly two fists space between the knees) and bring the upper body far forward with floor slightly diagonally stretched out arms. Bring the hands to the floor. Maintain this position during the entire exercise. Draw back the buttocks towards the ankles as far as possible without touching them while the hands maintain their position on the floor. Calmly push the upper body toward the floor. Keep the arms stretched out!

Exercise for the side of the back and side of the upper leg.

Stand roughly shoulder-width and try to imagine that during the exercise you are between two parallel walls. One imaginary wall is in front of you, the other behind your body. Thus you cannot move forward or backward, only to the left or right. Place the left hand just above the side of the left knee joint. This gives good support so that several muscles in the body can relax. (During a warm-up, this exercise might be done without this support because the goal is different. Here, one could place tension on the muscles in the rump rather than relaxing them as during a cooldown.) Calmly push out your right arm over your head to the left. If you want to increase the stretch, imagine pushing away something towards the left. Because the arm cooperates with the stretch, the stretched region will span from the hip to the armpit. Allow the head to follow along with the spine.

Undo

Exercise for the outer side of the forearm.

In karate, the lower arms are frequently used. Think only about the amount of times a fist technique is made, especially during the kimé-moments, during which the lower arms are tensed maximally in order to make a tight closed fist and stabilize the wrist for impact. It is important to balance the muscle tension by stretching them. Either sitting or standing, place the elbow of the stretching lower arm against the body. This allows the arm to relax a bit. Pull/press the right wrist down, as depicted in the photograph. Increase the stretch by exerting pressure upon the back of the right hand. Try to push down the wrist joint of the stretching lower arm while simultaneously pulling it in the direction of the fingers. Don't press through! This exercise can also be carried out in the opposite direction, during which the palm of the hand points upward and the fingers of the stretching arm are stretched and pushed downward. This will stretch the inner side of the forearm.

Exercise for the inside of the forearms.

Sit in seiza (on the instep, the shins and the knees, keeping roughly two fists space between the knees) and place the hands, fingers pointing towards the crotch, flatly on the floor. The arms should be stretched. Press the elbow joints calmly forward while the upper body moves very slightly in the opposite direction. Make sure the hands remain on the floor. This exercise can also be done without placing the hands on the floor. Straighten the arm to be stretched forward and pull the fingers of this arm/hand backward with your other hand.

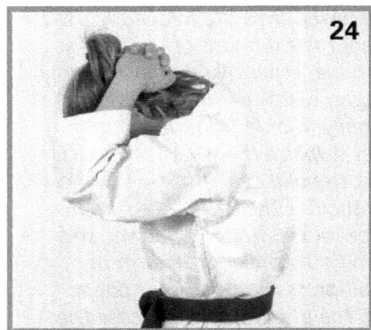

Exercise for the neck.

Grab the neck with both hands using the balls of the thumbs just behind and below the ears where the skull begins and the thickening of the neck provides good support. Push the head downward and simultaneously pull the head diagonally upward. This exercise can be done both sitting and standing. Never push the neck too far forward and downward! Always take extra care with exercises that involve the neck and spine.

Exercise for the side of the neck.

This exercise can be carried out both standing and sitting. Calmly bring the head sideways and downwards towards the right shoulder. The head is not turned! If the stretch is sufficient, it can suffice to do the exercise without the pressure provided by the hand. If an increased stretch is wanted, place the right hand on top of the head, as depicted in the photograph. The pressure applied to the head (in this case the pressure applied to the muscles of the left side of the neck), should be increased very calmly until one reaches his or her 'stretching limit'. When performing stretching exercises that involve additional pressure (in this case applied by the hand) one must be very careful. If exessive force is applied, pushing the stretch muscle past its 'stretching limit', then serious injury may result.

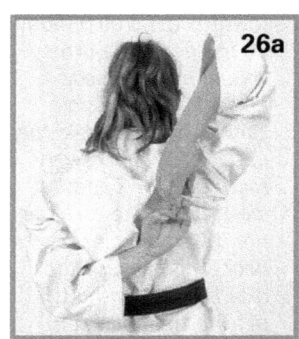 

Exercise for the back of the upper arm.

This exercise for the triceps can be done both standing and sitting. Although there are many variations, the one depicted in the photograph should be sufficient for most practitioners. If the right triceps is to be stretched, grab the right elbow joint with the left hand and position it next to the right-hand side of the head and push it backwards. The stretch can be increased if the body, especially the upper body/head, is stretched vertically. Switch arms and repeat. Variations include substituting the left hand by pushing against a wall in the same position, or by grabbing the right arm with the left via the backside. This last variation also stretches the shoulder muscles. When the stretch is extended to the shoulder joint, it is advisable to lightly stimulate this joint by calmly moving it in small circles with the stretched arm forward to backward and vice versa.

Appendices

> # Dojo-etiquette
>
> *By cultivating the primal power that is potentially present in all human beings, one can attain a focused mind that acknowledges our fellow man and the environment with deference and respect. Developing this power through the mind helps to balance body and spirit and create order within us all. Rituals help us navigate a landscape that contains the path to self-development.*
>
> Lex Opdam

Karate instruction typically takes place in a school, called a dojo in Japanese. More than just a school, the dojo is a sacred place where students devotedly follow a way to grow physically and spiritually. The dojo not only stands for the practical aspects of karate-do, but for the philosophical aspects as well. For the devoted student, the word dojo symbolizes a way of life. To stimulate atmosphere, solidarity, and concentration, and to express respect for the culture from which karate originates (and those who propagate this culture), there are a number of rules and rituals to be followed:

When entering the dojo:
 – bow before entering the (floor of the) dojo.
 – bow in the direction of the Sensei (teacher), or the Sempai (designated assistant instructor or eldest student) when the Sensei is not present.
 – bow to the altar of Dharma (when present), or to the symbolic front of the dojo.

At the beginning of the lesson:
 – the greeting-rite at the beginning of a lesson is normally lead by the Sempai. As a member of the group you respond to the Sempai's directives as follows:
 – "Shugo" or "seirets(u)," means line up in "Sempai" order, meaning in the Meibukan and most other Okinawan karate schools that the student with the highest rank stands in the front left corner and the student with the lowest rank stands in the rear right corner. All students stand in musubi dachi.

— "Ki otsuke," which means literally "take your Ki or energy and bring your full attention to the training and the present moment."

— "Seiza": first bring your left knee to the ground and then sit down in an attentive kneeling, with both hands on the upper legs.

— "Mokuso": kneel (or sit upright) in a relaxed posture, holding your left hand with your right hand (palms up) in your lap (at Dan Tien level), making a closed circle with both thumbs touching each other, and try to relax. If you find it difficult to relax, concentrate on your breathing.

Altar of the Headquarters of Meibukan in Naha-city, Okinawa.

— "Mokuso yame": open your eyes and slowly bring your attention to the outside world. Bring your hands on your upper legs again.

— "Shinzen ni (tai shite)": turn to the altar of Dharma.

"Rei": bow, placing both your hands on the ground in a diagonal way, where the tips of both your forefingers and thumbs touch each other.

When there is no altar:

— "Shomen ni (tai shite)": turn to the front of the dojo, representing the symbolic embodiment of the school's karate-do tradition.

"Rei": bow, as explained before.

— "Sensei ni (tai shite)": turn to the Sensei (teacher) or the person who leads the training when the Sensei is not present.

"Rei": bow, as explained above, saying: "Onegai shimasu."

— "Sempai ni (tai shite)": turn to the Sempai or the person with the highest rank.

"Rei": bow, as explained above, saying: "Onegai shimasu."

The Sensei or Sempai finally gives the sign to stand up, saying: "Kiritsu."

Put your right foot forward, raise yourself, and put your right foot back, so that you now are standing in musubi dachi. Never stand up or never sit down before the person on your left side (higher in hierarchy) is standing or sitting.

At the end of the lesson, repeat the above.

Short greeting:

Take a position in musubi dachi and bring your left hand opened to the level of your throat, bringing the right fist with the knuckles against the palm of the left hand, and say: "Onegai shimasu." The symbolic meaning of the two hands is: "no fight."

Another possibility is to stretch both arms along the body with the hands opened, bow and say: "Onegai shimasu."

This greeting can be done at the beginning of training, and is always done at the beginning of a new part of the training. It is also done each time you change training partners.

At the end of every part of the training, and when you leave the dojo, you bring the same greeting, this time saying: "Arigato gozaimashita."

The resting points for attention are called reigi. Other suggestions for proper dojo etiquette include:

– Be attentive to the training schedule, and strive to be punctual.

– Always take off your shoes before you enter the (floor of the) dojo.

– If a senior or a person with a higher rank is standing near the door, let this person go by first and do not push in.

– Prepare yourself in advance for the training session, including going to the bathroom and provisioning your body with adequate nutrition (food and water) before training. Eat only a light meal one hour before the training. Heavier meals two to three hours before the training.

– When addressing the teacher or senior practitioners, bow shortly and always use the title Sensei or Sempai, accordingly.

– Always be polite to instructors, seniors, and others.

– If you are observing a training session while seated, or sitting down during training, do not stretch your legs out and point the soles of the feet toward others, as this reflects a lack of respect. Do not lean against a wall, cross the arms, or behave in other negative ways as evidenced by body language. If you are physically able, sit down in seiza.

– Listen attentively and don't speak while something is explained. Only ask a question when the opportunity is given. Do not interrupt the teacher, unless the teacher has indicated that questions are welcome.

– If you understand an explanation, show this by bowing clearly. You can make it even more obvious by saying "Hai Sensei"—meaning "Yes, Teacher"—when the teacher asks if you understand.

– If the teacher asks you to demonstrate something, first bow shortly and then take your position in a general kamae (fighting posture) or in the requested posture.

– Always be focused and attentive when you are in the dojo, even during training breaks or when the lesson has not yet begun. Only chat in the changing rooms.

– Be attentive to further rules and current announcements within the dojo.

– In consideration of the dojo and your fellow students, wash your gi, or training clothing, regularly, and maintain adequate personal hygiene.

– Keep your nails short and neatly clipped on hands and feet, and do not wear any jewelry while training in the dojo.

– Never forget to do warm-up exercises, even if you are training alone.

– Train within the limits of your current physical constitution. Push yourself but never force yourself over your limits. You cannot train if you injure yourself!

– If you have an injury, let it heal first, but do try to observe training when possible.

– Do not take a very hot bath or shower immediately after training. Do not drink cold water during or just after training, as the shock may cause adverse health effects.

– If training gear, such as pads or chi'shi, is in disarray, take it upon yourself to tidy or organize the gear so that everything ends up in the right place.

– It is customary for all students to help clean the dojo regularly, regardless of seniority or rank.

– Do not forget to thank everyone who gives you advice or suggestions regarding karate.

– Never ask for a promotion, which is contrary to the spirit of karate-do. When the time is right, promotion will take place. Train karate-do instead of status-do!

– Should you have an urgent reason to speak to your teacher personally, explain this to the Sempai, who is the oldest of the class, or the designated assistant instructor. Always direct your questions to the Sempai first. Do not direct yourself to the Sensei directly during the lesson.

– Take care that the Sensei does not have to remind you of your dojo obligations. This shows a lack of respect, especially to the teacher.

If you have chosen to embrace karate-do, it is your obligation and duty to fully dedicate yourself to the training to the best of your ability. Only then can the teacher truly help you learn and progress. If you are lazy, impatient, or tardy, your progress will be limited, as will your teacher's attention. Try to be open and uninhibited during each lesson. Each lesson is a new experience and a new challenge. Remember that a cornerstone of this type of traditional training is repetition of technique, over and over again, thousands of times. Even if the same exercises are practiced each lesson, resist the temptation to think that you know all that you have to know, or have mastered the technique or the form. You cannot train effectively if "your teacup is full." Setting your sights on your ambitions or a final goal will cause you to stumble over the obstacles at your feet. Training while distracted by emotions, expectations, or frustrations, will not only prevent you from fully developing your karate, it also may lead to injury in training with your fellow students. If you focus on training in the exercise at hand, then you will surely achieve the best results.

> "In time of peace, karate should not be practiced as a way for its useful purpose, but karate should serve as a meaningful activity to train the mind. However, in times of danger and in fear of one's life, one can use karate to protect one's body and defeat the opponent. Although within our karate practice one does not use weapons, in case of emergency one can use a weapon to protect oneself."
>
> Chojun Miyagi, 1934

All civilized and industrialized nations have laws that concern self-defense. Some of these laws are very stringent while others may be lenient, but all have the same thread: that self-defense should be executed in direct proportion to the threat faced by the victim. Each jurisdiction regulates the amount of proportional response allowed to the amount of aggressive behavior.

NON-LETHAL AGGRESSION

For example, as a martial artist or trained individual facing someone attempting to harm you in a non-lethal way, such as a slap to the face, the proper response should be to deflect this attack and back away—and subsequently walk away. If your attacker is persistent, your next possible avenue of self-defense would be to seize and control the arm of the attacker to prevent further assault. In this same example, if your response is to escalate the violence to the point of excessive force, such as, for example, to break the arm of the attacker, this may no longer be considered self-defense but an escalation of the violence not in direct proportion to the provocation. In this case, the use of excessive force switches the role of the victim, who now becomes the assailant with many potential legal ramifications.

WEAPONS

Weapons can be divided into lethal (offensive) and non-lethal (defensive) categories. This is not to say that a defensive weapon isn't lethal! A broomstick for example exists in our everyday environment; however, should a broomstick be used in an aggressive manner, it could have deadly consequences. This same implement however, used in defense against a more lethal object, such as a knife, is more than reasonable in defense of life and loved ones. Most countries forbid the possession of certain, if not all, types of weapons, or require their citizens to have a license or permit to carry certain weapons.

PROTECTION OF PERSONAL PROPERTY

Most counties have laws that govern people's ability to protect themselves within their domicile. However, the common thread again is the proportional response to the threat. It always is best to flee a threat, and laws in some countries actually enforce this fact and frown upon violent defense of property. In the end, no one should endanger their lives in protection of inanimate objects or replaceable property. Keeping this thought in mind, the right to defend yourself and your family against a lethal threat should be paramount. If the ability to flee cannot be accomplished initially, one may try to defend oneself by deflecting physical attacks and verbally attempt to calm the attacker. If the attack is of such magnitude that these strategies fail to stop the attacker, then it is the responsibility of the martial artist to employ a proportional response in defense of life and loved ones. Intrusion into our homes aside, we should strive not to place ourselves into situations that represent a danger to us.

ENVIRONMENT AND OTHER FACTORS IN SELF-DEFENSE

Certain situations place us into certain conditions that may force us to make decisions that we may regret. Physical confrontation presents the "Fight or Flee" option in all of us. Ideally, our training attempts to teach us to recognize these dangers and not to place ourselves in confrontational or hazardous situations. Should this not be possible, however, proper training will, in most cases, provide the ability to safely extract ourselves from these types of threats. This proper defensive mechanism (response) should be:

- Flee the danger rather than confront it;

- If forced to confrontation, confront it passively and control it;

- If all else fails, defend yourself accordingly, to the extent allowed by law, and in direct response to the threat faced.

Not every situation is black and white and not every situation can be broken down, explained, or rationalized in simple terms. Obviously, each situation presents its own unique set of circumstances. Assailants can be drug induced or alcohol impaired, where their ability to judge right and wrong is clouded by the factor that is influencing their behavior.

In applying proportional response regarding drug-induced violent behavior, escalated methods may be needed to subdue the assailant. However, this same force may not be justified in the case of a person who is alcohol impaired. In addition, trauma, anger, undue stress, or past experiences all influence both the attacker and the victim. These factors may be known or unknown at the time of the threat, making the flee option the most desirable, and proportional response the best option when no other choice is available.

Hanshi Anthony Mirakian and Renshi Lex Opdam.

CLOSING

In a civilized society, only the authorities have the right to apply force, even deadly force, to end a confrontation or protect the public at large. However, the authorities have rules that govern the use of force in helping to bring a situation under control and reach a desirable conclusion that protects the public from harm.

This doesn't mean that, if threatened with lethal force, you shouldn't protect yourself. But you should take every precaution to protect your life, the lives of your loved ones, or innocent people who may ask your assistance as you await the arrival of the authorities.

The use of lethal force must be evaluated by the martial artist, and used only as the last possible, and very least desired option, to end a confrontation and protect life and loved ones.

The most desired outcome of any situation or confrontation should be protection of our lives and loved ones, with the preservation of ALL life as the desired goal.

Appendices

Vital Points

Over the centuries, warriors and martial arts practitioners have sought knowledge regarding physical "weak" spots or targets that might be employed to the fighters' advantage in battle or a physical confrontation. A number of fighting systems, especially those originating in India, China, and Japan, have increased their potency by incorporating techniques suitable for the manipulation of these spots. These "vital points" may correspond to the blood circulation in the body, nerve spots, joint structures and so-called energy flows that are of great importance to the functioning of the human body.

In some of the older traditional martial arts schools, "combat" art often was combined with medical science, not only to promote better understanding of health and to heal injury, but also to improve and refine fighting techniques. Some techniques were developed to paralyze or disable the body or a limb temporarily, while others produced their effect only after some time, depending on how and when they were executed.

Strangulation technique.

In addition to the techniques and attack spots that already are known to most students, there are many less common spots and techniques for manipulating joints, muscles, nerves, and blood vessels present within martial arts training. Such knowledge may interest anybody who wants to become proficient in the technical fighting applications, but, as with any discipline, an elementary base of understanding should be sought first, before one can assimilate more profound knowledge.

Starting in childhood, people may learn to fight in a playful way of romping about, or sometimes in a more serious way. We may experience a punch in the ribs, a kick in the groin, a blow to the head, or a similar injury while engaging in sports involving physical contact. This experience, combined with seeing violence in movies, television, video games, or perhaps daily life in a hostile or aggressive environment, gives us a general awareness of our physical vulnerability in a confrontation. We generally know that a kick in the groin will cause us to experience pain and immediate incapacitation, and that a punch to a relaxed stomach will cause a collapse and lack of wind for some time, both examples preventing an immediate or adequate defensive reaction. Most people can gauge the results of a certain fighting technique adequately enough, but martial arts practitioners can enhance their understanding with practical experience and additional theoretical knowledge.

By developing better knowledge of these attack spots, one cannot only make an attack or counterattack more effective, but also gain a better appreciation of the physical ramifications of such attack techniques on one's own body, and thereby develop a better defense.

When attacking an opponent's body, there always are many possible targets with different results. The drawings of "attack" spots shown here are suitable for beginning and intermediate karateka training. Technique results are not discussed here because they depend greatly on the power and speed with which the technique is executed, the angle of impact on the target, and the constitution of the body or body part that is hit. It is most important to remember that, as with the study of karate-do and the relationship between teacher and student, the same moral and ethical considerations apply when studying and learning techniques relating to the "attack" spots.

Front
1. Eye
2. Nose
3. Ear
4. Temple
5. Cheekbone
6. Jugular vein
7. Neck
8. Collarbone
9. Larynx
10. Trachea
11. Plexus Solaris
12. Ribs
13. Liver
14. Groin
15. Knee
16. Foot
17. Elbow
18. Wrist
19. Hair
20. Fingers

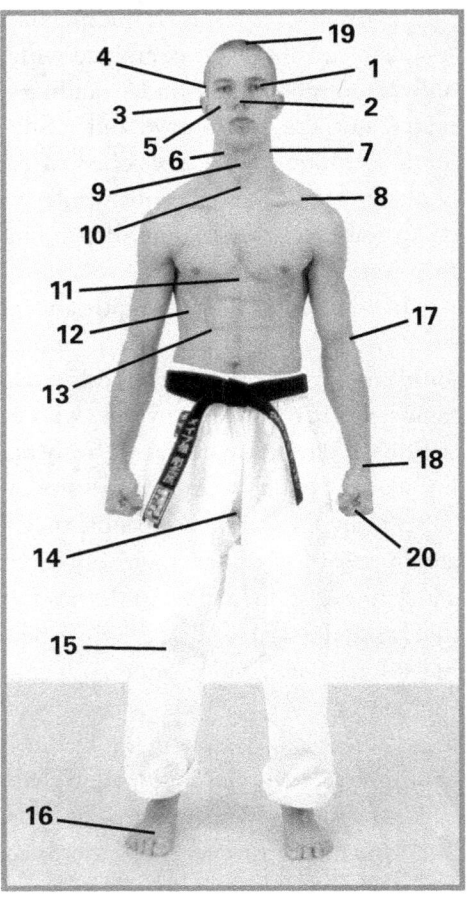

Appendices

Back
1. Ear
2. Neck
3. Kidney
4. Groin
5. Knee
6. Elbow
7. Wrist
8. Spine
9. Hair
10. Ankle
11. Fingers

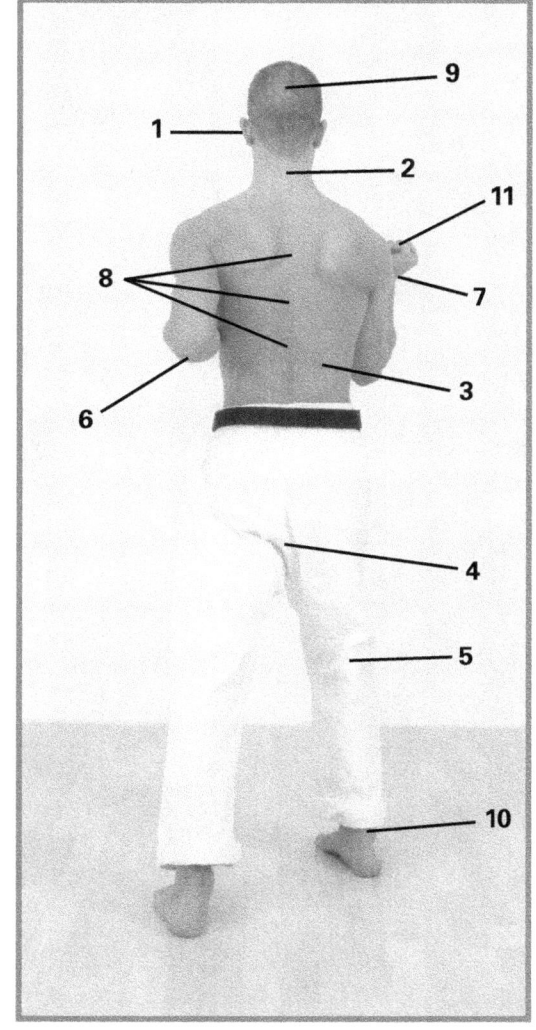

Goju Ryu Karate

Side
1. Ear
2. Neck
3. Kidneys
4. Groin
5. Knee
6. Elbow
7. Wrist
8. Armpit
9. Ribs
10. Temple
11. Hair
12. Leg muscle
13. Fingers

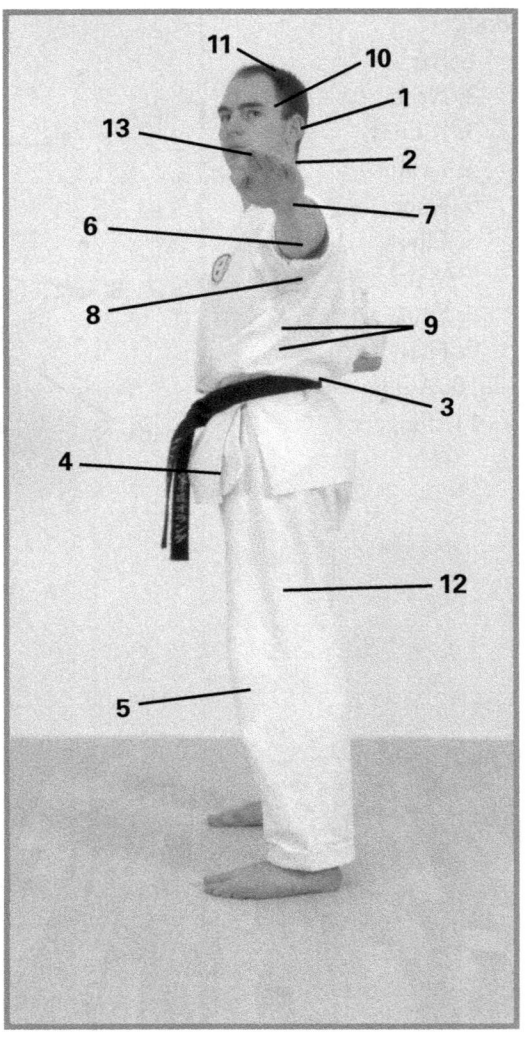

Appendices

Joints
1. Cervical vertebrae
2. Shoulder joint
3. Dorsa vertebrae
4. Elbow joint
5. Hip joint
6. Wrist joint
7. Knee joint
8. Ankle joint
9. Fingers

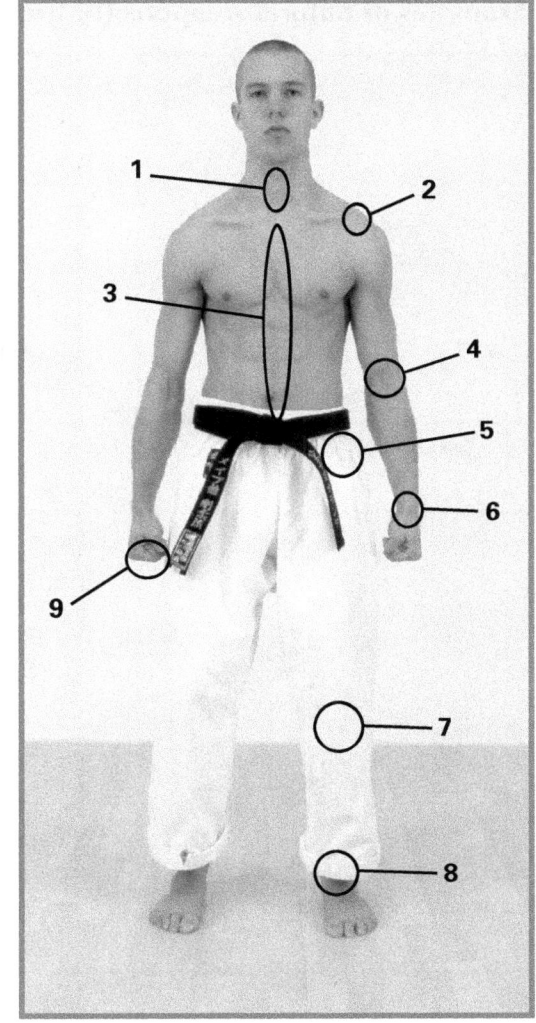

Examples of natural weapons (of the body)

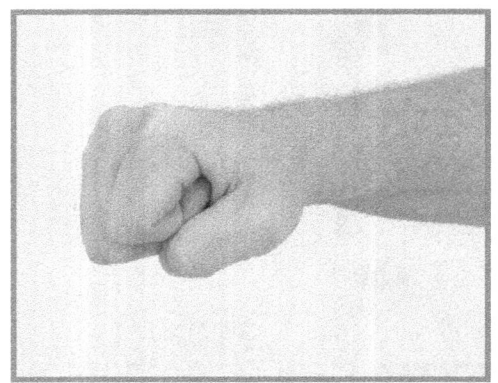
Seiken / front of fist.

Seiken Tsuki / straight front punch.

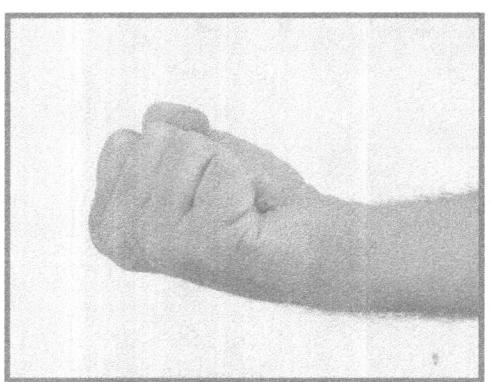
Ura Seiken / reverse front of fist.

Ura Seiken Tsuki / reverse front punch.

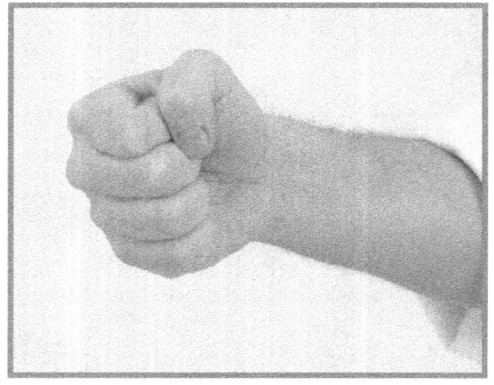
Tate Seiken / inward rotated fist.

Tate Seiken Tsuki / inward rotated punch.

Appendices

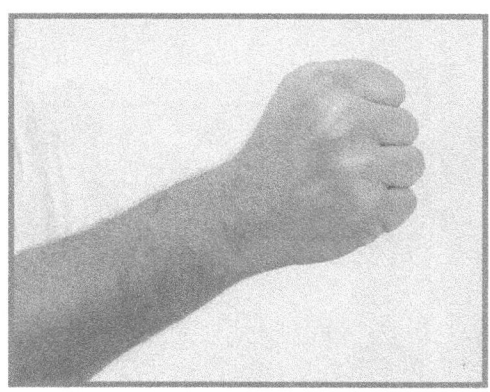
Tettsui / hammer fist.

Tettsui Uchi / hammer strike.

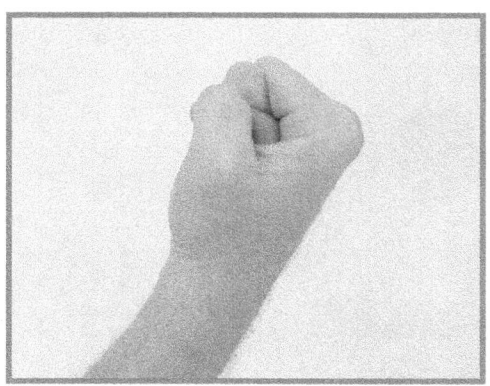
Uraken / back fist.

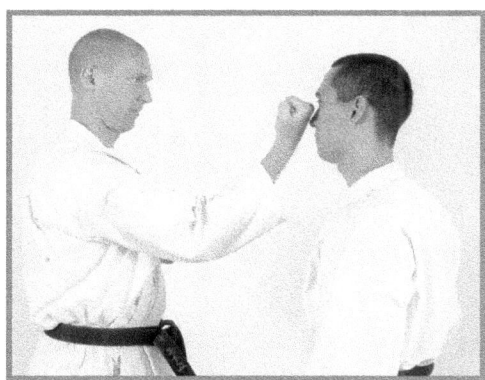
Uraken Uchi / back fist strike.

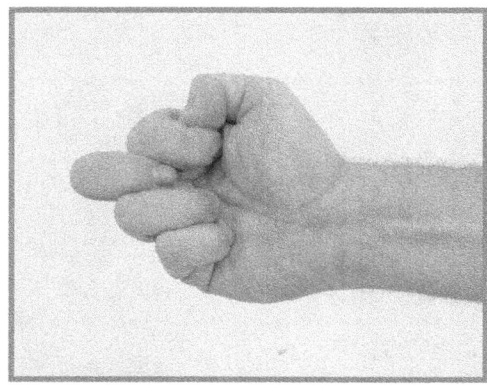
Nakadakaken / middle finger phalange fist.

Nakadakaken Tsuki / middle finger phalange punch.

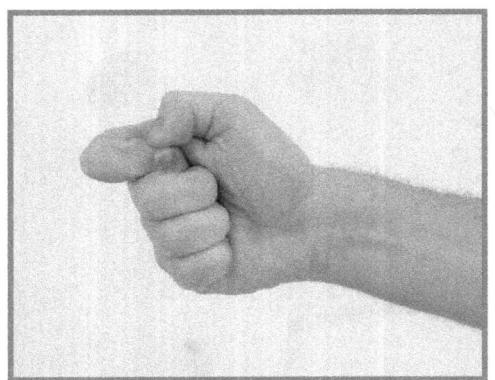
Keikoken / index phalange fist.

Keikoken Tsuki / index phalange fist punch.

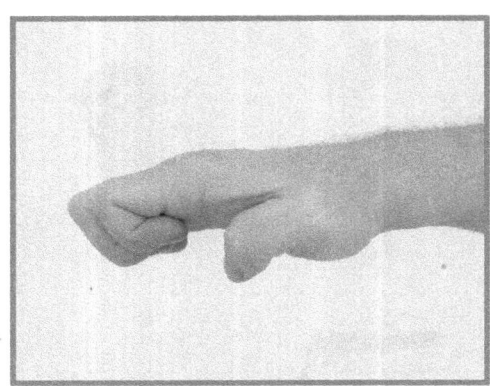
Kaikoken / phalange fist.

KaikokenTsuki / phalange fist punch.

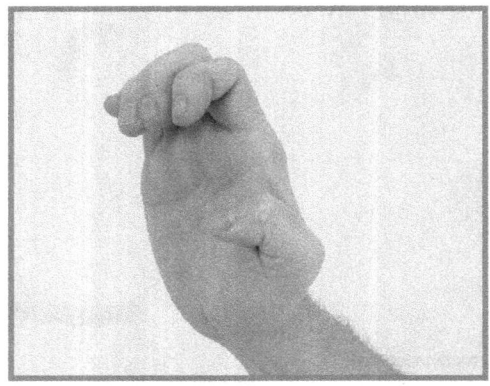
Washide / finger top claw.

Washide Hasami / finger top hook/pinch.

Appendices

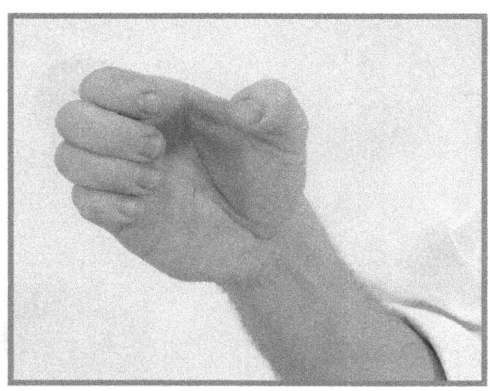
Yubi Hasami / finger pinch.

Yubi Hasami / finger pinch.

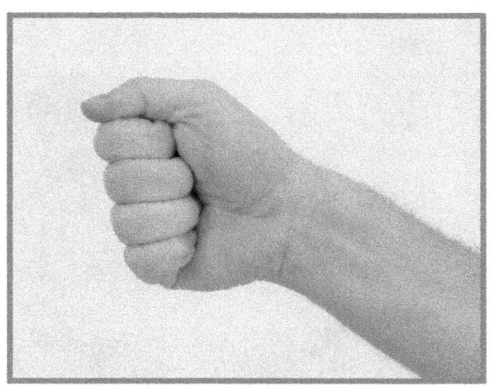
Boshiken / Thumb fist.

Boshiken Oshi / thumb fist push.

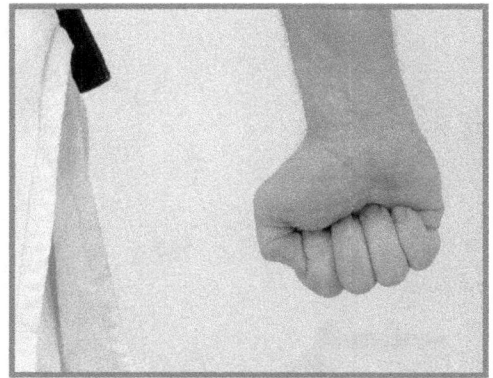
Heiken / flat fist.

Heiken uchi / flat fist strike.

Goju Ryu Karate

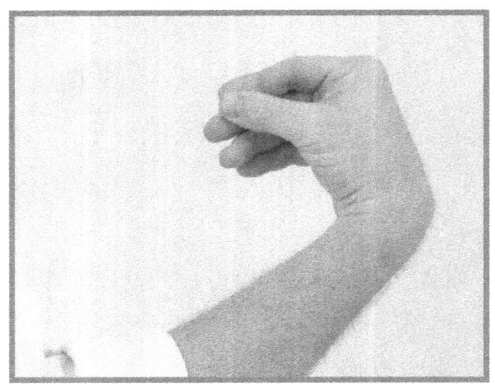

Koken / bent wrist.

Koken uchi / bent wrist strike.

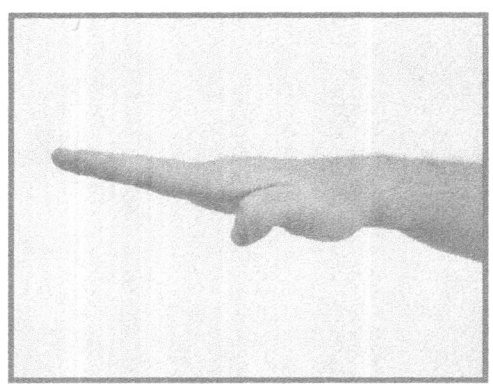

Nukite / spear hand.

Nukite / trust with the fingers.

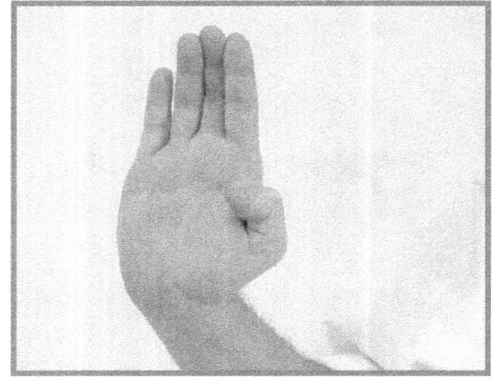

Shotei / palm.

Shotei Oshi / palm push.

Appendices

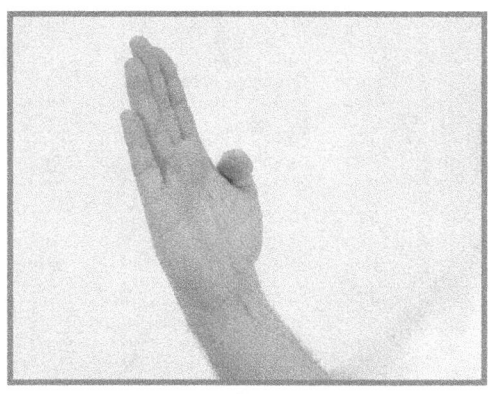
Shuto / knife hand.

Shuto Uchi / knife hand strike.

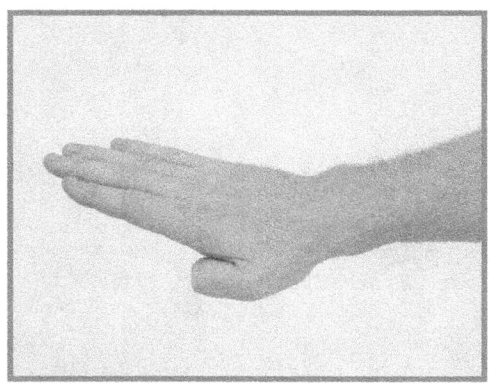
Haito / ridge hand.

Haito Uchi / ridge hand strike.

Hiji (empi) / elbow.

Hiji Ate / elbow strike.

Hiza / knee.

Hiza Geri / knee kick.

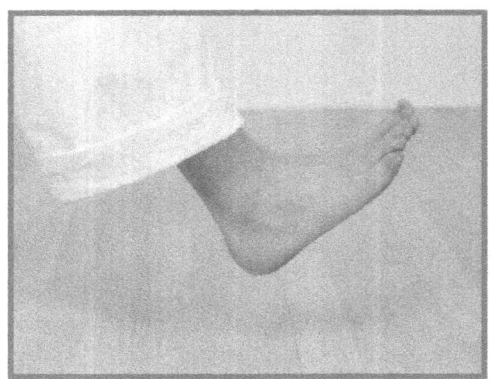
Kakato / heel.

Kakato geri / heel kick.

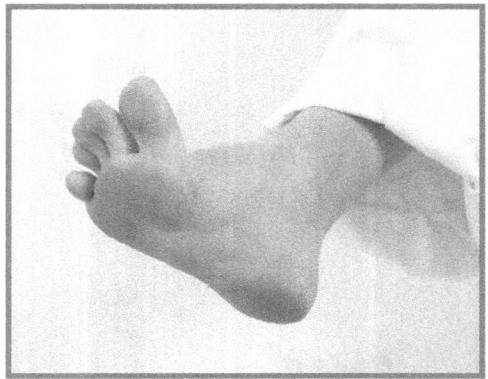
Josokutei / ball of the feet.

Josokutei Mae Geri / front kick with the ball of the feet.

Appendices

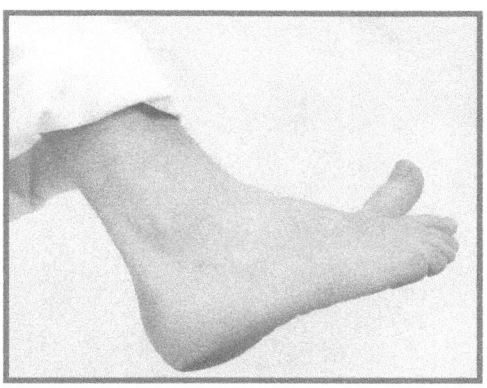
Sokuto / foot edge.

Sokuto Kansetsu Geri / foot edge kick.

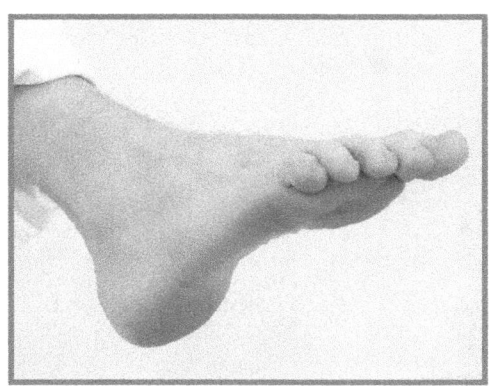
Tsumasaki / toe tip.

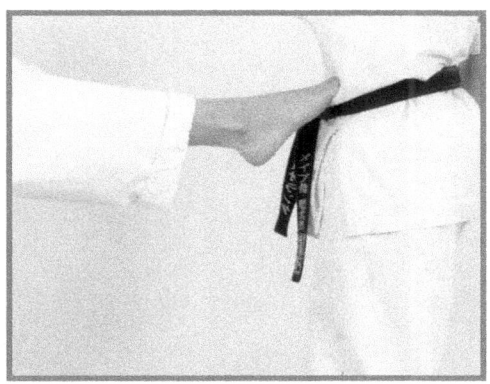
Tsumasaki Geri / Kick with the tip of the toes.

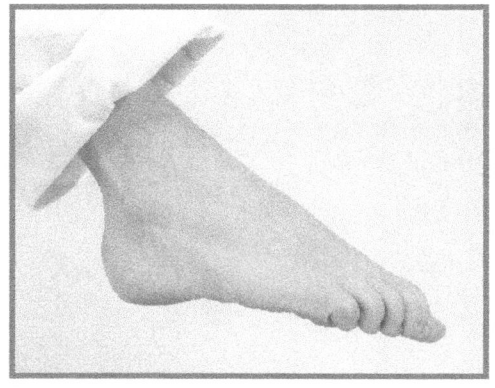
Haisoku / instep.

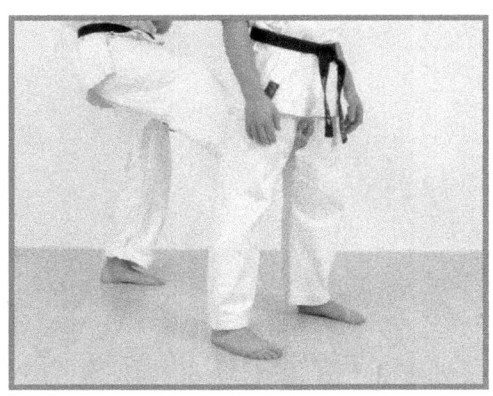
Haisoku Geri / instep kick.

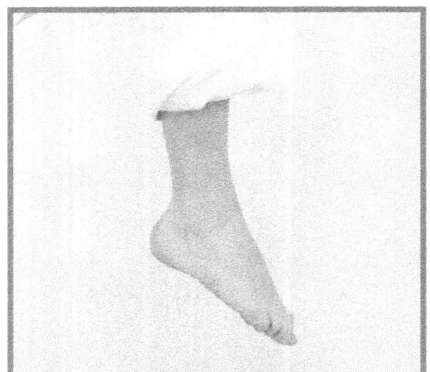
Sune / Shin.

Sune Geri / Shin kick.

Appendices

BASIC STANCES

Heisoku Dachi.

Musubi Dachi.

Heiko Dachi.

Hachiji Dachi.

Shiko Dachi.

Kiba Dachi.

Zenkutsu Dachi (frontal).

Zenkutsu Dachi (45 degrees).

Neko Ashi Dachi.

Kokutsu Dachi (frontal).

Kokutsu Dachi (45 degrees).

Renoji Dachi.

Benzoku Dachi.

Sanchin Dachi.

Koshi Dachi.

Ashi Mae Heiko Dachi.

Appendices

Lineage of Okinawan Goju-Ryu Karate Meibukan Association

Liu Liu Ko
Fuchow, Fukien, China

Kanryo Higaonna
(Naha-te) Okinawa

Chojun Miyagi
(founder, Goju-ryu) Okinawa

Meitoku Yagi
Okinawa

Yushun Tamaki
(Retired, inactive in the Meibukan, founder of his own organization)
(Okinawa)

Anthony Mirakian ———————————— **Alexander C. Opdam**
(Senior active student of   Headquarters Nijmegen
Grandmaster Meitoku Yagi)   Netherlands
(Watertown, MA, U.S.A.)   **Hing-Poon Chan**
                                                                        Headquarters Ottawa
                                                                        Canada

Shigetoshi Senaha
Founder of Okinawan Goju-ryu Ryusyokai
(Okinawa)

Meitatsu Yagi
(Okinawa)

Shosei Shiroma
(Okinawa)

Meitetsu Yagi
(Okinawa)

Kyoshi Nakamoto
(Okinawa)

Seisho Kuniyoshi
(Okinawa)

Kyoshi Horikawa
(Okinawa)

Masaaki Ikemiyagi
(Okinawa)

Masami Odo
(Okinawa)

Tadanori Shiki
(Japan)

Terminology

In this list only short explanations of the Japanese words are given. Mostly one explanation is given while more can exist. For more profound and detailed explanations other information sources have to be consulted.

GENERAL

ai	harmony
aiki	'harmonious meeting'
aikido	'The Way of Harmony'
bo	staff, wooden staff, long stick
bogu	protective armour
bojutsu	'The Way of the Staff (stick)'
bokken	wooden sword
bu	martial, military
bubishi	old text concerning martial arts and herbal medicine
budo	'The Way of Martial Art', martial arts in service of spiritual development
budo seishin	martial mind/spirit
bugei	classical Japanese martial arts
bugeisha	martial arts person
bujin	warrior
bujutsu	collective term for classical Japanese military arts until 1850 B.C.
buke	military caste
buki	weapons
bushi	samurai, warrior
bushido	'Way of the Warrior'
cha obi	brown belt
chikara	strength, power
chowa	harmony
chugi	loyalty
dan	level or step of degree (Black Belt)
do	'Way', discipline with a philosophical core with the ultimate aim to achieve enlightenment
dojo	place of practise of the Way
dojo kun	a set of statements and dojo rules that are intended to guide not only the training, but our everyday lives as well

dokyo	Taoism
domo	informal way of gratitude, way of saying thank you
eishin ryu/iaijutsu	original style of The Way of Drawing the Sword
embu	demonstration of martial arts
escrima	Philippine knife/stick fighting
fudo	stability
fudoshin	inviolably, inviolable mind, a state of mind that will not be distracted of external influences
gaman	persistence, perseverance
genshi	intuition
gi	uniform
giri	sense of duty coming from personal honour and pride
go	hard, external
gogyo	the five elements of the Chinese cosmology: fire, water, earth, wood and metal
gomen nasai	way of saying to be excused
goshin	self defence
hai	'yes'
hakama	culottes, skirt like trousers in some Japanese martial arts
hapkido	'Way of the coordinated power'
hishiryo	action without thought
hon(m)bu	headquarters
iaido	'Way of the Sword'
isshin-ryu	'One heart Method'
jeet kune do	'Way of the Intercepting Fist'
jo	short stick
jobajutsu	'Way of (horse)Riding'
jodo	'Way of the Stick'
ju	soft, internal
judo	'The Gentle Way'
jujutsu	'The Way of Flexibility'
jukendo	'The Way of the Bayonet'
jutsu	art
kai	association
kalari payat	old Indian fighting art
kali	predecessor of modern arnis, Philippine stick fighting

kama	sickle
kara	empty
karate	empty hand
karate-do	'Way of the Empty Hand'
katana	sword
kempo	Japanese name for Chinese martial arts in general
kendo	'Way of the Sword'
kenpo	'Way of the Fist'
ki (chi)	'spirit', mental and spiritual power or energy'
kiai jutsu	'Art of Kiai', energy meeting
kobudo	'Weapons Way'
kobu jutsu	'Art of Weapons'
kokoro	unity of heart and spirit
Kung Fu	'Hard Work', general meaning: Chinese martial arts
kyu	level, used as indication for levels below Black Belt
kyokushin kai	'Extreme Truth Association'
kyudo	'Way of the Bow'
mu	nothingness
mumen mushin	a clear mind
mumen muso	an empty mind
mushin	an open mind
naginate	'reaping sword', a curved-blade spear
naha-te	former name of the martial art from the town of Naha, Okinawa
nin	patience and perseverance
ninja	trained spies, assassins
Nippon	Japan
nunchaku	wooden flail
nyumonsha	acceptation of a student by a traditional school
nyunan shin	the readiness and potential to receive knowledge
o	great, important
obi	belt
orei	respect, etiquette
ori obi	coloured belt
reigi	etiquette
renmei	federation
ryu	style/system

ryuha	school, system, branches
sai	a pronged truncheon
seishin	spirit, soul
shinai	training sword made of bamboo
shorin-ryu	'Pine Forest Style'
shorin Matsubayashi-ryu	'Young Forest Style'
shorinji kempo	'Way of the Shorinji Fist'
shorinji-ryu	Style of the 'Shorinji Way'
shotokan	'Shoto's House'
shuri-te	former name of the martial art from the town of Shuri, Okinawa
t'ai chi ch'uan	'Great Ultimate Fist'
tameshi	experiment, testing
tameshi wari	test breaking
tanto	a short Japanese dagger
tatami	straw mat
te/ti	hand
teki	enemy
tomari-te	former name of the martial art from the town of Tomari, Okinawa
tonfa	handle, wooden weapon
tode	'Chinese Hand', an ancient name for Okinawan karate
Uchinan	Okinawa
Uchinanchu	inhabitant of Okinawa
Uchinanguchi	Okinawan language
uechi-ryu	'Uechi Way'
wa	peace, harmony, love
wado-ryu	'Way of Peace'
wu shu	term used in China to address China's fighting traditions in general
yang	positive
yin	negative

TITLES AND NAMES

budoka	person who follows the Way of the Martial Art
bujin	expert in the martial arts
bushi	warrior, samurai
dai sensei	respectable head teacher and style leader
daruma	Japanese for Bodhidharma

dojo-cho	dojo leader/head of a martial school with the rank of Sandan, 3th degree Black Belt with a minimum age of 25 year
hanshi	'model warrior', master with at least Kudan, 9th degree Black Belt
hanshisai	'perfect model warrior', grandmaster
honbu-cho	head leader/instructor of the headquarters of a school or organisation
judoka	judo practitioner
karateka	karate practitioner
karatedoka	practitioner in the art of karate-do
kohai	junior
kyosei	instructor with minimum rank of Black Belt
kyoshi	'master', a full teacher with at least the rank of Nanadan, 7th degree Black Belt
kancho	'master of the house', the senior karate-instructor
menkyo	license, certificate of recognition
renshi	'trained warrior', instructor with at least the rank of Godan, 5th degree Black Belt
sempai	'senior'
sensei	'honourable teacher', professor, doctor in an art form or discipline
shibu-cho	branch-head with a minimal status of dojo-cho and authorised to give instruction at a minimum age of 30 years
shidoin	assistant instructor with the minimum rank of brown belt
shihan	master instructor and dojo-cho with at least the rank of Godan, fifth degree Black Belt and head of a dojo
deshi	student
uchi deshi	'close by student'
yudansha	holder of a Dan rank (Black Belt)

CEREMONY

arigato gozaimashita	expression of gratitude: Thank you very much!
kata	style exercise, solo exercise
ki o tsuke	gathering attention/energy
kiritsu	raise up

mokuso	meditation, silent thoughts
mokuso yame	end of meditation
otegai ni rei	greet each other in respect by bowing
onegai shimasu	invoke question: Would you help me?
os/ush	greet to confirm solidarity (often used in martial arts)
seiza	stable sitting position (triangle posture)
sempai ni rei	greet the senior
Sensei ni rei	greet the teacher
shinzen ni rei	greet the altar
shomen	front (of the dojo)
shomen ni rei	greet in respect the front of the dojo as the symbolic embodiment of the persons that made it possible for you to practise the art
seirets(u) (shugo)	gathering, line up
za rei	kneeling greet
zazen	sitting meditation
zen	the discipline of enlightenment related to Buddhism

TECHNICAL
General

agari sagari	sag
antei	balance
anza	cross-legged
atagai	together, collective
atemi waza	techniques performed on weak and vital points
ateru	hitting, touching
ase	sweat, perspiration
arukikata	way or method of walking
barai	sweep
chakuchi	landing on one foot
chakugan	paying attention to
chidori ashi	crossing legs in movement
chiisai	small, little
chikai	close
chika ma (ai)	close combat distance
chikayori	covering distance
chimei	life threatening techniques
chokusen	in a straight line

choshi waza	harmonious techniques
chudan	middle level
embusen	floor pattern (foot pattern of movements)
gedan	low level
geri waza	kicking techniques
go no sen	reaction upon action performed by the one who is attacked
go waza	hard techniques
hajime	beginning, start
hara/tanden	energetic centre about 4 fingers below the navel between the front and back of the body
hantei	opposite
hayai	quick, fast
hidari	left
hikite	reaction arm, pulling back (of the arm)
hojo undo	supplemental training/exercise
ibuki	controlled breathing
ido	movement, locomotion
ido kihon	basic techniques supported by locomotion and shifting of the body
idori	sitting or kneeling defence
iki	breath
ikken hissatsu	killing with one single hit
in ibuki	internal breathing technique
ippon	single
Junan undo	stretch- and relaxation exercises
jodan	upper level
ju waza	soft techniques
jushin	centre of gravity
kamae	fighting posture
katsu	being helped, bring to conscious
keiko	training, instruction
ki	vital energy
kiai	bringing out energy by means of a shout
kihon	basic
kime	explosive focus of energy
koky donto	breathing
koshi	hip, waist
kotae	change
ko wasa	fighting techniques with small movements

kumite	fighting exercises
kyukei	pause
kyusho	vital point, vital spot/area
ma ai	fighting distance, range
mawatte	turning
migi	right
mochi	grip
morote	double, together
muchimi	focused eccentric and concentric muscle movement
muteiko	without resistance
naname	diagonal
nippon (nihon)	double (consecutive)
nujisashi	slow concentrated movement
o wasa	techniques executed with large movements
osea	control, repress
randori	free exercise, free-fight
renraku waza	combined techniques
renshu	practise, training period
sakeru	evade
sei	rest, inactivity
seiri undo (shumatsu undo)	cooling-down
semuru	attacking
semete	attacker
sonobu kihon	basic techniques performed from static position
sun dome	stopping before the target
tachi waza	techniques performed while standing
ukete	defender
wakuru	understand
waza	technique
yame	stop
yasume	to rest
yobi undo	warming-up, preparation exercises
yoi	ready, prepare
yokomuki	sideways
yoku	wide
zanchin	one thing, concentration, alert

Stances

benzoku dachi	scissor stance
dachi	stance
fudo dachi	free stance
hachi dachi	natural stance
heiko dachi	shoulder wide parallel stance
heisoku dachi	closed stance, feet straight together
iagoshi dachi	kneeling stance
kiba dachi	spread stance, horse stance
kokutsu dachi	backward stance
kosa dachi	cross stance
musubi dachi	open foot stance
naihanchi dachi	naihanchi stance
neko ashi dachi	cat stance
renoji dachi	L-shape stance
sanchin dachi	hourglass stance
shiko dachi	spread stance, sumo stance
zenkutsu dachi	deep front stance

Fighting postures

jigotai dachi	wide open stance
kamae	fighting posture
koshi dachi	squat stance
mu kamae	no fighting posture
neko ashi no kamae	cat stance fighting posture
sagi ashi no kamae	crane fighting posture
shinzentai no kamae	natural fighting posture
yoi no kamae	formal concentrated preparing fighting posture
saifa no kamae	specific fighting posture from Goju-ryu kata Saifa
seiryu no kamae	specific fighting posture from Meibuken kata Seiryu

Movements

ashi sabaki	foot movement, foot shifting
ayumi ashi	natural step
chakuchi	landing on one foot
fumi ashi	stamping, pounding foot
hiki ashi	retracting foot
kotai	backwards

Appendices

tsugi ashi	shifting step
suri ashi	avoiding step
taihiraki	body evading
taisabaki	body movement, displacement
tenshin	movement
yori ashi	second moving leg shifting after first leg motion (staying in the same front or back position)
zenchin	forwards

Body parts

ashi no ura / sokuto	sword side of the feet
ashi yubi	toes
atami	head
boshiken	thumb fist
daikento	knuckles of middle- and index finger
haito	ridge hand
haishu	back of the hand
haisoku	instep
hauri	hip
heiken	fist
hiji	elbow
hiza	knee
josokutei/chusoku	bal of the feet
kaikoken	crab fist, phalange fist
kakato	heel
kasokutei	side of the heel
keikoken	chicken beak fist, index phalange fist
koken	bent wrist
kote	wrist
nakadakaken	middle finger knuckle fist
nukite	spear hand
ude/kotai	forearm
uraken	back fist
seiken	fist
shuto	knife hand
shotei	palm
sokutei	sole of the feet
sune	shin
tettsui	hammer fist
tsumasaki	tip of the toes

Specific techniques

geri waza	kicking techniques
hazusa wasa	freeing techniques
hiki waza	pulling techniques
kansetsu waza	joint techniques
naga waza	throwing techniques
ne waza	ground techniques
osea waza	suppressing techniques
oshi waza	pushing techniques
shime waza	strangulation techniques
tsukamki waza	grip techniques
tsuki waza	punching techniques
uchi waza	striking techniques
uke waza	blocking techniques
ura waza	take over techniques

Punch, pinch and strike techniques

age tsuki	upward punch
awase tsuki	combined punch
choku tsuki	forward straight punch
furi uchi	sweep swing
furi tsuki	sweep punch
gyaku tsuki	opposite punch (with respect to legs)
haito uchi	ridge hand strike
hiji ate	elbow strike
hiraken uchi	flat fist strike
jun tsuki	equilateral punch
kagi tsuki	sideward hook punch
kata ate	shoulder push, shoulder support
kizami tsuki	jab
kinteki uchi	crotch strike
ko uchi	wrist strike
koto ate	a header
mawashi tsuki	angular punch, hook punch
nukite	finger strike
oi tsuki	front punch (with respect to legs)
ura ken uchi	back fist strike
ura tsuki	reverse punch,
shuto uchi	knife hand strike
shotei tsuki	palm punch

shotei oshi	palm push
tora guchi	tiger mouth grip
yama tsuki	mountain punch
yoko tsuki	sideward straight punch
yubu hasami	finger pinch
washide	bear claw (finger top hook)

Kicking techniques

hiza geri	knee kick
heisoku geri	instep kick
kakato geri	heel kick
fumikomi geri	stamping heel kick
furi geri	sweeping inside kick
keage geri	rising kick
kekomi geri	piercing, trusting kick
mea geri	front kick
mawashi geri	roundhouse kick
mikazuki geri	inward circular heel kick
ushiro geri	backward kick
sokuto geri	foot edge kick
sokutei harai geri	sole sweep
tobi geri	jump kick
tobi hiza geri	jump knee kick
yoko geri	side kick

Throwing techniques

ashi barai	foot sweep
ashi kake uke	foot hook sweep
ashikubi kake uke	ankle hook sweep
ashi tori	leg attack with hands
furi nage	swing throw
koshi nage	hip throw
tamoe nage	sacrifice throw

Defence techniques

age uke	rising block
haisoku barai	instep sweep/block
harai uke`	sweeping block
hari uke	bow and arrow block
hasami uke	scissor block

hiji uke	elbow block
hiki uke	pulling block
hiza uke	knee block
hojo uke	supporting block
kake uke	hook block
kosa uke	cross block
ko uke	wrist block
kuri uke	pulling elbow block
mawashi uke	circular block
nagashi uke	deflecting block
osea uke	suppressing block
otoshi uke	dropping block
shotei uke	sweeping palm block
shuto uke	knife hand block
sune uke	shin block
sukui uke	scoop block
sokutei osea uke	suppressing sole block
soto/yoko uke	outside block
uchi uke	inward block
ude/kotai uke	forearm block
uke/tsuki	shave, rebound block/punch
ura uke	pulling backhand block

Fighting drills

bunkai kumite	fighting applications in confrontation
dento teki bunkai kumite	traditional fighting applications in confrontation
ippon kumite	singular fighting drill in confrontation
kakete kumite	sticky hand fighting in confrontation
kakomi kumite	consecutive fighting drill in four directions
kumite	fighting drill in confrontation with one or more opponents
nihon/nippon kumite	twofold fighting drill in confrontation
randori kumite	free fighting
renzoku kumite	consecutive fighting in confrontation
sandan uke barai	three level fighting drill in confrontation
tanren kumite	'iron', contact conditioning in confrontation
yakusoku kumite	prearranged confrontation

Supporting training

chi'ishi	stone lever weight
ishi sashi	stone padlock
kongoken	iron oval weight
makiage kigu	wrist roller
makiwara	wooden striking post
nigiri game	gripping jar
sashi ishi	natural stone weight
suna bako	sand bucket
tan	barbell
tameshiwara	board breaking, breaking techniques on material
tetsuarei	dumbbell
tetsu geta	iron shoes
tou	bamboo bundle

COUNTING

ichi	one
ni	two
san	three
shi	four
go	five
roku	six
shichi	seven
hachi	eight
ku	nine
ju	ten

GRADUATIONS
Kyu-grades

ikkyu	first kyu
nikyu	second kyu
sankyu	third kyu
yonkyu	fourth kyu
gokyu	fifth kyu
rokkyu	sixth kyu
shichikyu	seventh kyu
hachikyu	eighth kyu
kukyu	ninth kyu
jukyu	tenth kyu

Dan-grades

shodan	first dan
nidan	second dan
sandan	third dan
yondan	fourth dan
godan	fifth dan
rokudan	sixth dan
nanadan	seventh dan
hachidan	eighth dan
kudan	ninth dan
judan	tenth dan

Physical appearance of the obi's

10th kyu	white belt
9th kyu	white belt & 1 green stripe
8th kyu	white belt & 2 green stripes
7th kyu	white belt & 3 green stripes
6th kyu	green belt
5th kyu	green belt & 1 brown stripe
4th kyu	green belt & 2 brown stripes
3th kyu	brown belt
2th kyu	brown belt & 1 black stripe
1th kyu	brown belt & 2 black stripes
Shodan	Black Belt
Nidan	Black Belt
Sandan	Black Belt
Yondan	Black Belt
Godan	Black Belt
Rokudan	Black Belt
Nanadan	Black Belt & 1 golden stripe
Hachidan	Black Belt & 2 golden stripes
Kudan	Black Belt & 3 golden stripes
Judan	Black Belt

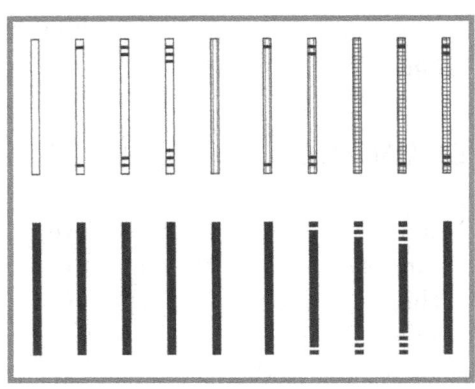

Physical appearance of the belts (obi).

Appendices

Suggested readings on Okinawan Goju-ryu Karate-do

Babladelis, **Paul**. *The Sensei Who Received Chojun Miyagi's Belt*. Article in Black Belt Magazine. 1992.

Bishop, **Mark**. *Okinawan Karate: Teachers, Styles and Secret Techniques*. 2nd edition. 1999.

Bishop, **Mark**. *Zen Kobudo: Mysteries of Okinawan Weaponryu and Te*. Charles E. Tuttle. Japan. 1996.

Bollinger, **Edward**. *On the Threshold of the closed Empire: Mid-19th century missions in Okinawa*. William Carey Library. Pasadena, California U.S.A. 1991.

Co, **Alexander**. *Five Ancestor Fist Kung-fu: The Way of Ngo Cho Kun*. Charles E. Tuttle Company. 1983/1996.

Corcoran, **John** / **Farkas**, **Emil** / **with Sobel**, **Stuart**. *The Orginal Martial Arts Encyclopedia: Tradition-History-Pioneers*. Pro-action Publishing. 1993.

Dollar, **Alan**. *Secrets of Uechi-ryu karate and the mysteries of Okinawa*. Cherokee Publishing. U.S.A. 1996.

Farcas, **Emil** / **Corcoran**, **John**. The Overlook Martial Arts Dictionary. The Overlook press. New York. 1983.

Funakoshi, **Gichin**. *Karate-do Nymumon: The Master Introductory Text*. Kodanshi International. 1988.

Funakoshi, **Gichin**. *Karate-do Kyohan: The Master Text*. Tokyo: Kodansha International. 1973.

Hokama, **Tetsuhiro**. *History and Traditions of Okinawan Karate*. Masters Publication. Canada.

Haines, **Bruce**. *Karate's History and Traditions*. Revised edition. Charles E. Tuttle. Japan. Third printing. 1997.

Higaonna, **Morio**. *The History of Karate: Okinawan Goju-ryu*. U.S.A. Dragon Books. 1995.

Jwing-Ming, **Yang**. *The essence of Shaolin White Crane; Martial Power and Qigong*. YMAA Publication Center. 1996.

Kim, **Sun-Jin** / **Kogan**, **Daniel** / **Kontogiannis**, **Nikolaos** / **Wong**, **Hali**. *Tuttle Dictionary of the Martial Arts of Korea, China and Japan*. Charles E. Tuttle Company. 1996.

Mattson, **George**. *The Way of karate*. Charles E. Tuttle. Japan. Third edition. 1998.

Mattson, **George**. *Uechiryu karate do -Classical Chinese Okinawan Self Defense-* Peabody publishing Co. U.S.A. 1974.

McCarthy, **Patrick**. *The Bible of Karate: Bubishi*. Charles E. Tuttle Company. 1995.

McCarthy, Patrick. *Classical kata of Okinawan Karate.* Ohara Publications. U.S.A. 1987.

McCarthy, Patrick. *Ancient Okinawan Martial Arts: Koryu Uchinada.* Vol. 1 and 2. Tuttle Publishing. 1999.

McKenna, Mario. *To'on-Ryu: A Glimpse into Karate-do's Roots.* Journal of Asian Martial Arts. Vol. 9 Number 3. U.S.A. 2000.

Nagamine, Shoshin. *The essence of Okinawan karate-do.* Charles E Tuttle. Japan. Fifteenth printing 1994.

Nagamine, Shoshin. *Tales of Okinawa's Great Masters.* Tuttle Publishing. U.S.A. 2000.

Opdam, Lex. *Tou'on-ryu; A Time Capsule of Okinawan Karate.* Interview with Mario McKenna. Meibukan Magazine, Number 5, 2005.

Opdam, Lex. *Karate-do, its purpose and responcibility.* Interview with Master Anthony Mirakian. Meibukan Magazine, Number 4, 2004.

Ravignat, Mathieu. *Commemoration booklet Dai Sensei Meitoku Yagi.* All American Meibukan-Canada. 2003.

Ravignat, Mathieu. *The History of Goju-ryu Karate.* Meibukan Magazine, Number 2 and 3, 2004, and Number 4, 2005.

Reid, Howard / Croucher, Michael. *The way of the Warrior.* Eddison/Sadd Editions. London.

Schoene, Mark. *The Golden Age of Okinawan Karate.* Interview with Master Anthony Mirakian. Fighting Arts vol. 66, 67, 68. 1990.

Smith, Robert. *Chinese Boxing: Master and Methods.* North Atlantic Books. 1974/1990.

Swift, Joe. *The Kenpo of Kume Village. Speculation of the Original Nafadi.* Meibukan Magazine, Number 6, 2005.

Toguchi, Seikichi. *Okinawan Goju-ryu: Fundamentals of Shorei-Kan Karate.* Ohara Publications Burbank. California. Third printing. 1977.

Toguchi, Seikichi. *Okinawan Goju-ryu 2: Advanced Techniques of Shorei-Kan Karate.* By Toshio Tamano and Scott Lenzi / Ohara Publications U.S.A. 2001.

Yagi, Meitoku. *"Otoko Meitoku no Jinsei Gekijo" ("The life drama of the man, Meitoku").* Japan 2000.

Yagi, Meitatsu. *Meibukan Goju-ryu Karate-do.* Japan. 1982.

Yagi, Meitatsu / Wheeler, Carl / Vickerson, Brock. *Okinawa Karate-do Gojyu-ryu Meibu-kan.* Canada. 1998.

Yamaguchi, Gogen. *Goju ryu Karate Do Kyohan.* Masters Publication, Canada. 1999.

Zundert, Willie. *On Walking the Teacher's Path.* Interview with Renshi Lex Opdam. Meibukan Magazine, Number 1, 2004.

Appendices

Contact addresses for the branches of Hanshi Anthony Mirakian

U.S.A.
Meibukan General Overseas Manager
Hanshi **Anthony Mirakian**
Kudan (9th Degree)
Contact:
151 Mt. Auburn Street
Watertown, MA 02472-1235
U.S.A.

Canada
Renshi **Hing-Poon Chan**
Rokudan (6th Degree)
Contact:
1864 Brousseau Cres
Orleans, Ontario
K1C 2Z3
Canada

Netherlands
Renshi **Lex Opdam**
Rokudan (6th Degree)
Contact:
Postbox 8, 6663 ZG
Lent
Netherlands

Interviews with Master Anthony Mirakian

The 'Golden Age" of OKINAWAN KARATE

Mark L. Schoene interviews MASTER ANTHONY MIRAKIAN

Karate pioneer **Anthony Mirakian** introduced Okinawan *Goju-ryu Karate-do* to the United States in 1960. A passionate and energetic exponent of traditional *karate*, **Mirakian** has taught what he calls "the true art" at his Okinawan *Karate-do* Academy in Watertown, Massachusetts for the past thirty years. He offers his students a mirror image of the training he received in Okinawa decades ago. **Mirakian** began his *karate* training when the U.S. Air Force stationed him in Okinawa in the early 1950's. He first studied under Okinawan *Goju-ryu Karate-*master, **Seikichi Toguchi** at the *Shoreikan dojo* in Nakanomachi, Okinawa. He also trained there with Okinawan *karate* master, **Ryuritsu Arakaki**. When *Sensei* **Arakaki** noticed Mirakian's passion and commitment to the art, he advised him to train under the foremost *Goju-ryu Karate* master on Okinawa, Grandmaster **Meitoku Yagi**, the top student and successor of the late founder of *Goju-ryu Karate*, Grandmaster **Chojun Miyagi**.

Grandmaster Meitoku Yagi promotes Anthony Mirakian to 8th Degree Hachidan (Kyoshi) at his home in Kume, Naha-city, Okinawa, on February 25, 1985.

Mirakian was the first Westerner taught by Grandmaster **Meitoku Yagi** and the first to receive a Black Belt from him. The traditional *karate* training at Yagi's *Meibukan dojo* was challenging and arduous, with four-hour workouts five nights a week. **Mirakian** was promoted to 3rd degree Black Belt before returning to the United

States in 1960. He is the senior active student of Grandmaster **Yagi**, who promoted him to 8th degree Black Belt in Okinawa 1985.

Sensei Mirakian's academy in Watertown, Massachusetts is the North American headquarters of the *Meibukan Goju-ryu Karate-do* Association based in Kume, Naha-city, Okinawa. In 1972 Grandmaster **Yagi** appointed **Mirakian** the Overseas General Manager of the *Meibukan* Association. His *dojo* offers Okinawan *Goju-ryu Karate-do* training in its purest form. **Mirakian** is an excellent example of the benefits of life-long *karate* training. He has beautiful *katas*, finely-honed techniques, and devastating power.

This interview took place in Mirakian's tranquil Watertown *dojo* after his regular three-hour Saturday evening workout.

You arrived in Okinawa in the early 1950's. How would you characterize Okinawan *karate* in that era?

This was "The Golden Age" of Okinawan *karate*. It was during this time that *karate* training first became available to Westerners, which caused a great impetus in the propagation of Okinawan *karate* to the Western world. During these years, Okinawan *karate* was taught in a traditional way as an art form of self-defense. The *karate* masters upheld the old standards and placed great emphasis on *dojo kun* (etiquette). They took pride in patiently teaching their national art to Westerners as well as Okinawans. *Karate* was presented in a dignified, strict manner. To a Westerner it appeared fascinating, challenging, and mysterious.

Do you think something has been lost as *karate* has been modernized?

Yes. Unfortunately much of the essence and spirit of traditional *karate* has been lost. Since the advent of *karate* championships, many practitioners are competing to win at any cost. This approach is not the traditional aim of Okinawan *Goju-ryu Karate-do*.

Original Shuri Castle built in 1188 and expanded in 1350 and 1422 in Shuri, Okinawa. The king of Okinawa and his family resided in the Shuri Castle which was considered one of the national treasures of Okinawa. Very often karate demonstrations were held in front of the Shuri Castle. This castle was huge and measured 1350 feet from east to west and 900 feet from north to south. This castle was destroyed during the Second World War in 1945.

Why Okinawa? How could an island so small and remote have produced the world's best known martial art?

That's a very interesting question. Okinawa had the perfect chemistry to develop the art of *karate*. The Okinawans had the time to devote to the martial arts. Theirs was a quiet and simple agrarian and fishing society, without distractions. Because Okinawa was alternatively dominated by China and Japan, Okinawans were forced to develop unarmed martial-art techniques to defend themselves against larger, stronger, armed foes. Also, they were forced to look inward, and develop an inner strength that characterizes the art. Okinawans are a civilized and peace-loving people, and these traits are reflected in the unique moral foundation of their art.

How long has *karate* been practiced in Okinawa?

For well over a thousand years. Certainly Chinese martial arts were practiced in Okinawa during the Tang Dynasty, from 618 to 906 AD. By the fourteenth century, oral traditions say that a *karate*-like art was being practiced there.

When you first arrived in Okinawa, how did you find a *karate* school?

Accidentally. A friend and I hired a taxi and asked the driver to take us to a *karate* school. He took us to a *judo dojo*. One of the students there directed the taxi driver to take us to the district of Nakanomachi. When we arrived, the school turned out to be the *Shoreikan Goju-ryu Karate-dojo* of Grandmaster **Seikichi Toguchi**.

What was Grandmaster Toguchi's school like in those days?

The training at Grandmaster Toguchi's school was intensive. We trained six days a week. The only day off was Monday. The training started at six o'clock in the evening and lasted until ten-thirty at night. The calisthenics alone lasted an hour and a half. Hard demanding calisthenics, performed in 85 to 100 degree heat and extremely high humidity. We would do all sorts of stretching, loosing-up exercises, and strength training. The assistants to *Sensei* **Toguchi** were very demanding. They expected 100 per cent effort from us.

There were about forty students in the *dojo*. The school was perhaps twenty-five feet wide and forty-five feet long, and it had a patio where we could work out. The *makiwara* (striking posts) were all outside. All the workouts were supervised by *Sensei* **Toguchi**. He was the only Black Belt in the *dojo*, but he was assisted by some of his advanced brown-belt students. They led the calisthenics and the basic drills.

I take it that a brown belt in those days was the equivalent of a higher rank today?

Yes. At the time, in the 1950's, brown belt was a highly respected rank. Some of the Okinawan brown belts were powerful and very skilled. I would say that many of the brown belts that I saw then would have to be considered the equivalent of fourth- or fifth-degree Black Belts today.

In what physical condition were the Okinawan students?

Most of the Okinawans, even the beginners, were in excellent physical shape. They didn't begin *karate* training in order to lose weight or to get in shape; they were physically fit to begin with.

What was the training for beginners at Grandmaster Toguchi's *dojo*?

The beginners were trained at a very slow pace. Black footprints extending fifteen or twenty feet were painted on the *dojo* floor. There were two sets, one for Okinawans, and one for the larger American servicemen. For three or four months, we trained by walking on the footprints back and forth, trying to learn *sanchin* stepping. We also learned basic techniques, like punching, blocking, kicking, and striking. The training was very repetitious. The *kata* we practiced were basic, *Gekisai ichi* and *Gekisai ni*. We practiced these for a long time. The pace was slow, but also physically intense. No idle talk was allowed, no socializing, no taking it easy.

Did the seniors 'lean' on the junior students and push them around, as one often sees in *dojo* outside Okinawa today?

That wasn't allowed. Advanced students weren't allowed to take advantage of a lesser student. They were there to help the junior students in a strict but friendly environment. There was a feeling of mutual respect and brotherhood in the *dojo*. In later years I noticed that this was part of Okinawan culture. They take great pride in the teaching of *karate*. *Karate* is their national art and heritage, their cultural contribution to the world. They take pride in presenting it in a civilized and dignified manner. There was no reason or excuse for needless injuries, brutality, or reckless wild actions.

What kind of *kumite* did you practice?

We practiced prearranged sparring (*yakusoku kumite*). We practiced one, three, and five-step sparring as well as *kata bunkai* (application) *kumite*. There was no free-fighting. When you practiced with the advanced Okinawans, you had to remain alert, because they were fast, strong, and skilled; they also had control. The

Goju Ryu Karate

One of the last known photographs of Grandmaster Chojun Miyagi taken in Okinawa circa 1950 with some of his karate students, seated in the center. Third from the left standing, Mr. Eiichi Miyazato; fourth from the left standing, Mr. Meitoku Yagi; fifth from the left standing, Mr. Seikichi Toguchi; sixth from the left standing, Mr. Eiko Miyazato.

attitude was very serious. The students practiced *kumite* as if their lives depended on it, as if a mistake could be fatal.

Was *makiwara* training part of the regular workout?

It was optional, but most students did a lot of it. It was common for Okinawans to have a *makiwara* in their back yards. The *makiwara* were very abrasive. The hitting surface was made of rice straw ropes, and it frequently would cut the knuckles.

One of the most advanced students of Grandmaster **Toguchi** was an Okinawan names **Sakai**. He wasn't large, but he was extremely powerful. He used to work out seven days a week. He would get up at six o'clock every morning and punch the *makiwara* hundreds of times. One day he cut his knuckles and bled so profusely during practice that he fainted. His wife had to come and throw a bucket of cold water over his head to revive him. He developed thick callouses on his hands, and had devastating punches and strikes.

Were you given tests for promotions?

Yes. From time to time we were asked to perform *kata* and *kumite* in front of *Sensei* **Toguchi**. No compliments were ever given. If we didn't meet his high standards, we would simply fail the test. I remember once a serviceman didn't get promoted, and asked him what part of his *kata* was wrong. *Sensei* **Toguchi** said to him in a very abrupt manner: "Everything was wrong".

Was there a moral code you were supposed to abide by?

Yes. *Sensei* **Toguchi** was very strict in not allowing his students to misuse the art. There was an American student there who got into a fight with three other servicemen in a bar. He beat them up badly. Later he bragged to one of the Okinawan brown-belt students that the techniques of *Goju-ryu Karate* were very effective in actual combat. When *Sensei* **Toguchi** heard of the incident he became very upset. The serviceman was told to never show up in the *dojo* again. Also there were a couple of skillful Okinawan *karate* students who fought with some Okinawans in the villages and were expelled by *Sensei* **Toguchi** for misusing the art of *karate*.

Did *Sensei* Toguchi ever perform *kata* for his students?

Yes. On the eight day of every month, *Sensei* **Toguchi** would have a ritual commemoration in memory of the founder of *Goju-ryu Karate*, Grandmaster **Chojun Miyagi**, who passed away on October 8, 1953. He would have all of us, from white belt to brown belt get up on the floor one by one and go through one *kata*. At the end, he would get up and demonstrate an advanced *kata*. We were amazed at the beauty of his movements, the precision, power, fluidity, and control.

Memorial Chojun Miyagi 1955.

Are any of your fellow students at Grandmaster Toguchi's *dojo* still practicing *karate*?

Yes. Today several masters in their own right. *Sensei* **Masanobu Shinjo** and *Sensei* **Zenshu Toyama** were both green belts at that time. Today both are highly ranked, highly respected masters. And *Sensei* **Katsuyoshi Kanei**, president of the *Jinbukan Goju-ryu Karate-do* Association, was also a student here. He is a very strong *Goju-ryu Karate* and *kobudo* (traditional weaponry) master and a fine gentleman.

Who was your second *karate* master?

Sensei **Ryuritsu Arakaki**. We met for the first time in *Sensei* Toguchi's *dojo*. He was an architect, a man in his mid-forties. He was a seventh degree Black Belt who had studied with **Chojun Miyagi** and **Seiko Higa**. I was fortunate that he befriended me, and treated me as a protégé. I would visit his house on Sundays and eat dinner with his family. It was a great privilege to be invited into an Okinawan home. We would talk about the history of Okinawan *karate*, **Chojun Miyagi** and his training in China, and the old masters. He took me around to various *dojo* and introduced me to many great masters I would never have had the opportunity to meet on my own. One day he took me aside and said: "I can see that you have a great passion and desire to train in *Goju-ryu Karate*. You should train with the foremost authority on *Goju-ryu* in Okinawa, Grandmaster **Meitoku Yagi**, the top, senior student of **Chojun Miyagi**". I was reluctant to do this as it was at least an hour's bus ride from my base to the **Yagi** *dojo*. But *Sensei* **Arakaki** was insistent. He said: "You must train under him."

How were you introduced to Grandmaster Meitoku Yagi?

Sensei **Arakaki** approached Grandmaster **Yagi** and recommended me to him. We visited him on a Sunday afternoon. I remember that day vividly. When we arrived, Grandmaster **Yagi** was in his *dojo* drilling holes in the wooden name tags which he hung on the rank-tag rack. His *dojo* was next to his house, with a small fenced patio for outdoor workouts. He offered us tea. My first impression was that he was a very serene master. I said to myself immediately, "Here is a man of great physical, mental, and spiritual powers." I sensed that I had met a great master.

After asking me questions for an hour, with *Sensei* **Arakaki** interpreting, Grandmaster **Meitoku Yagi** asked me to demonstrate a *kata*. When I finished, Grandmaster **Yagi** turned to *Sensei* **Arakaki** and said that I had a build like the great Chinese Kempo masters, like a spider. At that time I had a very sinewy body and weighed about 150lbs. My height was 5ft 11 inches. He said: "I will accept Mr. **Mirakian** as a student, and all I expect in return is a few words of gratitude." I was immensely happy. It was a great honor to have been accepted by

Grandmaster **Yagi**, because Grandmaster **Meitoku Yagi** was highly respected among the inner *karate* circles in Okinawa.

Did Grandmaster Meitoku Yagi have other Western students at his *Meibukan dojo*?

No. I was the only one, the first Western student that he taught. There were about fifteen or twenty Okinawans. As soon as I started training in his *dojo*, I could sense that the *karate* techniques and *kata* were practiced in a very natural way. Each student did *kata* according to his own physique and abilities. It wasn't as if someone handed you a suit and said "Wear it, even if it doesn't fit you." Although the *karate* students were not allowed to change the basic techniques, there was more flexibility than in other *dojo*. A tall student, for instance, wouldn't be required to go so deep into *kiba-dachi* (horse-riding stance) or *zenkutsu dachi* (forward stance) that he lost mobility.

Master Ryuritsu Arakaki.

What was the training schedule at the *Meibukan dojo*?

Grandmaster **Yagi** held 4-hour *karate* training sessions five days a week, Monday through Friday. Although the formal workout started at 7pm, the students would arrive earlier than that to work out on their own. I would arrive two hours before the workout, stretch, do calisthenics, hit the *makiwara*, and work with traditional Okinawan training equipment.

Grandmaster **Yagi** was the superintendent of the Customs House. He would come home from work in a suit. If you saw him in the street, you would take him for a university professor. He was a man of about 5'8", weighed a solid 180 pounds, with broad shoulders and very powerful hands and arms. He would come home at seven, and without eating supper, put on his *gi*, and the formal training would begin.

What kind of training equipment was used at the *Meibukan dojo*?

There was a *makiwara*, *chishi* (strength stones) of about five to ten pounds, stone jugs for developing a strong grip, free weights, and a heavy punching bag. There was a homemade barbell of perhaps a hundred pounds that had been made from two railroad wheels. These wheels had probably been used years before on the small railroads cars that ran through the sugar cane fields. But in the *honbu* (headquarters) *dojo*, there wasn't an emphasis on lifting heavy weights. My impression was that Grandmaster **Yagi** felt that excessive weight lifting would cause a loss of flexibility and speed. He stressed that punching against the *makiwara* was the best way to develop devastating power.

What was the atmosphere at the *Meibukan dojo*?

A very subtle spirit pervaded the *dojo*. When you stepped inside, it was as if you stepped into another era, another time, as if you were going back to the Shaolin monastery years ago. There was something mystical there, very difficult to express in words. A person had to be attuned to perceive this mood. There was very little speaking allowed. There was no socializing, no idle talk, no ego, no flexing of muscles of physical vanity. That would have been contradictory to the concept of the *dojo*, and was not allowed. The *karate* training consisted of a blending of physical, mental, and spiritual elements harmonized in a very smooth way. There was no harshness. The grandmaster led the class in a strict and disciplined way, but with a friendly attitude. The *karate* students felt very comfortable being taught by Grandmaster **Meitoku Yagi**.

Grandmaster Meitoku Yagi teaching his older son, Meitatsu (center) and an Okinawan student in his dojo in Kume, Naha-city, Okinawa, in the 1950's.

How was the formal workout structured?

The formal training started at 7pm and ran to 11pm. Grandmaster **Yagi** would lead the workout personally, with the assistance of his senior student, *Sensei* **Yushun Tamaki**, one of the finest *karate* instructors I have ever met.

All of the students would line up. There was a complete silence. We would begin by going through all the *Goju-ryu kata* to *Suparinpe*, one after each other. This practice was done very seriously, with tremendous concentration; the mind wasn't wandering, there was no wavering of the eyes. Once the student was training in the *dojo*, he had to be in command of his mind and in complete control of himself. Everybody responded to the commands at once. Everything was a drill in unison. There were no stragglers. We would always end the training with *Sanchin kata* and *Tensho kata*. Sometimes we would begin with *Sanchin* as well.

Would the junior belts step aside for the advanced *kata*?

No. Everyone, even white belts, did all the *kata*. But you must remember that the beginning Okinawan students had some awareness and appreciation of *karate* before they began training, since it was their national art. The beginners knew that just because they were allowed to go through the advanced *kata* didn't mean that they had mastered them. They were only familiarizing themselves with some of the movements. I was told by masters in Okinawa that to begin to perfect a single *kata* would take two to three hours a day for three to five years, and sometimes as long as ten years. The Okinawan students understood this.

How were you taught the *kata* at the *Meibukan dojo*?

Grandmaster **Meitoku Yagi** would usually take me aside and teach me the movements of the *kata* once. While he was performing the *kata* I would follow him. It was a great honor to be taught by the Grandmaster, and it was taken as a sign of respect that you would give absolute concentration, and learn the basic movements on the first try. I watched like a hawk. There's a saying in Okinawa that the master speaks only once.

The *kata* were taught in a systematic and logical way in the *Meibukan dojo*. *Sensei* **Yushun Tamaki** led the *karate* class in the practice of the *kata*, and the students followed him. When we went through the *kata* for the first time each evening no corrections were made. But as we kept

Master Meitoku Yagi and his top student Yushun Tamaki performing kumite.

practicing the *kata* over and over, Grandmaster **Meitoku Yagi** and *Sensei* **Yushun Tamaki** would make corrections to each *karate* student. The *kata* were taught slowly and patiently step by step to the *karate* class. Generally, once a student was shown the *kata*, he was expected to correct the movements himself. When I was learning the *Tensho kata* I had a wrong move for one to two months. Finally after paying closer attention to some of the advanced students practicing the *Tensho kata* during one of the workouts, I noticed the right movement of the hand and corrected it myself. This was a very difficult technique to learn, because it was performed fast. Leaving a person to discover and refine techniques by himself has a great built-in value. A student who has to do this becomes highly observant, one of the most important factors in mastering *karate*. You must remember that there is a Buddhist tradition in Okinawa: To make spiritual progress, you must search for yourself.

Where the students ever asked to perform *kata* in front of the class?

Twice a week or so, Grandmaster **Meitoku Yagi** would have us sit down quietly on the sides of the *dojo*, and one by one we would perform *kata*. The atmosphere in the *dojo* was so calm that you could hear a pin drop. We would get a chance to see the *kata* of every student, their strengths and flaws. We benefited from the relaxed contemplation of each other's *kata*. There was never any praise given.

Anthony Mirakian practicing the Saifa kata in the honbu dojo in Okinawa with Shigetoshi Senaha in the 1950's.

Did Grandmaster Yagi perform *kata* in his *dojo*?

On occasion. They were the finest *kata* I have ever seen in *Goju-ryu Karate*. It was beauty in motion. The perfect balance of hard and soft. He had tremendous power, control, and speed. I remember his *Sanchin* in particular. It didn't have the extreme tension you see in some practitioners. But when he tensed his body, it was impressive and deceptive; like tempered steel covered by velvet.

What followed the *kata* in the workout?

After we finished going through the *kata* we would practice many different types of *kumite* that had been adapted from the breakdown of the *kata*. We would also practice combinations of striking, punching, kicking, blocking, and counter-punching. We would practice many patterns, *jo-chu-ge*, *chu-ge-jo*, *ge-jo-chu*, many different techniques done in a very fast, sequential manner back and forth across the *dojo* floor.

Then we would practice *ippon kumite* (one-attack sparring) at close range, with one arm length between attacker and defender. At this range, given the skill and speed of the students, there was no margin for error. We paid close attention. We had to develop lightning fast reflexes or we would get hit. The emphasis was

A young Anthony Mirakian practicing the Sepai kata in the honbu dojo in Okinawa with Shosei Shiroma in the 1950's.

on watching the pupils of the opponent's eyes. We watched closely enough so we could always see the punch telegraphed by the eyes. This was a form of active meditation, and much better than sitting meditation. The outside world did not exist, we couldn't worry about the past or future. Only the split-second counted, this made the mind very strong, it developed tremendous power of concentration. We practiced against various students, so we constantly had to adjust and readjust according to the makeup of the opponent.

I was a weapons technician in the U.S. Air Force, and every day I had to move 3 to 5 tons of heavy equipment by myself. And then I trained in *karate* 4 to 6 hours per night five nights a week. This schedule made me very strong. But even with my strength and good training I had difficulty in blocking the punches of some of the Okinawan students. In three-step sparring against Mr. **Tamaki**, I was able to block his first punch, and then his second, but on his third punch he had so much momentum and power that most of the time I had to just get out of the way or get hit.

There would be many repetitions of techniques, hundreds of punches, strikes, blocks, kicks. The workouts varied from day to day, but we always did the basics, covering the same techniques again and again and again. There was a heavy emphasis on fundamentals, *kata*, and *Sanchin*.

We practiced *kake-uke* most evenings to develop good stance, strength, and balance. (This is the middle blocking exercise where the student link wrists, a relative of pushing hands done in a *sanchin* stance). This was not practiced as a full strength tug of war, as seen in some other *dojo* today, but done in a softer, systematic, balanced way. I believe this to be one of the best *Goju-ryu Karate* exercises.

I remember many times practicing against Mr. **Tamaki**. When I tried to exert too much strength on the palm of his hand, he would sense that I was rigid and off-balance, and sweep me to the floor. I had apprehension at first, and my mind wasn't as calm as it should have been. Eventually I learned that if I remained calm, without any preconceived ideas, I could sense when he was going to try to sweep me, and just lift my foot up. This taught me a fundamental principle that you have to relax both your body and mind to detect changes in your opponent.

Kake-uke was originally used to pair up highly skilled practitioners for *kumite*. If one student could not move the arm of another student in *kake-uke*, or could not hold his stance, he would not be allowed to engage in *kumite* with that student. The feeling was, if he couldn't handle the other student in *kake-uke*, he would not be able to block his punches either, and could be seriously injured.

Your students practice the arm toughening drill called "koteki-tai". Was that practiced at the *Meibukan honbu dojo*?

No. That has been introduced in the *Meibukan dojo* in the past twenty years. This arm-pounding exercise originated in Taiwan, from Taiwanese *Kempo*. Before that, the students would toughen their arm by practicing forearm strikes on the *makiwara*, by hitting their forearm against the trunks of the banyan tree, and by blocking each other's punches.

How did the workouts end?

Every workout ended with *Sanchin*. Before *Sanchin*, however, we practiced the exercise that I call the flexible horse. Each of us would count one hundred times. Usually there were twenty or more students, so we did at least two thousand flexible horses. It was hot and humid there, especially in the summer, so by the time we finished, we were soaking wet. Sweat would run down our faces, into our eyes, and cover the floor. I wouldn't dare wipe the sweat from my eyes because if I did, all of the Okinawan students would give me dagger-looks as if to say "You are doing something that is improper. Can't you take a little physical punishment? Don't you have the mental fortitude to ignore discomfort?"

After *Zazen* (sitting meditation) and bowing to the master, we would take off our uniforms and go outside to dry off. The China Sea was only a half a mile from the *dojo*, and sometimes there would be a cool breeze. In about ten minutes it would dry up our shorts and we would be able to put on our clothes. Then we would walk three miles to the bus terminal and ride the bus home.

Could you describe the flexible-horse exercise?

Yes. We started in an upright position with the feet twice shoulder wide apart. Both arms were outstretched touching each other in front of the chest with the palms up. Then we dropped into a horse-riding stance (*kiba dachi*) while bringing the palms of both hands to the outside of the knees. Next, we trust up into an upright standing position, bringing the hands to the sides of the upper body in closed fists, while momentarily tensing all the muscles of the body.

Anthony Mirakian practicing the Saifa kata in Okinawa in the honbu dojo with Shigetoshi Senaha in the 1950's.

You are renowned for conducting hard, demanding workouts in your *dojo* lasting many hours. Were the workouts in Okinawa harder when you trained there?

Although the *karate* workouts at my *dojo* are very intense, the training in Okinawa was even more rigorous. They were continuous workouts. There was rarely a break. When *karate* practitioners talk about the training in Okinawa in that era, they always talk about how hard it was physically. They talk about the many hours of daily training, the relentlessness of the workouts, the endless repetition of techniques. But many students never grasped that it wasn't the physical element that was most important. It was the way the training was conducted, it was the mental intensity that counted. When you trained in the *dojo*, nothing else mattered. The emphasis in the *dojo* was in developing tremendous powers of concentration in a relaxed environment. The goal was to develop the mental concentration and physical power to be able to move in and stop an opponent with a single technique, one punch, one kick.

What was Grandmaster Meitoku Yagi's approach to *makiwara* (striking post) training?

Grandmaster **Yagi** felt that *makiwara* training was the best method of developing a devastating punch. The *makiwara* were in the patio of his *dojo*, which was surrounded by a seven foot fence for privacy, so no one could view the workouts from the outside. There were six *makiwara*. How much you hit them was left to your own discretion, but most of us practiced diligently. The *makiwara* were about three feet from the fence. One of the students would tie a stick to the top of the fence and suspend a string with a stone attached to the end of it, like a plumb line. The *makiwara* all had a certain amount of give, a few inches. The student would position the string so the stone hung perhaps three inches behind the *makiwara*. Then we would hit the *makiwara* and try to move the stone. When we were able to move it easily, we would move the string further back. Then we had to put more power to the punches.

Sometimes Grandmaster **Meitoku Yagi** would practice very short punches on the *makiwara*. He would stand with his feet parallel in front of the *makiwara*, and hit it with a punch about one inch. There was one particular *makiwara* that was made of seasoned pine wood, and had little give in it. I punched this *makiwara* on occasion, but had difficulty in bending it. One night I was going to hit it, and couldn't find it. Then I noticed it had been broken off cleanly at the base. I asked Mr. **Yushun Tamaki**, Grandmaster Meitoku Yagi's top student, what had happened. He said that *Dai Sensei* had come out the evening before just as it was getting dark. He positioned himself in front of that *makiwara*, made a loud sound like "unh!", and broke the *makiwara* with a blow of just one inch. Still I wonder all these years later what sort of an awesome punch that must have been to break off the *makiwara* from that very short distance. When Grandmaster Yagi's son, *Sensei* **Meitetsu Yagi** visited my *dojo* in Watertown, Massachusetts several years ago, he said that his father had developed 100% of internal power over his many years of training.

Is it necessary to develop calloused hands in *makiwara* training? Some old pictures of Grandmaster Chojun Miyagi, for instance, show him to have uncalloused knuckles.

You can also practice on the *makiwara* and not develop calluses. The tops of most *makiwara* in Okinawa were wrapped for eight to ten inches with rice straw rope, which would cut into the skin of the knuckles, leading to heavy calluses. But there are other ways to construct a *makiwara*. Sometimes they would cover the top with a blanket, leather, or piece of rubber, something that would not cut into the knuckles. It is possible to have normal-looking hands and still develop a powerful *karate* punch.

Anthony Mirakian shown outside his dojo with Sensei Meitetsu Yagi in Watertown, Mass. Anthony Mirakian's dojo is the North American Headquarters of Okinawan Meibukan Goju-ryu Karate-do.

Many people misunderstand *makiwara* training. They mistakenly believe that the goal is battering the hands and developing huge calluses. But the real emphasis is on strengthening the hand and wrist, so in case of having to hit someone, the fist will not buckle. Also, *makiwara* training encourages good stance. If your stance is weak, your punching techniques will also be weak. The *makiwara* exposes this. We did not hit the *makiwara* an equal number of times with each hand. I was told that if you are right handed, you should hit the *makiwara* three times as often with the left hand, and vice-versa for left handers. For example, being right-handed, if I hit the *makiwara* 500 times with the right fist, I would strike the *makiwara* 1500 times with the left fist. This way a student develops ambidextrous power.

Group of karate students in Master Meitoku Yagi's dojo on Okinawa in the 1950's. Front row, left to right: Mr. Anthony Mirakian, Mr. Tamaki, Master Meitoku Yagi, Mr. Yushun Tamaki and Mr. Shosei Shiroma. Standing in the back third from left is Mr. Meitatsu Yagi and next to him is Mr. Shigetoshi Senaha.

In the practice of *kata*, was there much discussion of the meaning of particular moves and their applications?

There was very little explanation of the meaning of the *kata*. And there was no discussion of terminology. There was very little talking at all. The emphasis in the training was in doing rather than discussing. Some of the simple applications of the *kata* were obvious to us. Sometimes Grandmaster **Meitoku Yagi** would ask Mr. **Yushun Tamaki** to attack him, and demonstrate an application. But many times, the applications were left to the student's imagination and inquisitiveness. This is a logical approach, which forces students to think. Some of the techniques in the *kata* are obvious: a strike here, a block there, a counter there. However, many of the applications are very difficult to figure out and are sometimes the opposite of what a *karateka* thinks. There can also be many applications from a single technique. I was told that masters in China would intentionally keep the advanced applications of their techniques secret, so other masters from other styles would not learn their hidden fighting techniques. Grandmaster **Yagi** was once asked if in *Goju-ryu Karate* there are any "*Gokui*" or "*Hidden*" as in other martial arts. "*Gokui*" are the deep innermost secrets that can be understood only by those who are training for a long time. "*Hidden*", are those secrets passed down and taught only to special students. The Grandmaster replied that there were no formal "*Gokui*" or "*Hidden*" in *Goju-ryu Karate*, but that every *kata* had "*Nanjiru Gokuden*", or secrets learned by yourself. These could only be understood by trial and effort. He said that the effort was more important than anything else. The long repeated efforts are the secrets. You learn by yourself, under your teacher's tutelage, little by little, through long repetitive training and hardship. He also pointed out that a beginner and an advanced student, when seeing the same technique or application, will understand completely different things.

My feeling is that a student with only a few years training should not worry about applications, but should instead work on basics. For someone who has been studying longer, say eight or ten years, it is healthy to ponder the meaning of the *kata* techniques. But one shouldn't lose any sleep over it. In an actual fighting situation, it is not the conscious applications that count, but the spontaneous subconscious reflex reactions that count.

What do you mean by that?

Karate is not a purely physical art. It has physical, mental, and spiritual aspects. The philosophy of Okinawan *karate*, and *Goju-ryu* in particular is that in training the body, the practitioner is also sub-consciously training richness that exists in true *karate*. As the body trains naturally, so does the mind.

For a beginner, all the movements are mechanical, and have to be done consciously, by repetition. The conscious and subconscious mind clash with each other. The student has to learn by highly repetitive efforts. There are no short cuts. The student has to think about keeping the footwork right, the body straight, the shoulders down, the eyes looking forward, and the breathing regular. After two or three years of this training, the movements become less mechanical. After ten or fifteen years, the movements become effortless and automatic. In the case of an attack, the practitioner will react spontaneously. The subconscious mind will take over, and the movements will be lightning fast. If the actions of the practitioner

A young Anthony Mirakian practicing the Sepai kata in the honbu dojo in Okinawa with Shosei Shiroma in the 1950's.

are conscious, they will be too slow, to the point of being mechanical. In the advanced practitioner, there is no differentiation between blocking and striking, or offence and defense. It is all included in one movement. This is the by-product of years of training the mind as the body is conditioned.

Grandmaster Meitoku Yagi (far left) in his dojo on Okinawa with one of his daughters, Chikako (center) and older son, Meitatsu (far right) in the 1950's.

What was Grandmaster Yagi like when he was in the *dojo*? Was he approachable?

I would say that he had a certain amount of approachability, but I would not approach him often, out of respect. But if I asked a question, he would often stop and call his senior student, Mr. **Yushun Tamaki**, and explain the particular movement. But sometimes he would not explain at all. Everybody respected him. There was a great esprit de corps, and there was also a sense of good, harmonious human relations. The *dojo* was not run in a high-handed manner. In some other *dojo*, I noticed, the masters kept aloof from the students and would get highly annoyed if someone asked about an application from a particular *kata*.

Was free-fighting practiced at Grandmaster Meitoku Yagi's dojo?

No. Grandmaster **Meitoku Yagi** was, and still is, very much opposed to free-fighting. There has never been free-fighting in traditional Okinawan *Goju-ryu Karate-do*. There have been some experiments, but they have been dropped. **Chojun Miyagi** himself tried the idea of freestyle sparring with protective equipment more than a half century ago. But he cast the idea aside because he felt no equipment could cover all the vital areas.

Grandmaster **Meitoku Yagi** felt that the emphasis in *Goju-ryu Karate* should be *karate-do*, *karate* as a way of life. He said that there was a spirit of *budo* in *karate* that is different from the spirit of sports.

Grandmaster **Yagi** felt that free-fighting takes the true essence away from *karate-do*. In free-fighting, *karate* becomes a sport, and true *karate-do* is not a sport.

That is why free-fighting was taboo. It detracts from *karate-do*, brings bad feelings into the *dojo*, and injuries to the students. We practiced very spirited pre-arranged *kumite* in Grandmaster Yagi's *dojo*, but not free-fighting.

Don't you think it is necessary to engage in free-fighting to achieve good fighting skills in the street?

No. Let's say a person has been practicing *karate-do* very diligently for five or ten years. After so much practice, a student should have developed good strong techniques and fast reflexes, and should be able to defend himself against any unprovoked attack.

Free fighting can hinder the development of good *karate* techniques, especially in Okinawan *Goju-ryu* where the emphasis is on ending a fight with a single devastating technique. Fighting in a ring and fighting in the street are altogether different situations. Many techniques are not allowed in free-fighting. Because of this, free-fighting can actually limit a practitioner.

Okinawan *karate* is meant to be a lifetime practice. Grandmaster **Meitoku Yagi** still practices every day at age 78. A student who regularly engages in free-fighting is unlikely to be able to practice *karate* for more than a few years. I don't allow free-fighting in my *dojo*.

Are any of your fellow students at Grandmaster Yagi's school still practicing today?

Yes. Several have become distinguished masters. The most prominent student in Grandmaster Yagi's *dojo* was **Yushun Tamaki**. Today he is a ninth degree Black Belt master. He has retired from the *dojo*, but still practices daily. He is the true embodiment of what a *karate* master should be, highly skillful and tremendously powerful, but also polite, humble, unassuming, and hard working. His *kata* and technical skills are exceptional.

Both of Grandmaster Yagi's sons were students at the *dojo* when I was there. The younger son, **Meitetsu Yagi**, was about nine or ten years of age in those days, but already a highly spirited student. He is an eight-degree Black Belt master today, a strong, skilled, and energetic *karateka*. He has a *dojo* in the village of Nagata. He came to teach in my school in Watertown, Massachusetts several

Anthony Mirakian visits Meibukan Goju-ryu Karate Master Yushun Tamaki, 9th Degree (Hanshi), the top student of Grandmaster Meitoku Yagi (shown in the centre in Naha, Okinawa, in 1985 with Meibukan Goju-ryu Karate Master Meitatsu Yagi (right).

years ago. My students became familiar with his favorite English word, "Endure!", which he would repeat throughout his demanding workouts.

The older son, **Meitatsu Yagi**, was in his early teens when I first trained with him. He was slender, and his movements were fluid and strong. Today he is a ninth-degree Black Belt master and was inaugurated as the Chairman of the All-Okinawan *Goju-ryu Karate-do* Association on June 25, 1989. He is a powerful master, with beautiful *kata*. He also came to teach at my *dojo* several years ago.

Sensei **Meitatsu Yagi** is a very strict and powerful *karate* master. In addition to being the chief instructor at the *Meibukan Honbu* (Headquarters) *dojo* in Kume, Naha-City, Okinawa, he is also the President of the Okinawan *Meibukan Goju-ryu Karate-do* Association. *Sensei* **Meitetsu Yagi** is the Vice-President and Grandmaster **Meitoku Yagi** is the Chairman of the Association.

Jinbukan Goju-ryu Karate Master Katsuyoshi Kanei (left), President of the Jinbukan Goju-ryu Karate-do Association, shown with Anthony Mirakian at Grandmaster Meitoku Yagi's 73rd Birthday celebration on February 10, 1985 in Naha-city, Okinawa.

One reads a lot of conflicting information about the practice of *Sanchin*. No other *kata* seems to cause as much confusion. How was *Sanchin* presented to you in Okinawa?

Sanchin is the *kihon kata*, the basic *kata*, of Okinawan *Goju-ryu*. It has many purposes. One of them is to train the practitioner in bringing forth strength. According to Chinese masters, the human psychic centre dwells in the *Dan Tien*, one and a half inches below the navel. This is referred to many Chinese Taoist texts as the spiritual cauldron. *Sanchin* emphasises strengthening of the *Dan Tien*. The *karateka* who practices *Sanchin* for many years will develop a strong physique and tremendous power, through enhanced flow of *Chi*, the immaterial substance of life and energy. *Sanchin* will calm a student, develop composure, and enhance self-control. It also has many physical benefits, such as controlled breathing and the ability to withstand an opponent's attack. It is very important in the development of fighting skills. If a person pants and loses control of the breath, he will lose control of his techniques and ultimately of himself. Another purpose of *Sanchin* practice is to harden the entire body through dynamic tension breathing.

I remember a demonstration in Okinawa over thirty-two years ago by a master who had an extremely powerful *Sanchin*. His breathing sounded like the roar of a lion, and he exuded tremendous vitality and power. I asked an Okinawan friend who he was. It turned out that he was a master who only practiced *Sanchin*, no other *kata*. He was in his late fifties and had been practicing *Sanchin* eight times in the morning and eight times at night for 35 years.

In my opinion, *Sanchin* is of the utmost importance for a *karateka* trying to master *Goju-ryu Karate*. If a person neglects *Sanchin*, it will affect his entire *Goju-ryu Karate* training. The teachings of *Goju-ryu* are founded on the *Sanchin* principles of the proper inhaling and exhaling of the breath and the expansion and contraction of the lower abdomen.

At Grandmaster Kanryo Higaonna's *dojo* (Editors note: **Kanryo Higaonna** was the teacher of **Chojun Miyagi**, the founder of *Goju-ryu*), the students performed nothing but *Sanchin* and basic techniques for the first three to four years of training.

Sanchin is normally practiced with three steps forward and three steps back, followed by one step forward and one back. At Grandmaster Kanryo Higaonna's *dojo*, it was sometimes performed with 15, 20, or 25 steps forward and the same back. This *karate* training based on *Sanchin* was very demanding.

Do you think a practitioner can damage his or her health through improper practice of *Sanchin*?

Yes. If a student doesn't practice *Sanchin* properly, he could hurt himself. A practitioner must have good sound instruction.

You saw many Grandmasters perform and teach *Sanchin*. Have you ever seen it performed silently, with no audible breathing?

No, never. The level of breathing sound varied from school to school, but I've never known it to be performed silently.

Anthony Mirakian (centre) delivers congratulatory speech at Grandmaster Meitoku Yagi's 73rd Birthday Celebration on February 10, 1985, in Naha City, Okinawa.

Was there more than one version of *Sanchin* practiced at Grandmaster Yagi's *dojo*?

Yes, there were two versions of *Sanchin*. Originally, the *Sanchin* that Grandmaster **Kanryo Higaonna** brought back from Fukien province in China was done open-handed. On various occasions, Grandmaster **Meitoku Yagi** would have us perform this version. But the *Sanchin* we practiced most was the closed-hand version Grandmaster **Yagi** learned from Grandmaster **Chojun Miyagi**.

Was the testing of *Sanchin* similar at the respective *dojo* of Grandmasters Seikichi Toguchi and Meitoku Yagi?

No. *Sanchin* testing at Grandmaster Toguchi's *dojo* was harder and more dynamic. There was a lot of pounding on the shoulders to keep them down. Also the testing of the legs was more intense. On the other hand, the testing at Grandmaster Yagi's *dojo* was slightly softer and more natural. There was more emphasis on posture and the proper positioning of the arm relative to the body. The hitting of the shoulders and legs was a little lighter. Great emphasis was placed on proper breath control as well as tensing of the whole body.

Anthony Mirakian visits the home of the famous Chinese Hung Master, Dr. Kwan Tak Hing in Hong Kong in the 1950's.

From your description, there seems to have been a powerful, unspoken etiquette in these Okinawan *dojo*. Was this discussed by your masters?

Yes. My second *Goju-ryu Karate* master, **Ryuritsu Arakaki** told me that if we take the morality, the ethics, and the meditative aspects out of *karate*, then we're left with only animal skills. In *karate*, he said, we learn to fight like lions, tigers, monkeys, cranes, bears, dragons, and the other animals from which we have adopted our fighting techniques. What balances this knowledge is the moral training imparted with the fighting skills. If you take the morality away from *karate* training, then you're left with something dangerously close to brutality. This is why *dojo kun* (*dojo* etiquette) is so important. No unseemly behavior, no rudeness, no harshness, no brutality was allowed in any of the Okinawan *dojo* I visited.

Grandmaster Kanryo Higaonna.

The true philosophical concept of Okinawan *Goju-ryu Karate* is to seek the way of virtue. In *karate*, through training the body and mind, we strive to cultivate the ideal human nature of physical, mental and spiritual unity. The Okinawan masters felt that students should strive to be virtuous, and pursue the ultimate goal, which is to win over any situation with a superior mental attitude, not with fighting skills alone.

Grandmaster **Kanryo Higaonna** was the leading Confucian scholar on Okinawa. In the Confucian Analects, there is tremendous emphasis on filial piety. Grandmaster **Kanryo Higaonna** stressed that his students should have respect for themselves, their fellow students, families, and life in general. *Dojo kun* reflects this aspect of *karate* training.

You mentioned that the atmosphere in Grandmaster Meitoku Yagi's *dojo* was peaceful and relaxed. This sounds quite different from many modern *karate* schools, where the training is held in a stressful, almost militaristic environment.

Yes. We trained with a very relaxed but alert state of mind. The master conducted the training with a soft, subtle hand. There was no militaristic atmosphere, no rudeness, no harsh commands. You were expected to train with the attitude of a hawk that was ready to pounce on its prey, with a heightened concentration stemming from a relaxed state of mind.

The most important aspect in *karate* training is the mental attitude of the student. If the student entertains fear, apprehension, rancor, he is likely to become stiff and rigid and slow in his movements. Nervousness and a disturbed emotional state will cloud judgement and perception of an opponent. The training at the *Meibukan dojo* cultivated a calm, tranquil, alert state of mind.

There is a story about **Yatsusune Azato**, the famous *Shuri-te* master who lived in Okinawa in the late nineteenth and early twentieth centuries. Some say his skills in *karate* and swordsmanship were unsurpassed. He once fought a duel against the most famous swordsman in the Ryukyu Islands, a tremendously powerful man named **Yorin Kanna**. He chose to fight unarmed, even though **Kanna** was armed with a long sword. **Azato** surprised **Kanna** by parrying his initial attack with a turn of the hand, and then with a lightning fast *karate* technique drove **Kanna** to his knees and ended the duel without killing him. He later told his students that **Kanna** was a swordsman of great skill who, because of his fearsome reputation, was able to terrify his opponents at the very beginning of duals, and go immediately for the kill. **Azato** explained to his students that if a practitioner refuses to be terrified and remains calm, victory can be achieved. It is not easy to remain calm and unperturbed in stressful situations. To develop a calm, undisturbed mind requires many years of training.

The famous Chinese Hung Master, Dr. Kwan Tak Hing demonstrates a movement. Photo taken in Hong Kong in the 1950's.

Did you have a change to view non-Okinawan martial arts during your years in Okinawa.

Yes. I traveled extensively in Japan, Taiwan, Korea, and Hong Kong. I have an avid interest in the history of the martial arts. I visited many martial arts schools, observed a variety of styles, and met prominent masters. I still keep in touch with many of them today. For instance, I met the eminent *Hung* Master and famous Chinese actor Dr. **Kwan Tak Hing** in Hong Kong in 1958. I still keep in touch with him today and value his friendship greatly. He visited and demonstrated his *Hung* style of Chinese martial arts in my *dojo*. His demonstration was so impressive that my students still recall his outstanding techniques and forms. He demonstrated all of the Shaolin Monastery animal movements.

Detractors of Okinawan *karate* maintain that Okinawa was a cultural backwater and that it was the Japanese who breathed life into Okinawan *karate*. Harry Cook wrote in 'Fighting Arts' (no. 47, page 64): "Nineteenth century *karate* was not of a particularly high standard...the Japanese added new techniques, organized and rationalized the

Appendices

The late Goju-ryu karate Grandmaster Seiko Higa (far left) performs a kumite from the Kururunfa kata with one of his students in the city of Itoman, southern Okinawa.

Two of Grandmaster Seiko Higa's students perform kumite.

structure of the art and basically revitalized what had been an moribund provincial peasant art."

How would you respond to this?

I would say that this is not true. These claims are based on a limited knowledge of Okinawan *karate*. There is merit in what the Japanese and other outsiders have done for Okinawan *karate*. They have helped make *karate* popular, and it is now practiced all over the world. There have been some external changes in Okinawan *karate* attributable to outside influences. But the essence of Okinawan *karate* has not been changed. It was and is extremely rich and powerful.

Karate is a pure Okinawan traditional art. It is part of the Okinawan culture. Throughout the world, Japan is called the "home of *karate*." But in Japan Okinawa is called the 'home of *karate*."

Mirakian's students visiting Okinawa standing left to right, front row, Paul Zarzour, Sandan; Master Anthony Mirakian, Master Shigetoshi Senaha Kudan; Sensei Hidenobu Tamaki, Vice-President of Master Senaha's dojo, Godan; Sensei Kinjo, Instructor of the Itoman Meibukan dojo, Godan; second row: Joseph Flynn, Sandan; extreme right, Mark Allio, Nidan; third row: Alexander Stewart, Nidan; and Frank Cohen, Gokyu, August 18, 1990.

In Okinawa, *karate* has been practiced for over a thousand years. Outside of Okinawa, *karate* has been practiced since 1923. Now where do you think the vast store of knowledge would be? The Okinawans are true masters of the art, with a deep knowledge and repertoire. Okinawans are humble, peace-loving people. Like the Chinese, they refrain from ostentatious display, wild claims, and ego trips. They do not brag about their knowledge or skills. These traits are assets in most cases. But they can also be liabilities, in that the Okinawan *karate* masters often don't bother to refute the excessive claims of others. There are many *karate* masters making great claims for themselves who have far less skill than the great Okinawan *karate* masters such as **Juhatsu Kiyoda**, **Seiko Higa**, **Meitoku Yagi**, and **Shinken Taira**, who were not interested in promoting themselves.

As far for those who would say that nineteenth century Okinawan martial arts were not of a particularly high standard, this is based on hearsay, from the reports of travelers and old photographs. Did these people ever stand in front of **Ankoh Itosu**, **Kanryo Higaonna**, or **Yatsusune Azato** in combat? Nineteenth century Okinawan *karate* masters were extremely powerful. Their skills were highly sophisticated and deadly.

But until 1902, the art was taught in complete secrecy, and it was taught only to the select few. Outsiders traveling to Okinawa obviously wouldn't be shown these secret arts. And you can't judge the skills of masters by photographs.

The only way to find out about the history of Okinawan *karate-do* is by going to Okinawa and studying with the masters. The history of Okinawan *karate-do* is not in books. I was fortunate to be in Okinawa in the golden era of *karate*, when *karate* was slowly being presented to the outside world. I lived there in an era when Okinawan *karate* masters were beginning to selectively teach their unique art of *karate-do*.

Many outsiders went to Okinawa to study *karate*. But many of them studied Okinawa *karate* for a relatively brief period, sometimes as little as a few months. They might have learned a small part of the art, and then gone back home. Many of them, because of their limited knowledge, eventually came to a stumbling block and could progress no further. This does not mean that the art is not sophisticated, but that many practitioners have incomplete and limited knowledge of it.

You met many great Okinawan *karate* masters. How do these masters compare to modern *karate* practitioners?

There is no comparison whatsoever. These great Okinawan *karate* masters are in a class by themselves because they trained intensively their entire lives, day in day out, year after year. They were highly motivated to perfect and master their art. For modern practitioners, there are many distractions, and less time is spent training.

According to the masters you studied with in Okinawa, under what circumstances should *karate* be used?

They taught that a *karateka* should use his *karate* fighting skills only when there is no alternative whatsoever. Grandmaster **Meitoku Yagi** said that in Japan if someone spit in the face of a *Samurai*, the *Samurai* would bring forth his "*Budo*" (martial arts spirit) and cut the person's head off with his *katana* (sword). But in Okinawan *Budo*, he said, there is a saying that "if someone spits in your face, just wipe it off. That's all."

One must use *karate*, he said, only when one's life is in peril. This is a moral principle of *karate* that is emphasized in Okinawa. The philosophy at the *Meibukan dojo* was to avoid any situation which could lead to a physical confrontation.

By employing a superior mental attitude a *karate* practitioner can find many ways of defusing a confrontation before it becomes a fighting situation.

Once during the late 1930's, Mr. **Meitoku Yagi** was in a tea house with his friend Mr. **Ryuritsu Arakaki**. Already at that time Mr. **Yagi** had a reputation as a prominent *karate* practitioner. An Okinawan ruffian happened to be there and decided to challenge Mr. **Yagi** to fight. He dropped into a low stance in front of Mr. **Yagi** and shouted: "I am going to fight you." Mr. **Yagi** looked him up and down, and in a very calm, posed manner said: "With that stance?" The ruffian suddenly lost all his confidence, and fled the tea house.

Kanryo Higaonna with his granddaughter.

What philosophical and ethical concepts were passed down to Okinawan *karate* practitioners?

The great Okinawan *Naha-te* Grandmaster, **Kanryo Higaonna** left an important philosophical saying for future generations: "Those who train in the great Okinawan art of *karate* should help others. Never seek trouble and refrain from arguments and senseless fights."

The founder of *Goju-ryu Karate*, Grandmaster **Chojun Miyagi** taught his students the ethical philosophy of avoiding any serious incidents or confrontations that could lead to a fight. Also he said ; "Do not hit anybody and do not let anybody hit you."

The *karateka* should strive to have a very calm and unperturbed nature, and avoid situations where it might be necessary to resort to physical confrontation. The greatest form of self-defense is to avoid situations where self-defense will be necessary. Discretion is the better part of valour.

Could you explain the meaning of the practice of *karate-do*?

Traditionally on Okinawa, *Goju-ryu Karate* is taught as *karate-do*, as a "way of life." *Do* is the Japanese pronunciation of the Chinese ideograph Tao (pronounced dow). Tao, or the "way," is the dominant idea of all Chinese philosophy, the foundation of the ancient Chinese world-concept. All things are dissoluble interrelated, and influenced by each other. In *karate-do*, the training will influence the practitioner, and the practitioner will influence the training. The balance between the *karateka* and his art is influenced by the manner and presentation of the training. *Karate-do* seeks, therefore, to attain that most harmonious joining so the *karateka* will follow the true philosophical concept of *karate* as a way of life.

The practice of *karate-do* is training with the awareness of *Jingi* (humanity, morality, and an ethical code of conduct). It is very dangerous to teach *karate* with-

Appendices

Group picture taken in Grandmaster Meitoku Yagi's dojo in Okinawa in the 1950's. Front row, left to right: Shosei Shiroma and Meitatsu Yagi. Standing in the back, left to right: Anthony Mirakian, third from left, Yushun Tamaki; in the center in black gi, Grandmaster Shinken Taira; Grandmaster Meitoku Yagi, and Mr. Tamaki.

out teaching the *Do* (the way). *Do* is the true philosophical concept of *karate*, as it teaches the importance of moderation.

There is a saying in Okinawa that "If the heart is right, then the hand will be right." The *karate* masters of Okinawa emphasize setting the heart of the student right from the beginning. In the traditional long, slow, patient approach, the true essence of *karate* is not distorted.

Did you study *kobudo* (traditional weaponry) under the eminent Grandmaster Shinken Taira?

Yes. Grandmaster **Meitoku Yagi** invited his good friend Grandmaster **Shinken Taira** to his *dojo* to instruct the students in *Kobudo*. He was a famous *kobudo* master, a man of very high reputation. He was in his sixties when I studied with him, but still moved quickly and adroitly. He was graceful and strong,

Group picture taken in Grandmaster Meitoku Yagi's dojo in Okinawa in the 1950's. Front row, left to right: Mr. Tamaki, Grandmaster Shinken Taira (Master of kobudo), Grandmaster Meitoku Yagi, Mr. Yushun Tamaki. Standing in the back second from the left: Meitatsu Yagi, Anthony Mirakian and Shosei Shiroma.

and his techniques were flawless. He was a great master. We studied mostly the *sai*, *tonfa*, and *bo*. Grandmaster **Shinken Taira** was a traditional Okinawan master, firm and strict, but also a jovial and friendly man.

It was enjoyable studying under him. He took a liking to me and was very gracious. He asked me to teach his *kobudo kata* in the United States when I returned.

Most Okinawan *kobudo* masters have a background in *karate*. Was Grandmaster Shinken Taira associated with a particular *karate* style?

Yes. He has studied *Shorin-ryu* going back to Grandmaster Funakoshi's time. He was a student of **Kentsu Yabu**. He didn't elaborate about his *karate* training. He did mention that he used to work out with Grandmaster **Funakoshi** in his youth. He taught me some *Shorin kata* on the side. I learned *Kusanku kata* and *Chinto kata* from him.

"Hard and soft" are among the most difficult concepts for martial artists to understand. These are frequently discussed in *Goju-ryu Karate*. What is your interpretation of these terms?

When a *karateka* starts talking about hard and soft, he starts falling into dualistic thinking. The hard and the soft are not separated in true *Goju-ryu Karate*. The hard and the soft are harmoniously interwoven. It is very difficult to tell when one leaves off and the other takes over. There is hardness in softness and softness in hardness. They complement each other.

Many masters in Okinawa spoke to me about the hard and the soft aspects of *Goju-ryu Karate*. The hard external side of *karate* is easy to understand and practice. The soft side is deceptive, elusive, and more difficult to develop.

When a *karate* student who has developed the soft internal side of their art goes through the *kata*, you can notice something different about their performance, something mysterious that is difficult to put a finger on, something unique that denotes a superior mastery. There is a different emotional state in the practitioner. There is something that is not sheer physical strength. Something not based solely on muscular contraction and expansion, but based on inner force, the circulation of *Chi*, which has an explosive devastating power.

"Hard and Soft" can only be understood through long practice. In *Goju-ryu*, the practice of *Sanchin* and *Tensho* enhance the development of soft internal powers.

When I was training in *Goju-ryu Karate* at the *Meibukan dojo*, I witnessed Grandmaster Meitoku Yagi's mastery of the hard and soft aspects of *Goju-ryu Karate* when he taught and demonstrated the various *kata*. His mastery, especially of the soft inner aspect, was superb. His top student, Master **Yushun Tamaki**, also showed great inner strength when performing *kata* and techniques.

Is it true that some martial art techniques do not require power or physical force?

No. I do not believe that such a thing exists. I had the honor of meeting Dr. **Cheng Man-ch'ing**, the great *Tai Chi Chuan* master. Dr. **Cheng Man-ch'ing** was taught by the famous Chinese Grandmaster, **Yang Cheng-fu** in Shanghai. Dr. **Cheng Man ch'ing** told me that he once asked **Yang Cheng Fu** to practice pushing hands with him. He said that while they were practicing, **Yang Cheng Fu** put his hand on Dr. Cheng Man-ch'ing's throat. The hand felt like soft velvet. Suddenly Dr. **Cheng Man ch'ing** was propelled more than ten feet backwards against the wall, hitting with so much force that he was knocked-out for half an hour. He said that was the first and last time he asked to perform pushing hands with his master!

Dr. Cheng Man-ching (who died in 1975), famous t'a-chi-ch'uan master of the Yang style, demonstrates a technique.

Even in soft techniques strength is applied. There is no such thing as magic. Although the internal energy (chi) looks like magic to the untrained eye, it has great power and physical force when brought forth.

Do you think *karate* training can increase extra-sensory perception?

Yes it might. Master **Ryuritsu Arakaki** told me that some *karate* masters do possess extra sensory perception. He said that one day when he and Mr. **Meitoku Yagi** were training with Grandmaster **Chojun Miyagi** during the late 1930's, he and Mr. **Yagi** were walking together in a park in Naha. Mr. Meitoku Yagi was a few feet in front of him, so Mr. **Arakaki** began thinking to himself, "What could

Grandmaster Meitoku Yagi at his 73rd Birthday Celebration held in Naha City, Okinawa, on February 10, 1985.

Mr. **Yagi** do if I suddenly hit him from behind? There is nothing he could do since he is walking in front of me." At that precise moment, Mr. **Yagi** turned around, looked at Mr. **Arakaki** straight in the eye and said: "What do you have in mind? You want to punch me, don't you?"

Another incident was described to me by Mr. Yagi's younger son, **Meitetsu**. He said that when his father was a police officer around 1938, Mr. **Yagi** arrested an Okinawan for disturbing the peace and causing trouble in a business district in Naha. When he took him to the police station, the man threatened to kill Mr. **Yagi**. Six months later, Mr. **Yagi** was walking home late at night on a dirt road. It was pitch dark and the road was lined with heavy bushes on both sides. The Okinawan, whose name was Mr. "N." was waiting in ambush with a knife behind the bush. When Mr. **Yagi** was about 20 feet away, he stopped and shouted: "Mr. N. You are hiding there with a knife and you want to kill me don't you?" The man was unnerved by the fact that Mr. **Yagi** could sense the danger without even seeing him, and run away. When I was training in Mr. Yagi's *dojo*, I repeatedly had the feeling that Mr. **Yagi** could sense my innermost thoughts. He has extra-sensory powers developed by his *karate* training.

What was the attitude of the Okinawans towards foreign students in the 1950's?

The Okinawan were skeptical, and with good reason. The *karate* masters wanted to know the true intentions and characters of all their students. The masters were very observant, and I felt I was watched very closely at first. Eventually, after I proved that I could handle the physical and mental rigours of the training, I felt accepted. I had to show that I was sincerely and honestly interested in learning the art of *Goju-ryu Karate-do*.

I remember one time I represented the *Meibukan* at a large martial arts demonstration in Ginoza, Central Okinawa in 1958, with over 2,000 people in attendance. I was the only Westerner participating. When I got up to perform *Shisochin kata*, the crowd began booing and whistling. But when they saw me performing, and recognized that I was a serious student, they quieted down. When I finished, they gave me one of the biggest ovations of the day. Some of the attending Okinawan *karate* masters approached me after the demonstration and commended me on my performance. Okinawans were very gracious and friendly once they saw that you had a respectful and sincere attitude towards their national art of *karate*.

What differences do you find in the way Okinawans and westerners approach *karate*?

In Okinawan, and in Asia in general, one of the goals of *karate* training is to minimize ego. In the West, unfortunately, the emphasis in much of martial art training is in building the ego, which is quite the opposite of the training in Okinawa. There's a saying in Okinawa that when the rice grain is plentiful, the stalk bows. When empty, it stands tall. This saying is analogous to the Western saying, "An empty barrel is apt to make the most noise."

Chojun Miyagi and Gichin Funagoshi (both sitting in front).

The Okinawans are generally more disciplined, patient, motivated than westerners in their approach to *karate* training. Also, the Okinawans have an initial advantage as *karate* is their national art. Therefore, the Okinawans have a better awareness of the goals of *karate* training than Westerners. In the beginning, self-imposed discipline will make the *karateka* feel uncomfortable and restricted. Okinawans understand and accept this, while most Western *karate* practitioners are unwilling to endure this initial hardship. After a while, of course, the self-imposed discipline brings tremendous inner freedom and harmony to the practitioner.

What were the major styles of *karate* practiced in Okinawa when you lived there?

The major, official styles of Okinawan *karate*, as recognized by the *Zen Okinawa Karate-do Renmei*, were *Goju-ryu*, *Uechi-ryu*, *Matsubayashi Shorin-ryu*, and *Kobayashi Shorin-ryu*. These were the four pre-eminent styles. This is true still today.

Were the relations between the major styles friendly?

Yes. I frequently attended the meetings of the *Zen Okinawa Karate-do Renmei* in Naha City, where the leading masters and their top students would come together and discuss matters of mutual concern: how best to enhance and present the development of Okinawan *karate*, how best to present it, standards of etiquette,

Anthony Mirakian representing the Meibukan Goju-ryu karate school demonstrates the Goju-ryu Shisochin kata at the Annual Martial Arts Event in Ginoza, Central Okinawa, in 1958.

and standards of promotion. I attended these meetings with my second *karate* master, **Ryuritsu Arakaki**, and also on occasion with Grandmaster **Meitoku Yagi**. These were very polite, dignified gatherings. The masters were courteous to each other and presented their views in a dignified, respectful manner.

Did you meet the leading masters of the other styles?

Yes. I met many of them. The head of the *Kobayashi* style of *Shorin-ryu* was the late Grandmaster *Chosen Chibana*. I met him several times at the Okinawa *Karate-do Renmei* meetings. These were held at the *dojo* of Grandmaster *Shoshin Nagamine*, who was the head of the *Matsubayashi* style of *Shorin-ryu*. I also visited the *dojo* of Grandmaster **Kanei Uechi** many times.

Grandmaster Kanei Uechi.

How did you happen to visit Grandmaster Nagamine's *dojo*?

I was invited *by Goju-ryu Karate* master **Ryuritsu Arakaki** to attend one of the meetings. At that time, master **Arakaki** introduced me to Grandmaster **Nagamine** and I also met many of his students.

Did you ever visit his *dojo* again?

Yes. I would visit his *dojo* periodically, as the meetings of All-*Okinawan Karate-do* Association were held there. I was the only Westerner present at these meetings. As time went on, I became friends with many of his *karate* students. Some of them were brown- and black-belt students who were very impressive and powerful. Grandmaster *Nagamine* is one of the most respected and skilled grandmasters on Okinawa, and it was a great honor to have met him.

Shoshin Nagamine, Grandmaster of Mastsubayashi Shorin-ryu Karate, second from the left, with some of his Okinawan karate students. Photo taken in Naha, Okinawa, in the 1950's.

What were the workouts like at his *dojo*?

The practice at his *dojo* included a lot of weight lifting. They had a full range of barbells, and other free weights, and they practiced many different weight-lifting techniques. Grandmaster *Nagamine* told me that he encouraged his students to engage in strength building as well as *karate* training. Even though the students were muscular, I noticed they had excellent speed and reflexes. They were very powerful *karateka*. I still remember seeing one of Grandmaster Nagamine's top students, **Omine**, throwing sequences of punching techniques. I could hear the sound of his punches breaking the air all the way across the *dojo*.

Was free-fighting practiced there?

No. Everything was pre-arranged. The emphasis in the *karate* training was very traditional, the *kata*, the drills, the pre-arranged *kumite*.

How was the training at the *dojo* of Grandmaster Kanei Uechi?

I visited the *dojo* of Grandmaster **Kanei Uechi** in Futenma City many times. He is a highly respected and very powerful grandmaster. *Uechi-ryu* and *Goju-ryu Karate* systems have a natural affinity. They both were influenced by the martial arts of Fukien Province in China, and have a common geographical background.

The *Uechi-ryu karate* training was very intense, and the students were superb *karateka*. They have a controlled form of free-fighting, using classical *Uechi* techniques. They exercised enough control that they stopped their techniques short of full contact.

What was your impression of their unusual method of kicking ... I'm referring to their toe kicks?

Their toe kicks were devastating, very impressive. They toughened their toes by hitting them against baseboards and other hard objects. I saw one student break five wooden boards held by another student by kicking just with his big toe.

I've seen films of their *Sanchin* testing. Perhaps it was only because of the camera, but it looked extremely hard. Were the students really being tested that hard?

Yes. It was hard. I remember seeing two-by-two boards broken over the students' arms, legs, and abdomens. I saw Grandmaster **Kanei Uechi** testing the *Sanchin* by hitting the students in the abdomen with hard punches thrown out of a horse stance. The students looked rugged and highly conditioned. It appeared as if their entire bodies had been hardened through the *Sanchin* training and testing.

Did you meet other eminent *Goju-ryu karate* masters?

Yes, several. I met the late Grandmaster **Seiko Higa** many times. He was an excellent teacher and had been the assistant of Grandmaster **Chojun Miyagi**. When I met Grandmaster **Higa** he was in his late fifties. When he performed the *Goju-ryu Kata*, he had great power, speed, and control. As a master gets older, the techniques do not depend as much on physical technique as on internal strength.

Master Seiko Higa.

The two most famous students of Grandmaster Kanryo Higaonna were Chojun Miyagi and Juhatsu Kiyoda. Did you ever meet Grandmaster Kiyoda?

Yes. I had the great honor of meeting him in Beppu, Kyushu in Japan. He was in his early seventies when I met him, and he was an extremely powerful man. His posture was erect. He had a strong voice, and his eyes were very sharp and penetrating. He was a large man. I saw a photograph of him in his younger years, and he was over six feet tall and perhaps 180 to 190 pounds. He had a very muscular build.

Appendices

Juhatsu Kyoda in traditional clothing in 1937.

Grandmaster **Kiyoda** told me that the study of *kata* should be supreme. He told me: "The true *karate* practice of *kata* is true *karate*." I will never forget those words. I also met his son who was over 6 feet tall and around 200 pounds. They showed me their photograph album which went back many years. They had a variety of group photographs with Grandmaster **Kanryo Higaonna** that included **Juhatsu Kiyoda**, **Chojun Miyagi**, **Kenwa Mabuni**, **Higa Seiko**, and many other great Okinawan *karate* masters.

There was one particular photograph of **Juhatsu Kiyoda** wearing the traditional black uniform used in Okinawan festivals. He was holding a thick wooden pole about six feet long. I asked his son what Grandmaster **Juhatsu Kiyoda** was doing. He said that in Okinawa around 1920 when practicing *karate*, two advanced students would sometimes be paired in a controlled version of free-fighting; fighting designed to practice the techniques of a specific style. When the students engaged in the *kumite*, two masters would stand on either side of them, and when the action got too fierce and there was the possibility of severe injury or even death, the masters would cross the poles in front of the students and end the fight. He said that this was a very fierce form of *kumite* practiced only by highly trained *karateka*.

The foundation of *Goju-ryu Karate* was laid by Grandmaster Miyagi's teacher, Grandmaster Kanryo Higaonna, who trained in China for over twenty years.

Is there one particular Chinese style to which *Goju-ryu* is related?

Yes. Okinawan *Goju-ryu Karate* is related to Chinese *Chuan-fa* style. **Kanryo Higaonna** sailed to Foochow in Fukien province, China, when he was fifteen. There he met the famous Chinese *Chuan-fa* Grandmaster, **Liu Liu Ko** with whom he studied for over twenty years. **Kanryo Higaonna** became Grandmaster Liu Liu Ko's top student. Little is known about the actual style that **Liu Liu Ko** taught. Some *karate* masters say it was the *Hung* style; others say it was another style that had been indigenous to Fukien province for over one thousand years.

Who was Grandmaster Liu Liu Ko?

There isn't much written information on Grandmaster **Liu Liu Ko**. I was told that he was of the Chinese nobility and had been tested to become the equivalent of a knight three different times. He failed the imperial test at age 37 and again at age 50. On his 73rd birthday he was tested again, before the Emperor of China after walking hundreds of feet carrying a rock weighing 180 kilos strapped to his back. When Grandmaster **Liu Liu Ko** arrived in front of the Emperor, he performed *Sanchin kata* and passed the test. Then he was knighted by the Emperor. Grandmaster Liu Liu Ko's training was said to have been very arduous. Anyone who aspires to practice *karate* must keep in mind the Chinese character *"Nin"* which means "to endure." There is no easy way of attaining mastery. It was through this long and difficult kind of training that Grandmaster **Kanryo Higaonna** was able to develop his exceptional skills. In 1890, he returned to Okinawa and began teaching in Naha. His skill, knowledge, and dedication soon became legendary.

When he returned to Okinawa from China did Grandmaster Higaonna make changes to the Chinese martial art that he learned from Grandmaster Liu Liu Ko?

Yes. Grandmaster **Higaonna** did make changes to the Chinese martial art that he learned in Fukien Province, China. Even though the style that he mastered in China was superb, he felt the need to revise and adapt some of the techniques to make his art suitable to the Okinawan lifestyle and culture. Also, Grandmaster **Higaonna** for some unknown reason changed the name of the highest *kata* from the Chinese pronunciation *Yepatlinpa* (meaning 108) to *Suparinpe*.

Was Grandmaster Higaonna a strict *karate* master?

Yes, a very strict teacher. He would not allow or teach any student with a violent nature in his *dojo*. He was very selective as to whom he accepted.

His training was very strenuous. The *Sanchin kata* was practiced for three to four hours during each session. A new student was taught only the *Sanchin kata* for as long as three to four years before going into another *kata*. While practicing the *Sanchin*, some of the students would collapse from sheer exhaustion. That was the intensity of Grandmaster Kanryo Higaonna's training.

The *Sanchin kata* taught at that time by Grandmaster **Higaonna** was performed open-handed. When Grandmaster **Higaonna** demonstrated his *Sanchin* breathing *kata*, he would occasionally allow four Okinawans to try and dislodge him from his standing position while performing. They could not move him. When he finished the *Sanchin kata* the floor where he stood would be heated by the friction of the gripping of his toes.

Appendices

Who were Grandmaster Higaonna's top students?

His top students were **Juhatsu Kiyoda**, **Chojun Miyagi**, and **Kenwa Mabuni**: **Miyagi** founded *Goju-ryu Karate* from *Naha-te*; **Kiyoda** founded *Toon-ryu*, a *karate* system named after the first character in Grandmaster Higaonna's name, and **Mabuni** founded *Shito-ryu karate*.

Kenwa Mabuni and Gichin Funagoshi.

Anthony Mirakian seated next to the great Okinawan Karate Grandmaster Juhatsu Kiyoda, founder of Tou'on-ryu Karate and one of the famous students of Grandmaster Kanryo Higaonna, circa 1958, in Beppu, Japan.

Did Grandmaster Miyagi make any changes in the *Naha-te* system that he inherited from Grandmaster Higaonna?

Yes. Grandmaster **Miyagi** studied with Grandmaster **Kanryo Higaonna** for thirteen years, and upon his master's death went to China for two years to conduct further research into the martial arts. While he was in China, he met and befriended the Chinese White Crane Master, **Go Ken Kin**, and traveled around with him to several provinces studying with a number of great Chinese masters.

When **Chojun Miyagi** returned to Okinawa, he decided to take the art of *Naha-te* and expose it to scientific scrutiny. His approach was very critical, and he discarded the techniques that did not meet strict scientific standards. **Chojun Miyagi** incorporated many Chinese martial arts techniques which he had learned while while in China to the *Naha-te* system of Okinawan *karate*. He refined the

The founder of Goju-ryu Karate, Grandmaster Chojun Miyagi.

existing *kata* and developed his own *kata Gekisai* 1 and 2 and *Tensho*. **Chojun Miyagi** designed the auxiliary exercises, *kata bunkai kumite,* and other forms of *kumite* that are performed in traditional *Goju-ryu Karate* training *dojo*. He modernized the training and developed the structures that we still follow. He also changed the practice of open-hand *Sanchin* to closed-hand *Sanchin*.

What is known of Master Go Ken Kin?

He was a Chinese White Crane Master whom Master **Miyagi** met in Fukien province, China in 1915. They traveled together for two years visiting and training with Chinese masters of various systems of *Chuan-fa* (*kempo*). Master **Go Ken Kin** introduced Master **Miyagi** to many great Masters. In 1936 Grandmaster **Miyagi** visited China again and studied Chinese martial arts at the *Seibu Dai Iku Kai* (Great Gymnastic Association, Pure Martial Arts Spirit) in Shanghai.

Years later Master **Go Ken Kin** moved to Japan and lived there under the name **Yoshikawa**. He passed away in 1940 in Japan at the age of 55.

There are many versions of the origin of the name *Goju-ryu*. Where did the name come from?

From the old Chinese book *'Wu Pei Chih'* ('Army Account of Military Arts and science') by **Yuan-i Mao**, published in 1636. Grandmaster **Miyagi** named the system of *karate* "*goju-ryu*' which appears in the sentence: The successful method requires both give and take (*go-ju*)." When Grandmaster **Miyagi** was asked why he gave this specific name to his style of *karate*, he replied that *goju* defines the hard and soft nature of his style.

Grandmaster **Miyagi** named his style of *karate Goju-ryu* around 1932. He was teaching and promoting *Goju-ryu Karate-do* up to the time of his death on October 8, 1953 at the age of 65. He was called the last great samurai warrior of Okinawa because of his legendary strength and skill as well as his intense dedication to the martial arts.

On what principles did Grandmaster Miyagi base the foundation of *Goju-ryu Karate-do*?

Grandmaster **Miyagi** subjected the art of *Naha-te*, as received from Grandmaster **Kanryo Higaonna** to strict scientific examination. Originally, a martial arts expert was trained for killing an enemy with one blow. *Karate* as such was unsuitable for the contemporary world. **Miyagi** studied the basic "*go*" of *sanchin* and the six rules and formed the "*ju*" or *tensho* form, thus combining soft and hard movements. He also organized the auxiliary movements designed to help develop *karate* techniques by strengthening the body through calisthenics. He organized these exercises in preparation for practicing the *kaishu kata*. Thus, he determined the theory for the practice of *karate* and organized it as a martial arts educational subject, an art of self-defense, and as a spiritual exercise.

Grandmaster **Miyagi** spent his entire life contributing to the improvement and proliferation of *karate-do*. Before his intervention, *karate* had been considered a very mysterious practice, but by using a scientific approach, **Miyagi** created, through his *Goju-ryu Karate-do*, a clearly defined and universal platform for the art which gave it a basis for mass acceptance.

Grandmaster Chojun Miyagi.

Did Grandmaster Chojun Miyagi receive any awards for his contribution to *karate*?

Yes. In 1936 he received a medal for "Excellence in the Martial Arts" from the Ministry of Education of Japan.

Did he hold any official positions?

Yes. In 1928, Grandmaster **Miyagi** traveled to Japan and instructed *karate* at the Kyoto Imperial University, Kansai University, and Ritsumeikan University, Kyoto. **Miyagi** is credited as the first master to introduce *karate* on an international level. (Editor's note: i.e. outside of Japan). In 1930, Grandmaster **Chojun Miyagi** became chairman of the Okinawan-*ken Taiiku Kyokai Karate-do* (Okinawan Prefecture Athletic Association *Karate* Division).

In 1934 he became permanent officer of the Okinawan branch of *Dai Nippon Butokai* (Great Japan Martial Virtues Association). As a result of his great efforts, *karate* was first recognized officially as one of the martial arts of Japan with the formal establishment of the *Dai Nippon Butokai*, Okinawa Branch, in November 1933.

In May of 1934, **Chinei Kinjo**, editor of the Okinawan newspaper *Yoen Fiho Sha*, invited Grandmaster **Miyagi** to Hawaii. There he gave lectures and taught in order to promote Okinawan *Goju-ryu Karate-do*. He returned to Okinawa in February, 1935.

In May of 1937, Prince **Moriwasa Nashimoto**, Commissioner of the *Dai Nippon Butokakai*, authorised **Miyagi** with the headmaster of *Shinto shizen-ryu* (*jujutsu*) and the headmaster of *kushin-ryu* (also *jujutsu*) to form the *Dai Nippon Butokai Karate Jukkyoshi* (Great Japan Martial Arts *Karate* Teachers' Association). They inspected and regulated *karate* throughout Japan until the dissolution of the association. In 1937, **Miyagi** received the *Kyoshi* degree from the *Dai Nippon Butokai*.

Goju Ryu Karate

Rare photograph showing Grandmaster Chojun Miyagi standing fourth from the left in his Japanese kimono. The Grandmaster had just come back from Hawaii where he taught karate for almost a year. To his left are Master Nakamoto and Mr. Senaba. In front of Grandmaster Miyagi (seated) is Master Shiroma and first on the left seated is Mr. Anzama. Photo taken around 1935.

In 1946, Grandmaster **Miyagi** was promoted to an Official of the Okinawan *Minsei Taiiku Kan* (Okinawan Democratic Athletic Association). In 1953 **Miyagi** was instructing at the *Ryukyu* Police Academy in Naha City, Okinawa.

What is the origin of the term "*karate*"?

Originally this Okinawan fighting art was simply called "*Te*". Then the Okinawans made a strict distinction between their native art "*Te*" and "*Tode*", which meant "Chinese hand" for the Chinese art of *Ch'uan Fa* or *Kempo*. The Chinese ideograph "*To*" of "*Tode*" means "Chinese" or "*Tang*" (The *Tang* dynasty ruled China from 618 to 906 AD). A tremendous cultural revival occurred during the *Tang* dynasty which was symbolic of the Chinese culture and enlightenment. Since Chinese culture was highly respected in Okinawa, anything labeled "Chinese" was regarded as superior.

The word "*To*" is very elegant and raises the value of everything it is applied to. There is a certain snob appeal in calling anything "*To*". Gradually, the Okinawans came to apply the term "*To*" to all "*te*", especially those of Chinese influence. According to Grandmaster **Miyagi**, *karate*, written in this way is the special word used only in the *Ryukyus* and it came from the Chinese *Ch'uan-fa* (*Kempo*).

Chojun Miyagi (sitting) shortly after his return from Hawaii.

When was *Tode* changed officially to *karate*?

On October 25, 1936 a *karate* symposium sponsored by Mr. **Choju Ota**, Chief Editor of the *Ryukyu Shimpo* Newspaper, was held in the Showa Kaikan, at Naha City, Okinawa. Among the Okinawan *karate* Grandmasters present were **Kentsu Yabu, Chotoku Kyan, Chomo Hanashiro, Chokei Motobu, Chojun Miyagi, Juhatsu**

Kiyoda, **Chosen Chibana**, **Mashige Shiroma**, **Asata Koyoshi**, and **Eijo Shin**. At this conference it was agreed that the Okinawan martial art which previously was called "*Te*" or *Tode*" be called *karate* or "empty hands." From 1936 on the practitioners of this Okinawan martial art began simply to refer to it as *karate*, using the ideograph meaning empty hands. In this way the emphasis shifted from technique alone to spiritual values as well.

At what age did Meitoku Yagi start his training with Grandmaster Miyagi?

Meitoku Yagi was 13 years old when his paternal grandfather took him to Grandmaster **Miyagi**, who was thirty seven years old at the time. His grandfather told Grandmaster **Miyagi**, "**Meitoku Yagi** is a descendent of the leading *samurai* of Okinawa and the first minister of the three ministers of Okinawa, **Jana Oyakata**."

His grandfather also said: "**Meitoku Yagi** has Okinawan *samurai* blood in him, and I think he will be able to take your place some day in

Original Courtesy Gate on the grounds of the Shuri Castle on Okinawa called Shurei-no-mon built in the 19th century in honour of a Chinese diplomat. This gate was destroyed during the fighting on Okinawa during the Second World War.

the future, so please teach him your *karate*." That is how **Meitoku Yagi** was able to start training under Grandmaster **Miyagi** in 1925.

Who was his ancestor Jana Oyakata?

He was a very important official in Okinawan history. He was so influential that he escorted the king of Okinawa when the king had to go to the Peace talk after the defeat of the Okinawans by the *Shimazu* clan of Satsuma Province, Japan at the conflict of *Keicho* in 1609.

Was it Meitoku Yagi's own decision to start training in *karate*?

No, it wasn't. He didn't have any intention of starting to train in *karate*. But he had to follow the order of his grandfather.

I gather he came from a strict, traditional background?

Yes. Grandmaster **Meitoku Yagi** has been a life-long resident of Kume village. The Okinawans said they were more afraid of the people from Kume than the military. This was because the religion of the people of Kume was Confucianism. They were very strict and had a discipline exemplified by the saying: "Stay three feet away from the master, but don't step on his shadow."

Did Grandmaster Miyagi have a formal *dojo* when Meitoku Yagi started practicing *karate* in 1925?

No. According to Grandmaster **Yagi**, Grandmaster **Miyagi** did not have a formal *dojo*; he taught *karate* in his backyard, and when it rained, he taught inside his home.

You studied with the senior student of Grandmaster Miyagi and met many of his other students. How did they describe the Grandmaster as a person and a teacher?

Grandmaster Miyagi's nickname in Okinawan dialect was "*Busama-gunku*" or "*Samurai*" **Miyagi**. He was a very demanding and strict teacher. **Meitoku Yagi** began studying with him at the age 13, after undergoing an eight-month proba-

Shuri Castle 1937. Instructor Shinpan Shiroma instructs Shuri City Elementary School of the Okinawan Prefecture.

tionary period, during which he had to perform chores around Chojun Miyagi's house and backyard.

Grandmaster **Meitoku Yagi** said that Grandmaster **Chojun Miyagi** had fierce eyes. "When you saw them." he said, "you wouldn't be able to say a word. You would never dream of telling him something that wasn't true."

Grandmaster **Miyagi** was hard on his students. While doing *Zazen* (sitting meditation) he would not allow his students to relax as some their *karate* teachers would; instead he would make the students sit and meditate for one to two hours without moving.

Sanchin was taught one step at the time. Sometimes a single movement would be practiced over and over again for several months, nothing but one movement for hours a day. When **Meitoku Yagi** would go to the communal bathhouse, people would see the bruises and welts on his shoulders from *Sanchin* testing and say: "Aha, you have been training with **Chojun Miyagi**."

Photograph taken in front of Gokokuji Temple in Japan around 1930. On the left is Mr. Tadashi Yamashiro, center is Mr. Masagumo Itokazu, and on the right is Grandmaster Chojun Miyagi. Grandmaster Chojun Miyagi learned calligraphy from Mr. Tadashi Yamashiro, a scholar and master calligrapher.

Grandmaster **Chojun Miyagi** placed great emphasis on developing the character of his students. He only kept those students who had high moral ethics.

He was a strict disciplinarian. One day one of his students arrived for *karate* training with a towel wrapped around his neck, singing a popular song. Grandmaster **Miyagi** expelled him from the school. The student tried to apologize for his careless behavior, but Grandmaster **Chojun Miyagi** felt that if a student behaved in front of him in such a careless and disrespectful way, then he would do even worse things away from the master's presence.

Grandmaster **Meitoku Yagi** said that an average person could not have tolerated the very intense *karate* training given by Grandmaster **Miyagi**. You had to be highly motivated. Grandmaster **Miyagi** would often tell his *karate* students: "Lions push their cubs over a cliff, and they raise only the cubs that are able to struggle back up the cliff. That's how I teach here in my *dojo*."

Grandmaster **Miyagi** taught only those students who could withstand the rigors of the training. If a student dropped out, he made no effort to draw him back.

What were Grandmaster Miyagi's favorite *kata* and techniques?

I was told in Okinawa that Grandmaster Chojun Miyagi's favorite *kata* was *Shisochin*. He had exceptionally powerful open-hand techniques, especially *nukite* (finger-tip strikes). Open-hand techniques take much longer to master than closed-hand techniques. His other favorite *kata* were *Sanchin* and *Tensho*. Grandmaster **Miyagi** had very strong punching and kicking techniques. His punches and kicks had an explosive power. He was said to have superhuman strength.

Grandmaster **Miyagi** was renowned for having a vice-like grip. It was said that he could put his hand on a four to five pound piece of raw meat and squeeze it into a hamburger. When he was in China, I was told that he dropped his wallet in a rickshaw. When he went back to get it, the rickshaw driver refused to hand it over and tried to strike him. Grandmaster **Miyagi** instantly grabbed the forearm of the driver and squeezed so hard it paralyzed his arm, forcing the driver to give the wallet back.

Bust of Grandmaster Chojun Miyagi, founder of Goju-ryu karate, permanently installed in the Police Department Gymnasium (Old Budokan Martial Arts Exercise Hall) on Okinawa on October 8, 1963.

Did Grandmaster Miyagi teach different versions of the *kata* to students according to their level of development?

Yes. As Grandmaster **Chojun Miyagi** kept teaching, he kept refining the *kata*. Also, he taught beginners simplified versions of the *kata*. Later, as they practiced longer and learned more, they were taught more refined, advanced versions. Therefore, in evaluating the levels of any *Goju-ryu kata*, you have to know how long the master studied with Grandmaster **Chojun Miyagi**. He taught slowly and patiently. Clearly, someone who studied with him for a few years would not have *kata* and techniques as sophisticated and advanced as someone who studied and practiced with him for decades.

Who was the top student and successor of Grandmaster Chojun Miyagi?

Grandmaster **Meitoku Yagi** was the top student and successor to Grandmaster **Miyagi**. He studied with him from 1925 to 1953. He learned the most sophisticated versions of the *Goju-ryu kata* and techniques. The *Meibukan Goju-ryu kata* of Grandmaster **Yagi** are unique. They have a flair, elegance, and fluidity all of their own.

Grandmaster **Miyagi** passed away on October 8, 1953. Ten years later, in 1963, his widow and family gave the Grandmaster's *karate* uniform and his Black Belt to Mr. **Yagi**.

According to a speech given on the Twenty-fifth Anniversary of the death of Grandmaster **Miyagi** on October 8, 1978, his daughter, **Suruki** said that her family had decided to give her father's *karate* uniform and Black Belt to Mr. **Yagi** because he contributed the most and trained the longest with Grandmaster **Miyagi**. She said: "Mr. **Meitoku Yagi** was with my father for the longest time practicing *karate*. I think my father would be glad to see Mr. **Yagi** getting his uniform."

Grandmaster Meitoku Yagi shown seated in his office.

Party in Naha-city, Okinawa, honouring Anthony Mirakian on his promotion to Black Belt, Third Degree (Sandan). Seated in the front, left to right: Mr. Fukuji, Mr. Mitsugi Kobayashi, Mr. Anthony Mirakian, Mr. Meitoku Yagi and Mr. Seikichi Toguchi. Back row, standing left to right: Mr. Tamaki, Mr. Shinken Taira, Mr. Yohena, Mr. Seikichi Higa, Mr. Ishimine, Mr. Ryuritsu Arakaki, Mr. Higa, Mr. Yushun Tamaki and Mr. Sunabe. Photo taken in November, 1959.

I understand the Japanese Government gave Grandmaster Meitoku Yagi an award.

Yes. On April 29, 1986, Grandmaster **Yagi** received the Imperial Award, Fourth Class Order from the late Emperor Hirohito in Tokyo. This award was in recognition of his great achievements in the field of *karate*.

Grandmaster Meitoku Yagi (rear center) with some of his karate students and Okinawan Karate Masters during his 73rd Birthday Celebration on February 10, 1985, in Naha City, Okinawa.

Who promoted you to Black Belt?

Grandmaster **Yagi** promoted me to Black Belt. Before I left Okinawa, I was promoted by him to *Sandan* (3rd degree Black Belt). Grandmaster **Yagi** promoted me to *Haichidan, Kyoshi* (8th degree Black Belt) in Okinawa in 1985.

What was the occasion for your visit to Okinawa in 1985?

I was invited by *Sensei* **Meitatsu Yagi** to participate at a special celebration in honor of his father Grandmaster Meitoku Yagi's 73rd birthday on February 10, 1985. As the United States representative of *Meibukan Goju-ryu Karate-do*, I attended this event and gave a congratutory address and performed the '*Seiunchin*' *kata* on that day. My wife, **Helen** and my daughter, **Doreen** presented Grandmaster **Yagi** with flowers during the ceremony. Representatives from the United States, Japan, Brazil, and India were present for this birthday celebration as well as many prominent Okinawan masters. Grandmaster, **Kanei Uechi**, **Shugoro Nakazato**, **Shoshin Nagamine**, and **Shinho Matayoshi** all attended. The son of the late Grandmaster **Chojun Miyagi**, **Ken Miyagi**, was there, as was the son of the late Grandmaster **Seiko Higa**, **Seikichi Higa**. Hundreds of practitioners demonstrated *kata* and *kumite* in front of thousands of spectators. Afterwards a gala reception was held for special guests. This was a major cultural event in Okinawa, with radio, television, and press coverage.

What rank do you hold now?

Ninth degree Black Belt (*Hanshi*). Grandmaster **Meitoku Yagi** promoted me to the very high rank of *Kudan, Hanshi* (9th degree Black Belt) in Okinawa on October 21, 1990.

Why did you visit Okinawa in 1990?

To attend and participate in the 30th Anniversary celebration of the founding of the Okinawan *Goju-ryu Karate-do* Association. It was held on august 18, 1990 at the *Shimin Kaikan* in Ginowan, Okinawa. I was accompanied by my *karate* students who also demonstrated at this important event.

Are you the first person to receive the high rank of 9th degree Black Belt (*Hanshi*) from Grandmaster Yagi?

Yes. Outside of Okinawa, I am the first and only one who has received the 9th degree from Grandmaster **Yagi**, the Chairman of the *Meibukan Goju-ryu Karate-do* Association.

Your *dojo* in Watertown, Massachusetts is known as the most traditional Okinawan *karate* school in North America. Have you made many changes over the years in the way you teach karate?

No. I haven't made any changes. Basically I am teaching in the same way I was taught at the *Meibukan Honbu dojo* in Okinawa. I also keep the same attitude that permeated Grandmaster Yagi's *dojo*, - of respect, cooperation, discipline, and hard work.

Could you describe the benefits of traditional Okinawan *Goju-ryu Karate* training?

Anthony Mirakian performs Seiunchin kata at Grandmaster Meitoku Yagi's 73rd Birthday Celebration on February 10, 1985 in Naha-city, Okinawa.

Traditional Okinawan *Goju-ryu* training is very strenuous and disciplined. It develops a very strong foundation of fighting skills in the *karate* student and emphasizes the repetitious practice of basic *karate* techniques, *kata*, and *Sanchin* training. Because of these intense requirements, it develops and produces the best long term results in the *karate* practitioner. Traditional day-to-day, continuous *karate* training strengthens the body, improves the health, cultivates the mind and develops an indomitable human spirit in life. Grandmaster **Chojun Miyagi** used to say that winning and losing are part of each other. "Don't be afraid to fail one day " he said, because the next day you might win." Life is a constant struggle, and traditional Okinawan *Goju-ryu Karate* training will prepare a person to face that struggle, to deal with life's ups and downs, in a very confident way.

Note: This interview was originally published in the magazine "Fighting Arts" No. 66, No. 67, No 68 (1990).

Eric Tuttle interviews
Sensei Anthony Mirakian

Note: The questions of this interview were supplied by *Sifu* **Eric Tuttle** of the Kingston Twin Mountain *Kung Fu* Club in Kingston, Ontario, Canada. *Sifu* **Tuttle** has been a good friend of *Sensei* **Mirakian** for the past 15 years. *Sensei* **Mirakian** has graciously supplied all the answers to **Hing-Poon Chan** of the GTKA during his visit to Ottawa between September 2nd to September 4th and September 20th 1997.

Sensei Mirakian, for what purpose are you visiting Canada?

I traveled to Canada at the invitation of *Sensei* **Hing-Poon Chan** to visit and teach Okinawan *Meibukan Goju-ryu Karate* at his *dojo*, the Gloucestor Traditional *Karate* Association in Ottawa, Canada.

Who is your representative for the Okinawan *Meibukan Goju-ryu Karate-do* Association in Canada?

Sensei **Hing-Poon Chan** is my newly appointed representative in Canada.

From left to right: Sensei Hing-Poon Chan, Sensei Lex Opdam, Sifu Kiem Hou-Lee and Matthew Ravignat after a Chin Na work-out, Canada, Ottawa 1997.

Why did you choose *Sensei* Hing-Poon Chan as your representative in Canada?

I chose *Sensei* **Hing-Poon Chan** to be my representative in Canada in order to promote and expand genuine Okinawan *Meibukan Goju-ryu Karate-do* throughout Canada under my guidance. *Sensei* **Hing-Poon Chan** visited and trained diligently at my *dojo* in Watertown, Massachusetts, U.S.A., where I carefully observed his dedication and attitude towards the art of Okinawan *Meibukan Goju-ryu Karate-do*. Because of the loyalty, skill, and sincerity which he has demonstrated, I am very confident that *Sensei* **Hing-Poon Chan** is well qualified to be my representative in Canada. Therefore, I have designated his *dojo*, the Gloucestor Traditional *Karate* Association in Ottawa the Headquarters for Okinawan *Meibukan Goju-ryu Karate* in Canada, and I welcome this new branch in my Association.

Is *Sensei* Hing-Poon Chan the first representative you appointed in your organization?

No. *Sensei* **Alexander C. Opdam** is my first overseas representative in the Netherlands. He is a strong, skillful *Meibukan Goju-ryu Karate* practitioner who trained very diligently under me. I designated his *dojo* as the Netherlands Headquarters for *Okinawan Meibukan Goju-ryu Karate*, and I am pleased to have this branch in Nijmegen, the Netherlands, in my Association.

Hing-Poon Chan receives his certificate 'Personal Representative' for Canada from his master Anthony Mirakian. Canada, Ottawa September 1997.

Your *dojo* in Watertown, Massachusetts, is the U.S.A. Headquarters for the Okinawan *Meibukan Goju-ryu Karate-do* Association. When did you receive that authorization and from whom?

I received authorization from Grandmaster **Meitoku Yagi** on March 15, 1961, establishing my *dojo* in Watertown (Okinawan *Karate-do* Academy, *Meibukan Goju-ryu*) as the U.S.A. Headquarters for the Okinawan *Meibukan Goju-ryu Karate-do* Association.

What was your rank when you left Okinawa?

When I left Okinawa at the end of November, 1959, I held the rank of 3rd degree Black Belt, *Sandan*, given to me by Grandmaster **Meitoku Yagi**.

What rank do you hold now?

Ninth degree Black Belt (*Hanshi*). Grandmaster **Meitoku Yagi** promoted me to the rank of *Kudan*, *Hanshi* (9th degree) while I was in Okinawa on October 21, 1990. I am the only *Meibukan Goju-ryu Karate* practitioner outside of Okinawa who holds this high rank.

What other position do you hold in the Okinawan *Meibukan Goju-ryu Karate-do* Association?

Grandmaster **Meitoku Yagi** appointed me Overseas General Manager for the Okinawan *Meibukan Goju-ryu Karate-do* Association.

Lex Opdam receives his certificate as 'Personal Representative' for the Netherlands from his master Anthony Mirakian. USA, Watertown 1996.

Was this an official appointment?

Yes. I was awarded a certificate dated March 6, 1972, given in accordance with the provisions of the Okinawan *Goju-ryu Karate-do* Association and signed by Grandmaster **Meitoku Yagi**.

Who became the legitimate successor of Grandmaster Chojun Miyagi, Miyagi's Okinawan *Goju-ryu Karate*?

Grandmaster **Meitoku Yagi** is the legimate and only successor of Grandmaster Chojun Miyagi's *Goju-ryu Karate*. Grandmaster **Meitoku Yagi** is the only one who was taught all of the *karate katas* by Grandmaster **Chojun Miyagi**. Also, he trained the longest with Grandmaster **Chojun Miyagi**, became the top student of Grandmaster **Chojun Miyagi**, and contributed the most to Okinawan *Goju-ryu Karate*.

Nowadays, some Okinawan *Goju-ryu Karate* practitioners in Okinawa are trying to revise historical facts and are distorting the truth about the rightful heir of Chojun Miyagi's *Goju-ryu Karate*.

A rare picture of karate instructors Yushun Tamaki and Meitatsu Yagi practicing Goju-ryu techniques at the honbu dojo on Okinawa in the 1950's.

Appendices

Is there a linage chart of Grandmaster Meitoku Yagi's *Meibukan* Association?

Yes. I have included a current official lineage chart at the end of this interview.

Who was the top karate student at the *Meibukan Goju-ryu dojo* on Okinawa while you were training in *karate* in the 1950's?

The top *karate* student was **Yushun Tamaki** who was an assistant instructor to Grandmaster **Meitoku Yagi** in the *Meibukan Goju-ryu Karate dojo*.

Could you describe the *karate* training you had with *Sensei* Yushun Tamaki in the *Meibukan Goju-ryu Karate dojo*.

The *karate* training with *Sensei* **Yushun Tamaki** was very intense, strict and powerful. He taught classes along with Grandmaster **Meitoku Yagi** who would oversee the entire *karate* training while *Sensei* **Yushun Tamaki** assisted. Occasionally, Grandmaster **Meitoku Yagi** would show the application of a *karate* technique by demonstrating with *Sensei* **Tamaki**.

Sensei Shigetoshi Senaha performing Seiunchin kata.

Master Yushun Tamaki.

What were the ranks of your classmates while you were training at Grandmaster Meitoku Yagi's *dojo* in Kume, Naha, Okinawa?

While I was training in the late 1950's at the *Meibukan Goju-ryu Karate dojo* in Kume, Naha, Okinawa, the ranks of my classmates were : **Yushun Tamaki**, 4th degree Black Belt (*Yondan*) ; **Shosei Shiroma**, 1st degree Black Belt (*Shodan*) ; **Meitatsu Yagi**, green belt ; **Shigetoshi Senaha**, white belt ; **Tsuioshi Nakasone**, brown belt ; and myself, 2nd degree black belt (*Nidan*).

After you left Okinawa what promotions were given to your former *karate* classmates by Grandmaster Meitoku Yagi?

In March, 1961, Grandmaster **Yagi** promoted **Yushun Tamaki** to 5th degree Black Belt (*Godan*), **Shosei Shiroma** to 3rd degree Black Belt (*Sandan*),

287

Shigetoshi Senaha and **Tsuishi Nakasone** to 2nd degree Black Belt (*Nidan*) and **Kyoshi Nakamoto** and **Meitatsu Yagi** to 1st degree Black Belt (*Shodan*).

Was Meitetsu Yagi training in the *Meibukan Goju-ryu Karate Honbu dojo* while you were training there?

No, **Meitetsu Yagi** was not training with us in *karate* while I was at the *Honbu dojo*. He was too young to be in the formal *karate* workouts.

Who is the most senior active Okinawan *Goju-ryu Karate* master in the *Meibukan* Association?

Since *karate* master **Yushun Tamaki** on Okinawa retired from active practice many years ago, I am the most senior active Okinawan *Goju-ryu Karate* master in the *Meibukan* Association. In Grandmaster Meitoku Yagi's *dojo* in the late 1950's, **Yushun Tamaki** was the most senior advanced student, and I was the next most senior student. **Shigetoshi Senaha** was much younger than I, and he was a white belt at the time. **Meitatsu Yagi** was a green belt and also much younger than I when I was a Black Belt.

Karate Master Meitetsu Yagi, Eight Degree (Kyoshi), younger son of Grandmaster Meitoku Yagi and Vice-President of the Meibukan Goju-ryu Karate-do Association. Photo taken in Watertown, Mass. in 1974. He is performing the Saifa kata.

How does Okinawan *karate* training in the United States compare with the *karate* training in Okinawa?

The training in the United States compares favorably with the training in Okinawa today. There are many good Okinawan *karate* schools in the United States, and there are many bad ones. However, the same thing is true in Okinawa. In many *dojo's* in Okinawa the *karate* training nowadays is not what it was in the 1950's when intensive and lengthy *karate* training classes were given. In my *karate dojo* in Watertown, Massachusetts, the training has remained hard, long, and strict. My training classes are three hours long, four times a week. Presently, in most of the schools in both the United States and Okinawa, the workouts are only 1 hour long and three times a week. When I visited Okinawa in 1985 and again in 1990, I noticed that the workouts had been changed drastically from the intense training of the 1950's. This change brought nostalgia to me, as most of the workouts of the 1950's were gone.

Appendices

How long has *karate* been practiced in Okinawa?

Karate has been practiced in Okinawa for over one thousand years. Okinawa (Ryukyu Islands) is the true home of *karate*.

What is your opinion of the present standards for Black Belt promotions in Okinawa and elsewhere?

The Black Belt promotions are being given by the *karate* instructors much too fast. Therefore, the ranks awarded to the *karate* practitioners are highly inflated and the recipients are often not properly trained, qualified, or deserving.

Hanshi Shigetoshi Senaha and Sensei Hing-Poon Chan at a seminar in London, Ontario, Canada, Summer of 1996.

What are your standards and how do you promote and rank the *karate* students in your *dojo*?

The promotions in my *dojo* are based on strict standards that the Okinawans maintained in Okinawa in the 1950's and early 1960's. My students must be well trained to be considered for promotion to Black Belt by me.

Group photograph of Anthony Mirakian with some of his students at his dojo, the Okinawan Karate-do Academy Goju-ryu, in Watertown, Massachusetts, U.S.A. Seated left to right: Edward Mills, Black Belt 1st degree; Carmen Stroscio, Black Belt 2nd Degree; Mark Allio, Black Belt 2nd Degree; Joseph Flynn, Black Belt 3rd Degree; Anthony Mirakian, Black Belt 8th Degree (Kyoshi); Paul Zarzour, Black Belt 3rd Degree; Mark Schoene, Black Belt 2nd Degree; Angelo Puzella, Black Belt 1st Degree. Back row standing left to right: Justin Curry, Devin Curry, Marcelo Rizzo, Gabriel Rizzo, Arthur Gianoukos, Edward Slattery, Almut Zeeck, Honoch Cohen, Jeffrey Burd, and Ari Gennetian.

What is the highest black-belt promotion you have given in your *dojo*?

In the over thirty-seven years that I have been teaching *Meibukan Goju-ryu Karate* in Watertown, Massachusetts, U.S.A., the highest rank that I have awarded is 4th degree Black Belt, *Yondan*. I have students who have been training with me for fifteen, twenty, twenty-five, and thirty years and who still continue to train. *Karate* should be practiced for live.

Hanshi Anthony Mirakian and one of his most senior student Paul Zarzour, observing Canadian representative Hing-Poon Chan.

On what do you base your ranking system?

My first requirement is that the student has good character. He must have proven his honesty and dedication to the art of *karate* and to me. The most important aspect of the training in *karate* in my school is not the final destination (the goal, the Black Belt) but the journey itself (the training).

What rank was required in Okinawa in the 1950's for a black-belt *karate* instructor to operate his own *dojo* in Okinawa *Goju-ryu Karate*?

When I was training in Okinawa the requirement was that a black-belt instructor had to be at least a *Sandan*, 3rd degree Black Belt, to be eligible to open and operate his own *dojo*. However, the instructor was required to continue his formal *karate* training with his *karate* master. In those times in the 1950's in Okinawa, a *Sandan* was a well-trained *karateka*; the equivalent of a 4th, 5th, 6th or even higher rank of nowadays.

When did you open your *karate dojo* in Watertown, Massachusetts, U.S.A.?

I opened my Okinawan *Meibukan Goju-ryu Karate dojo* in Watertown in 1960 when I had the rank of 3rd degree Black Belt, *Sandan*.

What are the requirements for your students to open and operate a *karate dojo*?

My first requirement is that the student must have received the rank of *Sandan* (3rd degree Black Belt) from me. My very strict *karate* training and promotion policies ensure that a *Sandan karate* practitioner is well qualified to teach, based on the very high standards of the *karate* training on Okinawa in the 1950's.

I also require that the *karate* student must have other qualities which are very important besides the training such as sincerity, honesty, and dedication to the art of *Meibukan Goju-ryu Karate-do* and to me.

Is there a moral obligation in the relationship of the *karate* student to his master in Okinawan *karate*?

Yes. There is such a principle which is known as *Giri*.

What is the meaning of *Giri*?

The meaning of *Giri* is duty, responsibility, and honor. In the case of the relationship of the student to his *karate* master, the student has a responsibility, debt, towards his master, because what the master is passing down to the student is something unique. The obligation which the student has towards his *karate* master is that no matter what the *karate* student will give or do for his master the student will never be able to repay the master for what the master has given the student.

Master Mirakian (left) and Sensei Lex Opdam (back) visiting Master of the South Chinese Hung Gar system Sifu Li Fen Feng (right) in Boston in the 90's.

Hanshi Meitatsu Yagi and Sensei Hing-Poon Chan at the Meibukan Honbu dojo in Naha, Okinawa, March 1994.

Weapons training (*kobudo*) has been incorporated into some *Meibukan Goju-ryu Karate* forms such as *Saifa* and *Shisochin*. Do you think training with weapons like *Bo* and the *Sai* using *Goju-ryu Karate kata* is good for practice?

Definitely no. *Kobudo* and *karate* should not be mixed as they are two different martial arts each with his own principles. Weapons training (*kobudo*) has its own characteristics, principles, and forms which are not exactly like *karate* forms; and the two martial arts should be practiced separately. *Karate* means empty hands. Practicing *karate kata* with weapons is a contradiction.

Did you have *kobudo* training in Okinawa?

Yes. When I trained in the *Meibukan Goju-ryu Karate dojo*, the late famous *kobudo* Grandmaster **Shinken Taira** was invited by Grandmaster **Meitoku Yagi** on many occasions to teach us *kobudo*, weapons training.

Is there free-fighting practice (*jiyu kumite*) in the training of Okinawan *Meibukan Goju-ryu Karate*?

No. Free-fighting was not practiced in the *dojo* of Grandmaster **Meitoku Yagi** when I trained in the 1950's, and it isn't practiced now. Grandmaster **Meitoku Yagi** never taught free-fighting.

Why wasn't free-fighting practiced in the *Meibukan Goju-ryu Karate dojo* in Okinawa?

Grandmaster **Meitoku Yagi** believed that the free-fighting in *karate* turned the art of self-defense into a sport, and traditional *karate* is not a sport.

To what do you attribute the present international growth and popularity of Okinawan *Meibukan Goju-ryu Karate-do*?

Hard work and dedication. I have spent thirty-seven years working for the expansion and promulgation of Okinawan *Meibukan Goju-ryu Karate-do*. I am

Hing-Poon Chan (standing at the back; fourth from the right) after his Goju-ryu Shodan examination in the winter of 1971, Hong Kong.

proud that I have succeeded in making the name of Grandmaster **Meitoku Yagi** well known and in making *Meibukan Goju-ryu Karate-do* internationally recognized.

Who was the famous Okinawan master whom you had the honor of meeting while you were training in Okinawa?

I met many great martial art masters while I was in the Orient, but one of my greatest experiences was meeting the late legendary Okinawan *karate* Grandmaster **Juhatsu Kiyoda** while I was visiting in his home in Beppu, Japan. Grandmaster **Juhatsu Kiyoda** was *sempai* (senior) to Grandmaster **Chojun Miyagi** and was one of the three top students of *karate* Grandmaster **Kanryo Higaonna**. Grandmaster **Juhatsu Kiyoda** was the founder of *Toon-ryu karate*. He named his style in honor of his Grandmaster **Kanryo Higaonna**.

Instructor Juhatsu Kiyoda instructs 2nd Junior High School in 1937.

How was the style named *Toon-ryu*?

One of the Japanese characters in Grandmasters Kanryo Higaonna's last name is pronounced *Toon*.

Is *Toon-ryu* being practiced today?

Yes. *Toon-ryu* is being practiced in the city of Beppu in the southern island of Japan and elsewhere. There are Okinawans who have been taught *Toon-ryu karate* by the late Grandmaster **Juhatsu Kiyoda**. I had the honor of personally meeting some of them while I was in Okinawa.

Is *Toon-ryu karate* identical to *Goju-ryu Karate*?

There are great similarities in both styles; but, those who trained with Grandmaster **Juhatsu Kiyoda** claimed that his style was the closest style to Grandmaster Kanryo Higaonna's *Naha-te* which Grandmaster **Higaonna** brought from Fukien province, China, around 1890.

What is your advice for the betterment of the Okinawan *Meibukan Goju-ryu Karate-do* Association?

My advice to the practitioners of *Meibukan Goju-ryu Karate-do* is to adopt the strict standards of the *karate* training of the 1950's. Therefore, we need harder *karate* training, more dedication, true respect, less politics, no divisive policies, and greater unity than prevails today. As the old saying reminds us, "There is strength in unity".

Note: This interview was originally published on the webpage of the Gloucester Traditional Karate Association (1997-2006).

Sifu Eric Tuttle and Sensei Lex Opdam.

Karate-do, its purpose and responsibility
An Interview with Master Anthony Mirakian

After a decade of intensive training in Okinawa, Anthony Mirakian introduced *Meibukan Goju-ryu Karate-do* **to the United States in 1960. Mirakian was the first Westerner taught by Grandmaster Meitoku Yagi, the top student and successor of Chojun Miyagi, the founder of** *Goju-ryu.* **Reflecting on a lifetime of practice,** *Hanshi* **Anthony Mirakian, 9th degree Black Belt, discusses the meaning of** *karate-do* **and the techniques of** *Meibukan Goju-ryu kata.*

—*by Lex Opdam*

Sensei, **could you give your definition of a martial system and a martial art?**

An art encompasses the philosophical concept of a specific system. Not only as a fighting method but as a way of life, as a philosophical concept. There should be a guideline for all our actions, our interrelations with relatives, friends and students. This is the art.

A system is a composite of techniques that does not have a binding ethical concept that an art form will have. The art form will bring the human element into it, the human spirit, and the physical, mental and spiritual concept.

There was a great Okinawan master called **Tode Sakugawa** who developed the *dojo-kun* more than 200 years ago. Okinawan karate is recognized and highly respected for this moral ethical aspect that the *dojo-kun* represents.

In a *dojo* a group of people are training with the same aim. Practicing with a joyful heart and a pure mind, without distractions, training highly spirited without any ego intentions against each other.

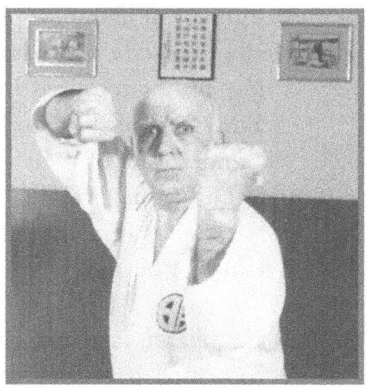

Sensei Anthony Mirakian, Okinawan Meibukan Goju-ryu Karate Master performs the Sepai kata.

Sensei, **how would you describe the role of the teacher in a martial art?**

An instructor in a system teaches purely physical movements. It doesn't go any deeper than that.

Teaching an art like *karate-do*, in our case Okinawan *Meibukan Goju-ryu Karate-do*, which includes aspects of spirituality, means that we are not just practicing the art for the sake of physical movements. The aim is to strive to develop a pristine human nature through hard intensive training, which is a challenge for a person mentally, physically and spiritually. An art goes into the inner aspects of the human being that is actively engaged by the continuous effort, devotion and dedication to the training the practitioner puts into it without egoistic feelings behind it. This process is guided by the teacher whose aim is to help the practitioner on this path.

In this process, you once said, the mind is our worst enemy.
Our mind is continuously in conflict. Being a human being, a social being living in society, we have our obligations and daily struggles and often are under pressure, challenging us to live harmoniously within an organized society. This is the existence of many people. But as soon as we have fulfilled harmonizing with societies demands, we then need guidelines to bringing us back to more self-realization and harmonized living. A lot of people live their lives on a terrestrial level, taking care of their body functions but their spiritual level is non-existent. They are not aware of their spiritual side and we should be careful with whom we are dealing with.

So, it is very difficult to teach something to someone when it is not part of his nature or his living.

***Sensei*, is there any difference in the way you teach here in your *dojo* and the way they teach in Okinawa?**
Yes, the way I teach is somewhat adopted in a cultural sense. We live in America and have an American way of live. If you live in Europe, for example the Netherlands, then there is also a cultural difference and this will influence the way of teaching. There is nothing wrong with that. This does not mean that the system has been altered. The way people think and live will be a living element for the practice of *karate* in that specific country.

I have also noticed that not all masters are as approachable as you are when people want to talk to their teacher outside the training.
This is my nature, as was my father's who was very approachable, friendly and generous. This can be said also for other masters in Okinawa, China, Japan or anywhere else who want to impart their knowledge in the right and friendly way to their students. But unfortunately there are also those who are not. When I lived in Okinawa I had the privilege to meet many masters and because of my nature and

search for information by the many questions I asked, I was granted information by the masters that I would not have received if my personality were different.

When you lived in Okinawa in the 50's you became very close to many Okinawans. One of them was Ryuritsu Arakaki. Was he approachable?

Master **Ryuritsu Arakaki** was very approachable. I would go to his home on the weekends especially on Sundays. And there in his home we would have very lengthy conversations, and he would try to explain to me the meaning of the martial art, *karate* especially. He told stories of how Okinawans went to China, and how they were taught, so I learned a lot about the martial art from my visits to his home. Master **Ryuritsu Arakaki** explained many things which otherwise I could not have ever learned if I had never met him. So meeting him was a very valuable experience.

Dutch and Canadian Meibukan practitioners performing Gekisai Dai Ichi Kata.

Anthony Mirakian performs Sepai kata.

Would you say that the American society is more goal oriented as opposed to the way of life in the Martial Arts which are a path in the way of life and not a goal?

Yes, American society is more goal oriented, they seem to chase the Black Belt. It is like when somebody is training and, this happened in my *dojo*, asks: "Could I use the knowledge of *karate*/ technical skill in daily life?" I replied with: "I don't think you should." The person then said, "Well then what good is it?" I responded, "When you have a pistol or a revolver with you, do you go around shooting people?' Americans are practical; they want to learn something they can use. Wealth, good health, convenience, poise, inner serenity, well being, all these are actually assets; qualities that are rewarding. A person doesn't have to have a trophy, that's more like feeding the ego. Some people like to think they can make Black Belt in a year, or a year and a half. If a Black

Belt means that, it means nothing. The Black Belt is a means to a beginning. Earning a Black Belt is a start of learning the art, not the end. The student embarks on a new aspect in life based on self-imposed discipline. The promotion to Black Belt is a certain amount of acknowledgement given by the teacher that the practitioner has reached a certain level. Now, he has to work to a higher level. I'm going to promote this student to a next level, now he is going to learn even more. See, so it's learning!

Actually, the most important aspect in the martial art is not the end goal, "the Black Belt", but the journey itself. It is like a person traveling from here to California. The final destination could be San Francisco, Los Angeles or San Diego. The most important thing is the journey to the person traveling. His journey and meeting so many people, enjoying and experiencing himself as he is training and learning. Being curious and learning, seeing different cities, different landscapes, this is the most important thing, not the final destination. So the journey itself is the most important aspect of *karate*. It is the training of *karate* that is the most important, not the Black Belt. When I started training *karate* I didn't have my aim on getting a Black Belt. I was practicing *karate* because I loved it. Regardless of whether I got a Black Belt. A person can have all kinds of Black Belts, but if his heart and enjoyment aren't in it, he is wasting his time. Even if I wasn't promoted to Black Belt, I would still practice *karate*. If a person is coming into my *dojo* and aims for the Black Belt, he is wasting his time. He should go some place else. Because if he wants the Black Belt, it means he's coming for the Black Belt and not for the training. The most important aspect of him being there is his training and what he is gaining from the training.

The belt is more a recognition from the master that after a certain amount of time the student has realized this level. A marker for what he has learned. But actually the most important thing is the beginning. That is why I understand that many grand masters in Okinawa, after a lifetime of dedication, would wear a white belt. Because they felt that after so many years, they do not know "anything". The artist of the artless art. They are going back to their original status that when actually in the beginning they were ignorant of the art and now in the end they are "ignorant" of the art again. I have only been teaching for 45 years of the over 50 years I have been practicing the martial arts and still I am not "scratching the surface." But, still there is something that is in the subconscious mind that if we, as a true martial artist, have to protect ourselves, it is there and that will never fade away.

You have a reputation of being strict and demanding when someone enters the *dojo* for the first time to workout. Training in your *dojo* also means that one has to train in a highly repetitive amount of basics over and over again. This is very demanding for

people, especially when you are not used to these kinds of workouts. This also means that not many students stay long. Could you please share your thoughts on these points?

Unfortunately, there are many people who practice the art with the right intentions, but do not know why or what they are doing, and unfortunately, there are many schools in America in which as soon as a person walks in off the streets he is taught to fight without explanation. Because teaching the method of how to block, how to punch, good stance, good body posture and movements takes a few years or even longer depending on the practitioner. It is very easy to get up in the morning and just start swinging, but that doesn't mean a person knows *karate*. A person should learn why he or she is practicing the art, starting from the a,b,c all the way up to z. That takes time. After a person learns that he goes his way, he goes off. It is difficult to teach *karate* to the American people; they don't have patience. In America everybody wants to learn everything now or quickly. It doesn't work like that. It took so many years for a master to develop that level of skill and it will take the student as long, or longer, to develop that same level of skill.

A young Anthony Mirakian practicing the Saifa kata in the honbu dojo in Okinawa with Shigetoshi Senaha in the 1950's.

Grandmaster Meitoku Yagi, Chairman of the Meibukan Goju-ryu Karate-do Association seated on the left with Master Anthony Mirakian, 9th Degree Hanshi in the Meibukan honbu dojo, Kume, Naha-city, Okinawa, Japan, Sept. 1, 1990.

Sensei, Chojun Miyagi has said he was not opposed to use certain titles like *Renshi, Hanshi* etc. but believed that a ranking system, like the system used in some of the Japanese martial arts would not be suitable for Okinawan *Goju-ryu*. It would distract and feed the ego. After his death in 1953 the Okinawan *karate* associations, including *Goju-ryu* schools, adopted the *Kyu-* and *Dan*-ranking system. In light of Chojun Miyagi's thoughts and that he did not want to incorporate the *Kyu-* and *Dan*-ranking, what are your thoughts on ranking, how do you personally see its purpose?

We don't know the way **Chojun Miyagi** thought. He thought that only members of the Japanese nobility were entitled to promote and award rank to practitioners of *karate*. He thought that the Japanese *Butoku-kai* were the only ones who could award rank. For that reason **Chojun Miyagi** did not award any rank to his students. I think when **Chojun Miyagi** died, this opened a gate for many people who had very little training from **Chojun Miyagi** to make ridiculous claims that they were top students of him. But the ones in the inner circle knew who was the top student of **Chojun Miyagi**. They knew **Meitoku Yagi** was his top student. Then there were some lesser students who claimed to be the top student. I think that if **Chojun Miyagi** had established some sort of ranking system, many of these claims might not have surfaced. Unfortunately, his untimely death left the possibility of unqualified people making all kinds of exaggerated claims.

How do you see the ranking within martial arts today, knowing that there are schools that do not use ranking?

It all depends on the school and the practitioners. When I was in Okinawa in 1990, I was talking to one of the Black Belts of *Sensei* **Senaha.** He said to me, "Mr. **Mirakian,** the ranking of *karate* in Okinawa is no good." I knew from where he was coming and I asked, "why?" He said, "Some have 8th, 9th, 10th degree, but they don't deserve half of that rank because they have never worked hard or practiced hard to deserve that rank." But now they are claiming all kinds of rank. The rank in Okinawa is highly inflated. There are many instructors and masters in Okinawa that are highly qualified and deserve their rank, but there are others who leave much to be desired.

How do you feel about the duality of rank then, feeding the ego of the person, where Zen principals in Martial Arts say the ego is to be shed?

Well, this is a difficult situation. It is very difficult to know exactly what is going on within the inner aspect of the practitioner's mind. A disturbed person could come and be respectful and polite to the master but that practitioner could have ulterior motivations. Well, the truth, like I always say, is like oil. It will eventually come to the surface. The true character of the practitioner will show in due time. It cannot be hidden forever. *Karate* is supposed to help develop the person into a better human being. That is the optimal situation. But if a person is of a bad character and a bad spirit, he will take this knowledge and distort it to accommodate his own selfish motivation of how to teach and turn whatever he knows into a money-making method. Rather than teaching the art to the right people, in the right way. What is the right way? To some people the right way is to confuse the practitioner… Ranking is sometimes delayed to bring forth the pristine and true nature of the practitioner.

Meibukan party held on August 28, 1990, in Kume, Naha City, Okinawa, standing left to right, Meibukan Goju-ryu Master Shigetoshi Senaha (Kudan), Meibukan Goju-ryu Master Anthony Mirakian (Kudan), Meibukan Goju-ryu Master Masaaki Ikemiyagi (Shichidan), and Sensei Souske Machida (Sandan), Vice-President of Sensei Ikemiyagi's dojo.

Sensei, you mentioned people making money with *karate*. What do you think about people who commercialize the art of *karate*?

The ones that are commercializing the art in my opinion are not teaching the true art. They are using the name of *karate* to suit their purpose. The worse they teach, the more people are coming to them because they have a certain image and ways to attract people to come to them to fool them. They even give kids of 10 or 12 years of age or even younger a Black Belt. That is a disgrace. Even a teenager of 16 or 17 years of age that has practiced 7 or 8 years has not developed a mental awareness for the realities of life. Once a person becomes an adult they might, without guarantee, develop awareness about the benefits of this intensive training and learn to respect it.

Today I have seen certain teachers and organizations charging money for grading tests and promotions, and those charges increase as the practitioner reaches "higher" levels. There are even schools that guarantee you that within three years you will become a "Black Belt" without ever having seen or met the prospective student!

Unfortunately there are people that make big money with *gassuku* and seminars. All they are really accomplishing, in most cases, is fooling the public with theses gimmicks. I do not make money with *karate*. If people want to be fooled it's their choice, but it is not my cup of tea, it is not the way I operate. Maybe to them I am too old fashioned, not practical, but I am not competing with anybody. If they want to do it like that they should do so, but they don't have to come to me and say that they teach the real *karate*, because they are not.

***Sensei*, when your students enter your *dojo* they bow before a shrine. Could you explain this ritual?**

Within the shrine there is a paper, upon which is written 'Respect towards the brotherhood of mankind". This is what Master **Meitoku Yagi** has written for me. This is a *dojo* shrine and is not directly dependent upon a religion. Bowing to the shrine and to the pictures of the masters is done out of respect. Without their existence we would not be practicing the art and in bowing to them we show our respect to them.

Anthony Mirakian representing the Meibukan Goju-ryu karate school demonstrates the Goju-ryu Shisochin kata at the Annual Martial Arts Event in Ginoza, Central Okinawa, in 1958.

When meeting a person one shakes hands to show that we have no bad intentions and come in friendship, that we have respect for each other. The bowing in the *dojo* means the same thing.

Sensei, before training you always burn incense. Is there a special reason for doing this?

Incense has, I would say, a purifying and cleansing effect in the *dojo*. It brings the right spirit to the environment. It helps the students realize that *karate* is not purely physical but it's spiritual as well. Incense is burned to honor the past masters, because, if it weren't for them, we would not be practicing that specific style of *karate*, or martial art. So incense is burnt in due respect to the masters and to bring spirituality to *karate* training because *karate-do* has spirit. It is not only the physical aspect but goes beyond the physical realm. It is a place for people's spiritual development because while the students are developing physically they are developing also mentally and spiritually.

Before starting the actual *kata*, one prepares oneself in the "*Yoi*" position. In this preparatory position, what is the exact purpose of bringing both fists next to the body, contracting all the muscles for a short moment, and performing these movements before opening up every *kata*? Is it correct to state that the reason for this is both a ritual and a preparation for the body and mind?

It is a preparation. You have to tense all of the muscles of the body and get ready from there on to start doing the *kata*. The movements are like a spring quality. You spring up and make the movements dynamic. Make the body like the coils of a spring. This "*Yoi*" position is for preparation pushing down like getting a feel of the floor and the feet really planted for tremendous maximum energy development and concentration.

Could you tell me why all the *Goju-ryu kata* start at the same spot as they do end? In the case of other Okinawan *karate* styles, like *Shorin-ryu* you see *kata* like *Naihanchi* that do not start at the same spot as they end. Is there a specific reason for this element of the *Goju-ryu kata*? Is it a philosophical approach or is it just a practical tool?

So many of the *kata* concepts remain the way that they were brought from China to Okinawa. Some *kata*, even in *Goju-ryu*, don't have the balance in that, what is done from the right is also done on the left.

Returning to the same spot has no deeper philosophical meaning. Its goal was for the symmetry of the *kata*. If the *kata* is correct, one should be ending up in the same place. It also depends on the steps that the student is taking. When the student takes a larger step and then the next one short, this can throw the *kata* off, and the student will not be able to end up in the same place. As far as *Shorin*, I am not a practitioner of *Shorin*. But it could be that some of the movements in *Shorin* have been eliminated or that's the way it was practiced.

Sensei Mirakian performing Naichanchi Kata.

Chojun Miyagi trained *Naihanchi* extensively. Is there a special reason why Chojun Miyagi did not put *Naihanchi* in his *Goju-ryu* system?

In *Shorin-ryu*, *Naihanchi* is like the *Sanchin* of *Shorin-ryu*, only they do it in a natural way with natural breathing while *Goju-ryu* emphasizes the deeper and dynamic breathing, rather than natural breathing.

Chojun Miyagi taught *Naihanchi kata*. Grandmaster **Meitoku Yagi** thought *Naihanchi* was such a good *kata* with good movement, that when we were training *Goju-ryu karate* in the 50's, we also trained *Naihanchi kata*. *Naihanchi* was a *Shorin-ryu kata*, so it wasn't incorporated into *Goju-ryu kata*; we had so many *kata* that were typical of *Goju-ryu*, so that *kata* wasn't affiliated with *Goju-ryu*.

Could you describe the reason why there are slow movements in some of the *Goju-ryu kata*?

Slow movements in *Goju-ryu karate* are typical of the system, which was founded by the late great Grandmaster **Chojun Miyagi**. Some of the movements in the *Goju-ryu kata*, like for instance in the *Seiunchin kata*, and to a certain extent in the beginning of *Seipai*, *Sanseru*, *Suparinpei* and other *Goju-ryu kata*, are done to develop more concentration in the movement and more awareness of the students while doing this movement. The physical explanation is that when a person is making a movement more deliberately, a person can spend more concentration on the movement and make it more correct.

Could this be applied to all kinds of movement or is it specific for certain schools?

This is typical, more typical of *Goju-ryu*, being hard and soft, slow and fast. There are other schools like *Tai Chi* or other certain internal systems that have slow movements and rhythm. Not everything is always done slow; certain movements are done slow to develop internal energy and inner strength. Suddenly these movements become fast and explosive. These forms also have rhythm. If everything is done at the same speed, then rhythm is lacking.

Sensei, in *Seisan kata* there is a movement where you push and you have a sort of up-down *Muchimi*. Is there a special reason for incorporating this movement? We see it in *Sanchin* and *Tensho kata,* but sometimes it is also found in other *kata* of our system. Is its purpose the same reason we practice it in *Sanchin kata,* to develop certain strength, energy and tension?

Yes, I think it is done for developing maximum energy in the movement and then slowly, I would say, transferring this energy into another movement. Going from one movement to the next one. So that's why it is done with a certain amount of speed and concentration. Then the movement can develop, or transition, with a sudden explosive surge of energy. This could be in the form of a kick or a punch, or as in the example of the *Seisan kata* last movements in an almost simultaneous and explosive kick/punch combination.

Sensei Anthony Mirakian, Okinawan Meibukan Goju-ryu Karate Master performs the Shisochin kata.

Sensei, we have six *Goju-ryu kata* including *Sanchin* and *Tensho* that start in a similar *Sanchin dachi* posture or the *Sanchin* guard stance. Obviously, seeing the background and origins of the *Goju-ryu* system, this seems to differ from the original Chinese versions. Is there any reason why Chojun Miyagi and/or Kanryo Higaonna changed the original versions, (except for *Tensho* which was created by Chojun Miyagi), adding or changing the first three *kata* movements as described?

It wasn't appropriate for **Kanryo Higaonna** to forward the system, as far as we could speak of a system, to the Okinawans exactly in the way he had learnt it in China because of cultural reasons. Okinawa is culturally different to the Chinese. The Okinawans don't fight like the Chinese and by nature are different from the Chinese. So that's why **Kanryo Higaonna** adapted what he had learned to suit the Okinawan culture, environment and Okinawan people's way of living.

Would you say that the opening of the *kata* is to incorporate Sanchin principals into the *kata*?

Well, all of the *Goju-ryu kata* have the inner aspects of the breath control of *Sanchin*. Like when you are doing all the movements they are done in a systematic, methodic way of inhaling and exhaling. It's done in a very quiet manner. It's like doing the *Sanchin*, but it is more silent with the concept of *Sanchin* behind it, of concentrating, and pushing the energy below the navel into the *Tan Tien* and tightening the strings of the chalice, the perineum, and the anus. Especially doing the *Sanchin* to create maximum energy. When one performs *kata*, it is done by moving the body with the concept of *Sanchin* behind it.

Most of the *kata* incorporate three steps in the opening movements. Is this done for the purpose of symmetry or is there a deeper meaning to these movements?

Well, that could be. It could be that there weren't that many steps and the Okinawans thought it was more beneficial to them to practice with those three steps. Maybe in the original *kata* there weren't the three steps, maybe it was less or more.

I believe that for cultural purposes they made it three steps. Most Chinese *kata* had highly repetitive movements. The Okinawans thought that rather than making it so repetitious, they preferred to concentrate on one or two of those specific techniques with maximum concentration and power. *Kata* with highly repetitive movements becomes very grueling and would lack energy. The Okinawans have always emphasized power. Power was always very important. Like the concept of one blow, one kill, to develop maximum energy in your movement, especially in the punch, so when attacking a person you eliminate this person with one blow. In actual combat, if your opponent is not defeated with one technique he might be able to fight back and reverse the situation.

You mean by stringing multiple techniques together, very quickly, the body cannot recover and quickly generate enough energy?

Then you are sacrificing power for speed. The Okinawans felt that speed and flexibility are very important, but they have always invested more in power. Okinawans are not built big. They are very strong by nature and felt that they were going to evolve *karate* to their own physiological make up. The Chinese are more slender, of course there are big boned Chinese, but generally they are slender people. Okinawans historic background, their nature, is that of farmers & fishermen. They worked in agriculture, cultivating the land and fishing from the ocean. So they were strong from the sort of labor they did. Over two to three hundred years ago, Okinawans would practice *karate* secretly during the night because it was forbidden by the Japanese conquerors of Okinawa. In that time they would practice their techniques on the *Gajimaru* tree, which is the Banyan tree, trying to break the *Gajimaru* shoots. The Banyan tree, which grows in Okinawa, grows shoots from some of the branches and the shoots reach the ground and then those shoots eventually become part of the main trunk of the tree. The Okinawan martial artists would try to break these *Gajimaru* shoots coming down from the branches to the ground with one powerful shuto, punch, kick or forearm strike, to develop maximum power. If they hit someone in actual combat with heavy armor they could penetrate the armor and kill the person.

It's been said that Chojun Miyagi greatly emphasized *Sanchin kata* practice and that it was extremely important to the development of the practitioners training. There have also been stories and writings that some people have practiced nothing but *Sanchin*. Is *Sanchin* more of a physical exercise for the body, teaching it to strengthen? Or is there a spiritual aspect to *Sanchin* that had Chojun Miyagi so embrace it as part of the training?

Well, the cultivation and preparation of *Sanchin* takes so much concentration. Because everything in life starts with breathing and ends with a breath. So the bringing of this energy in *Sanchin* is to raise the level of energy of the body. To maximize it. That is the concept of *Sanchin*. The concept of *Tensho* is to relax the level of energy in the body. They are two opposites. *Sanchin*, to increase and maximize the level of energy in the body and then *Tensho*, to relax the energy level. *Sanchin* has a spiritual value to it also. Because *Sanchin* is performed to develop a level of fighting spirit. To make a person gradually fearless in actual combat. That is the tremendous stress control that *Sanchin* is about.

Do the pauses in the middle of the movements of *Sanchin* carry any meaning other than a transition point?

Well, that is the concept of inhaling and exhaling, because the person is pushing the energy through the lower abdomen, to what is known as the *Tan Tien*. Pushing not only in the *Tan Tien*, but to the sides and the back of the body like a circle. The energy is not only in the *Tan Tien* but also in the lower *Tan Tien*, which is a few inches below the navel and to the sides and back of the body. These places are also expanding during *Sanchin* breathing, like an inner tube. The energy is not only in the front, but also in the back and sides as well.

If somebody performs *Sanchin* incorrectly, do they do their bodies more harm than good?

Yes, a person could actually hurt himself more than helping himself. Practicing *Sanchin* has to be a gradual process. A sign that the person has been cultivating and practicing *Sanchin* right is that when the body is relaxed it is soft like cotton or rubber. When the body is tense, the body should be very tight and hard. Also, the correct practice of *Sanchin* will develop the body to feel like steel covered with velvet. The actual appearance that a person would give is that his body is soft, but if a person touches that person's arm or body, he would realize that his body is very dynamic, tight and hard. It is very deceiving. Like for instance, watching Grandmaster Meitoku Yagi's biceps. They looked very supple and soft. He had well developed forearms, feet and fists. When Grandmaster **Meitoku Yagi** did his movements it was like iron covered in velvet. Once I took a magazine over to the

Karate Master Meitetsu Yagi, Eight Degree (Kyoshi), younger son of Grandmaster Meitoku Yagi and Vice-president of the Meibukan Goju-ryu Karate-do Association. Photo taken at Anthony Mirakian's dojo in Watertown, Mass. In 1974. He is performing Sanchin kata.

dojo, a bodybuilder's magazine with somebody on the front cover flexing his biceps. These biceps were 21 inches and Grandmaster **Meitoku Yagi** began mimicking the movement. You could tell that his biceps weren't that developed. But I have learned that he asked a Japanese soldier to take a rifle and hit him with it on the shoulder. The Japanese soldier broke his rifle butt over his shoulder and Grandmaster **Yagi** just shook it off as if it was nothing. He had very developed trapezes.

Chojun Miyagi seemed to have two variations of *Sanchin* and also there may have been more than one variation of *Tensho*. Do any other variations of *Sanchin* exist that were developed by Chojun Miyagi?

I don't think so. As far as I know, there was only one *Sanchin*. It was **Chojun Miyagi** who developed the deep breathing.

I remember going back to the 1950's, in Grandmaster Meitoku Yagi's *Meibukan dojo*. He practiced the *Sanchin* openhanded; similar to the way we hold our hands in the opening movements of *Shisochin kata*. When he did the movement it was done slowly, deliberately, with open hand and openhanded strikes, and it was done with dynamic tension. That's the way that we practiced it at the time. The format of the *kata* was the same like the regular *Sanchin* with closed fists, except this was open handed.

Appendices

Photo taken at 1st International Karate Championship, held in Long Beach, Calif., in 1964. Front row, left to right: Pat Burleson, Bruce Lee, Anthony Mirakian, Jhoon Rhee. Back row, left to right: Allen Steen, George Mattson, Ed Parker, Tatsuo Oshima and Robert Trias.

It is said that the open hand allows the _chi_ to flow through the arm faster and better than with the closed fist, which closes the _chi_. Is this correct?

Well, there is a certain amount of truth in that. Open hand techniques are always much faster than closed fists. When a person has open hands, they always have a longer reach. When a person is closing or making a tight fist with a hand, he is losing a few inches reach. So, Chinese martial arts favor open hand techniques, it was faster to manipulate and to operate, but also they had many various techniques that differed from the closed fist, like the panther punch, eagle eye punch and others. Those techniques were done for when you were facing a fast opponent. It all depended on the skill of the practitioner. If the practitioner was well skilled, he could use either technique. Open handed, or strike with the fingers or closed fist, depending on the level of knowledge and skill of the practitioner. But always open handed techniques are much faster than closed hand.

***Sensei*, if you could give advice to people starting the practice of *Sanchin*, what would be the appropriate way to do it? First the posture, then movement, then the technique, then the breathing, then the muscles focus?**

They should try to learn step by step. Good posture first, and then proper alignment of the body, where the head should be held, proper alignment of the arms and the feet, the relationship of the feet and the hands, then the breathing control which should be coupled with the movement of the hands. All this should be learned step by step. It is better to start slow, and develop a slow progress, rather than trying to learn everything all at once and then failing. So they should go step by step. In the beginning they should breathe as natural as possible. And then later on they can increase it. Young people are dynamic and have so much energy, they could apply so much strength and energy in *Sanchin* practice. Depending on when a person becomes old, their body loses some of that intensive energy and movements become softer by nature. Most importantly the practitioner should practice *Sanchin* under the strict supervision of a qualified *Sensei* to prevent harm to the practitioner.

Note: This interview was originally published in the magazine "Meibukan Magazine" Number 4, (2005).

Photo credits

Photo series and all digitalised photos

Copyright by: Lex Opdam
Photographer: Teun Meeuwesse
Performers: Tim Baartmans
                Maarten Arends
                Iwan Meij
                Pascal de Haan
                Rene van der Deijl
                Lèontine Veenhuis
                Els Honings
                Lex Opdam

Historical photos
Courtesy of Anthony Mirakian

Other photos
Other photos are from the private collection of Anthony Mirakian, Hing-Poon Chan and Lex Opdam. Photographers are Anthony Mirakian, Hing-Poon Chan, Lex Opdam, Teun Meeuwesse (page 19), Wil Koch (page 45) and Edward Mills (page 12, 295, 305).

Notes _____

Notes _____

Notes _____

Notes

Notes _____

Notes